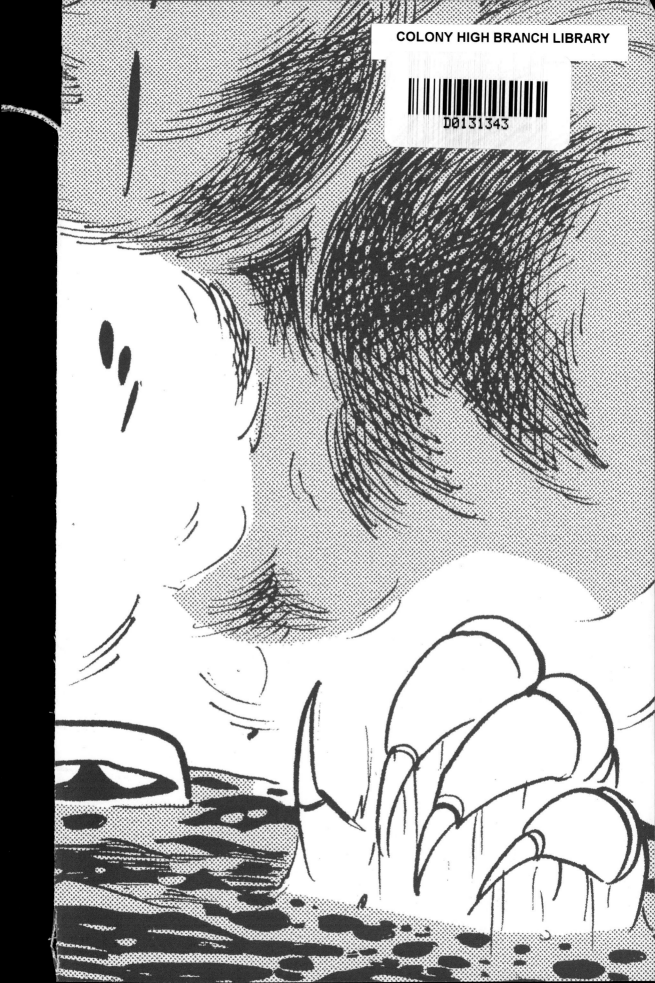

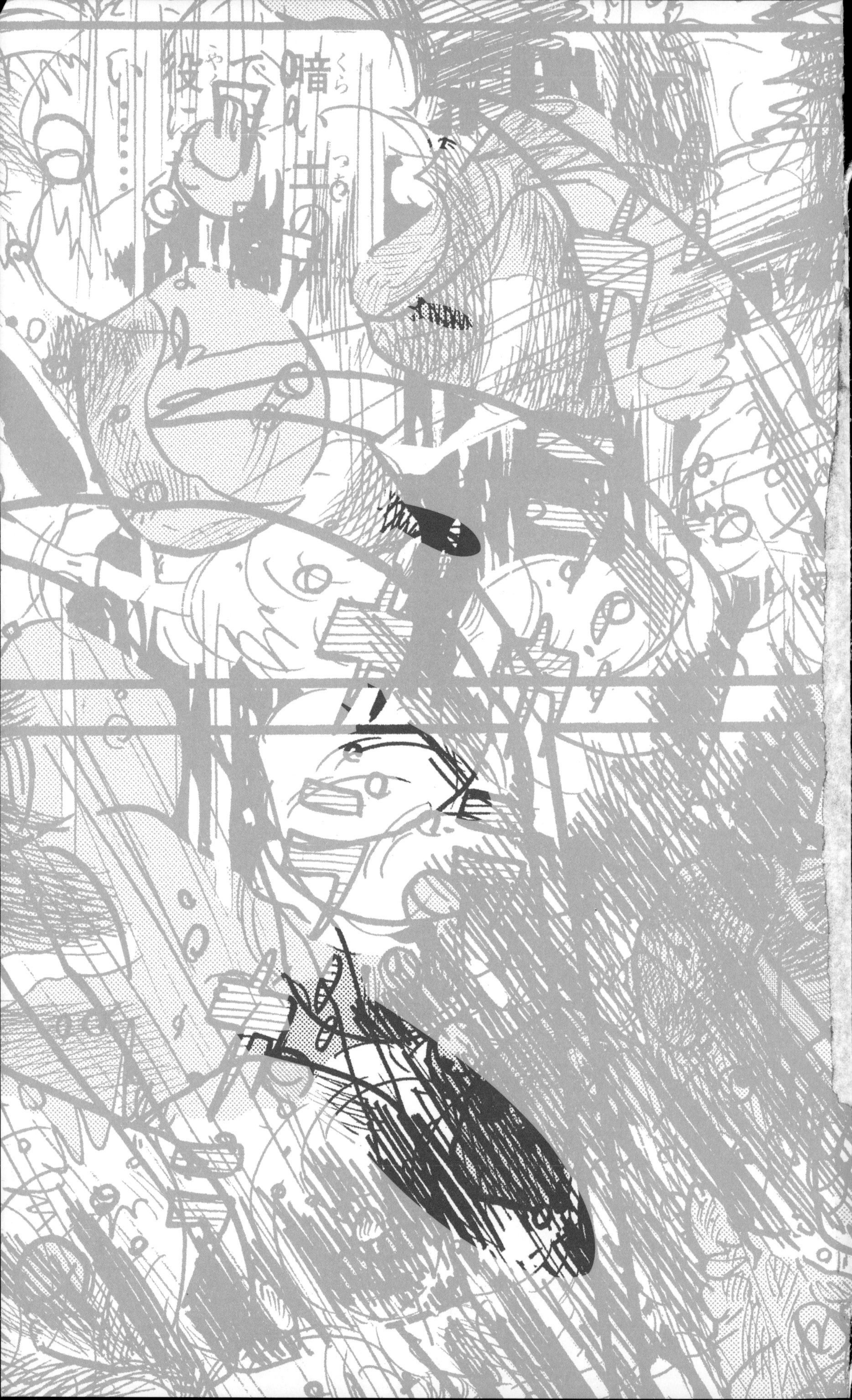
暗い
役に
い……

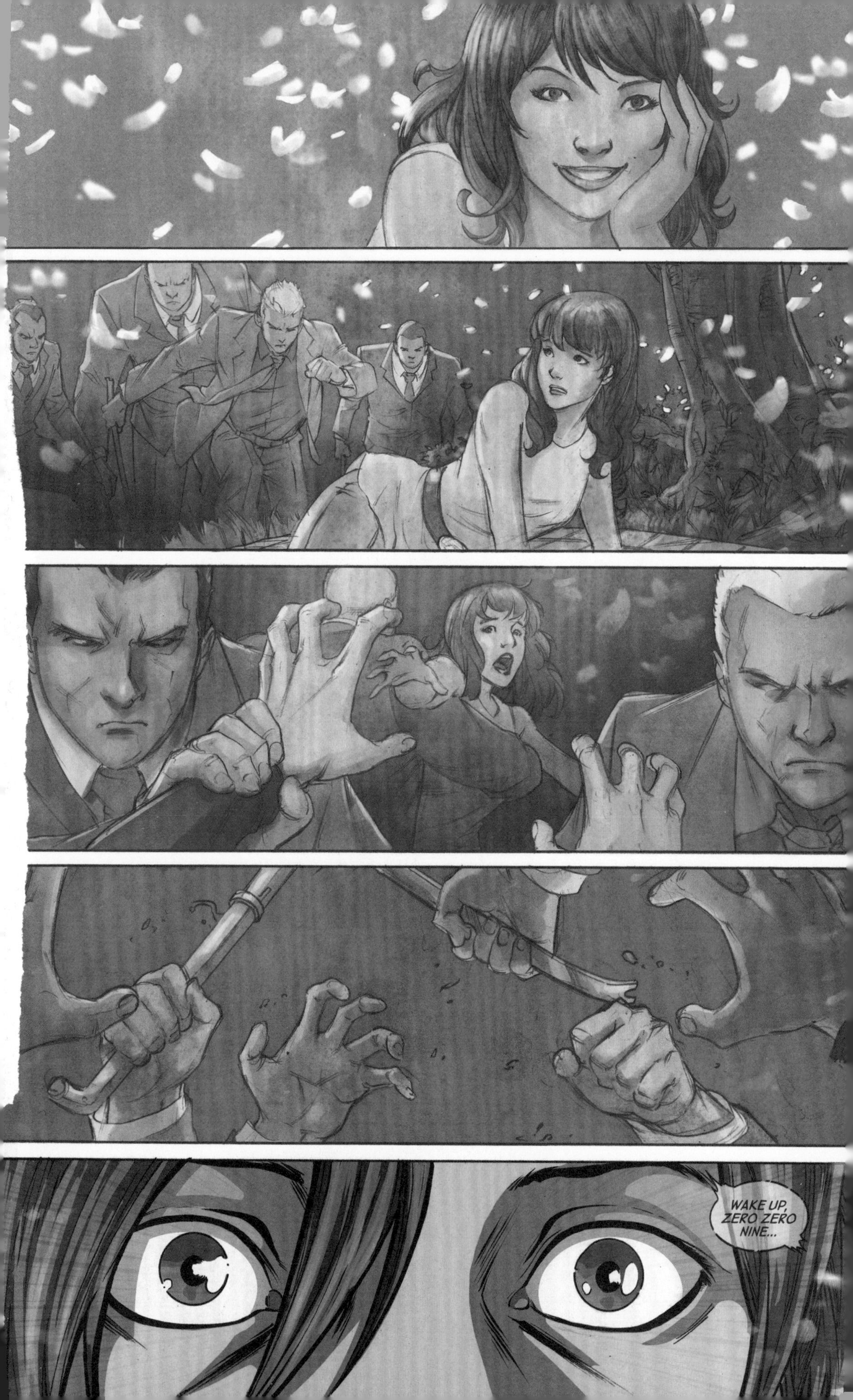
WAKE UP, ZERO ZERO NINE...

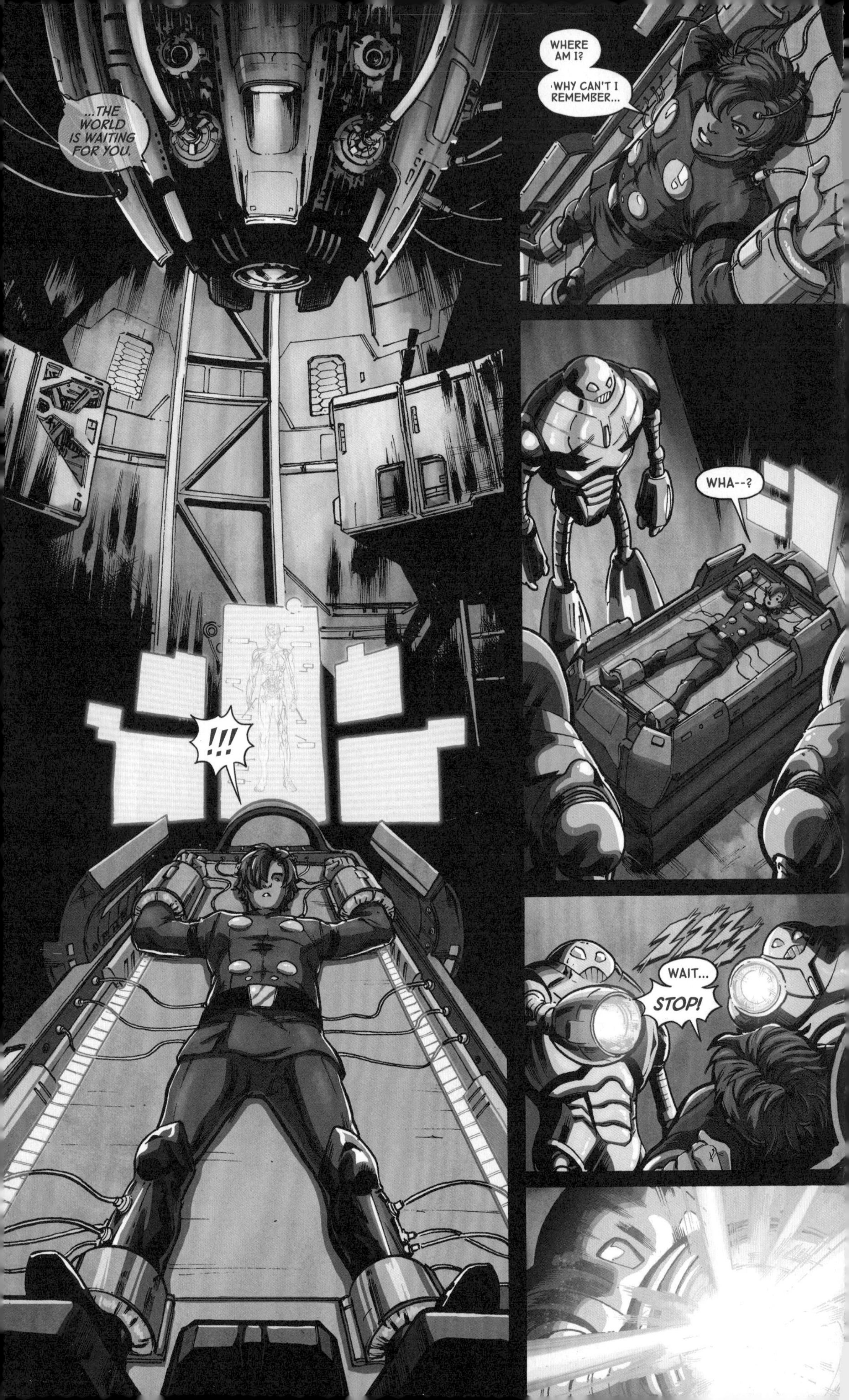
...THE WORLD IS WAITING FOR YOU.
!!!
WHERE AM I?
WHY CAN'T I REMEMBER...
WHA--?
WAIT...
STOP!

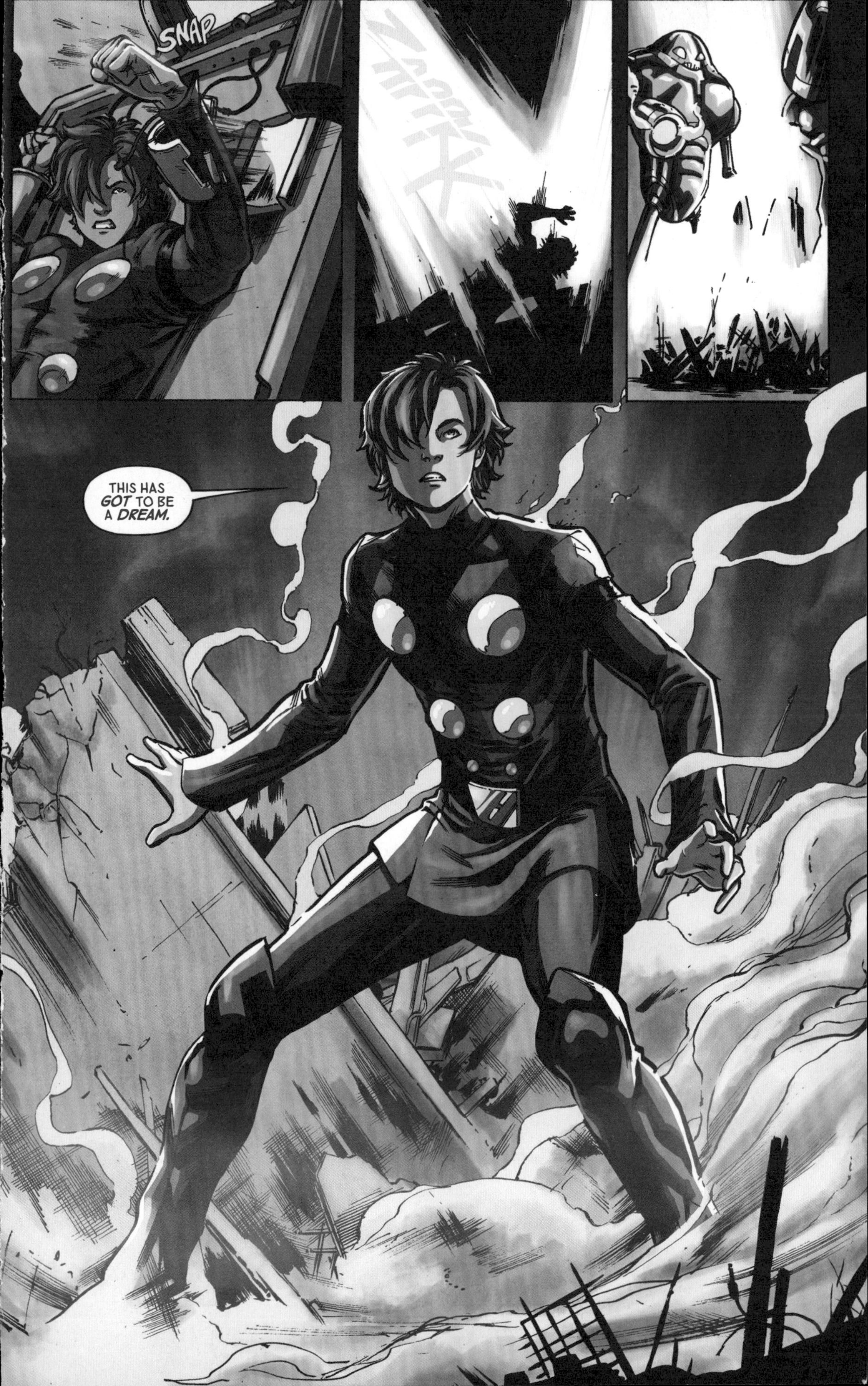
SNAP
ZARRRK
THIS HAS GOT TO BE A DREAM.

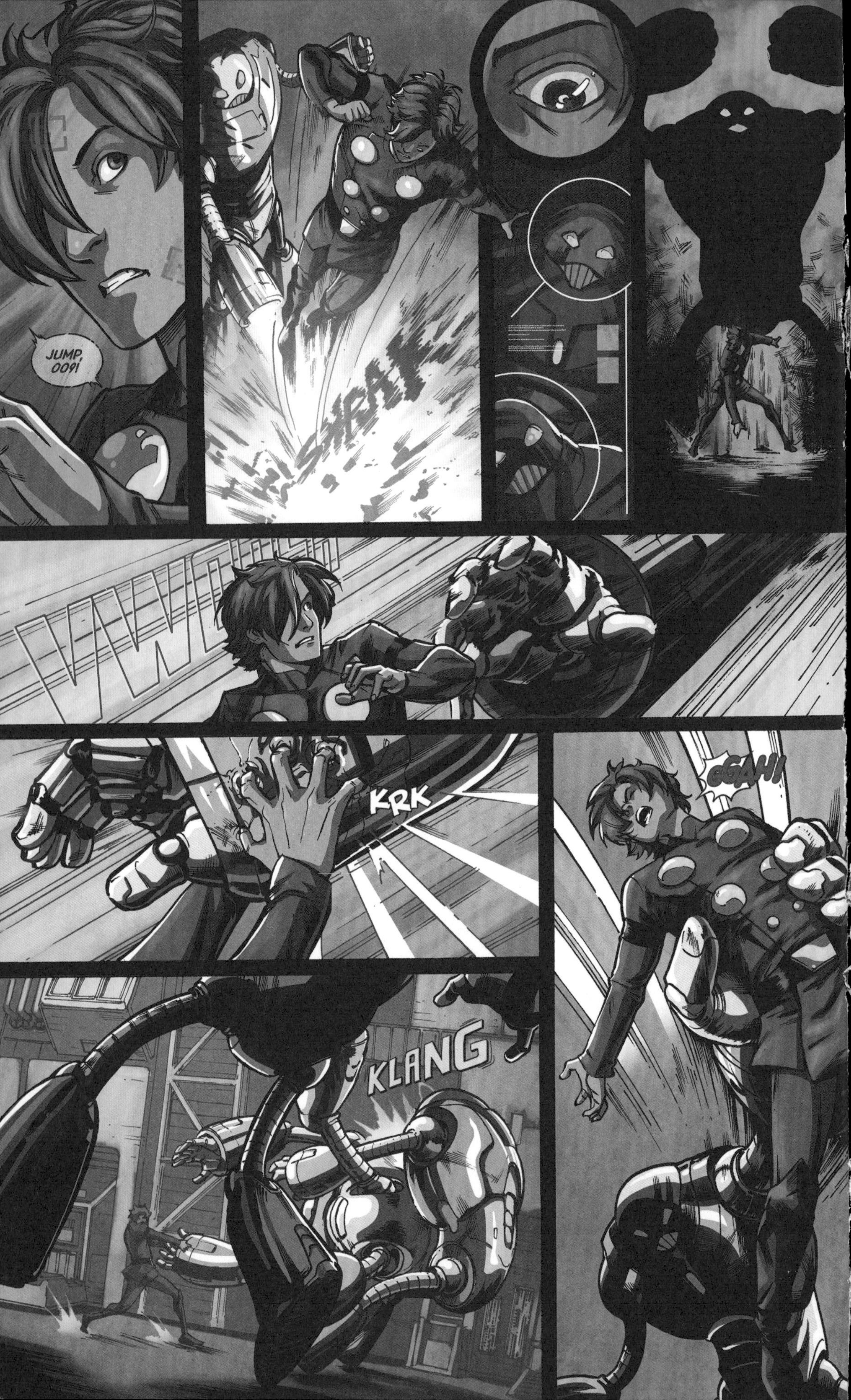
JUMP, 009!
SHRAK
KRK
KLANG
GAH!

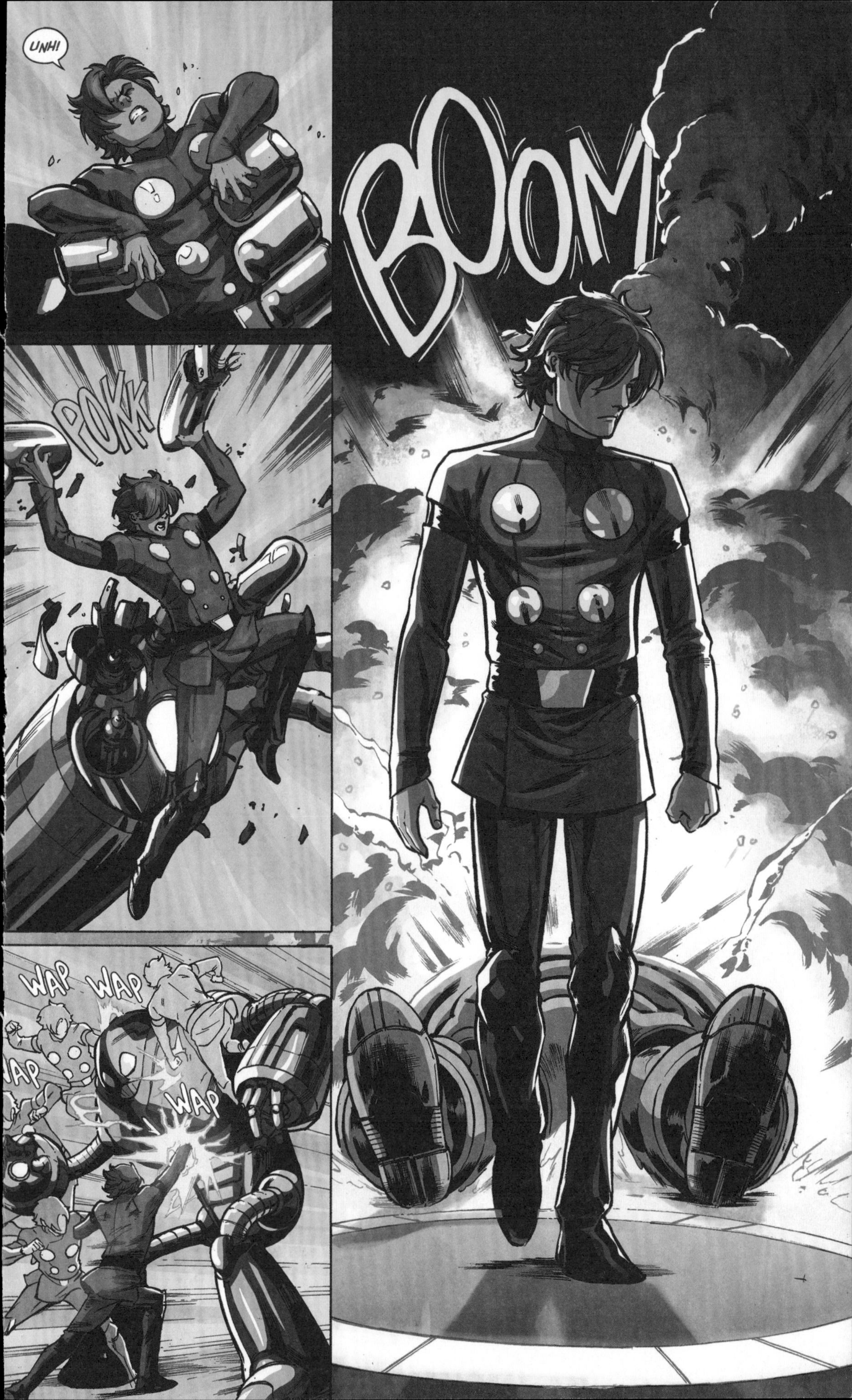
UNH!
POKK
WAP
WAP
WAP
WAP
BOOM

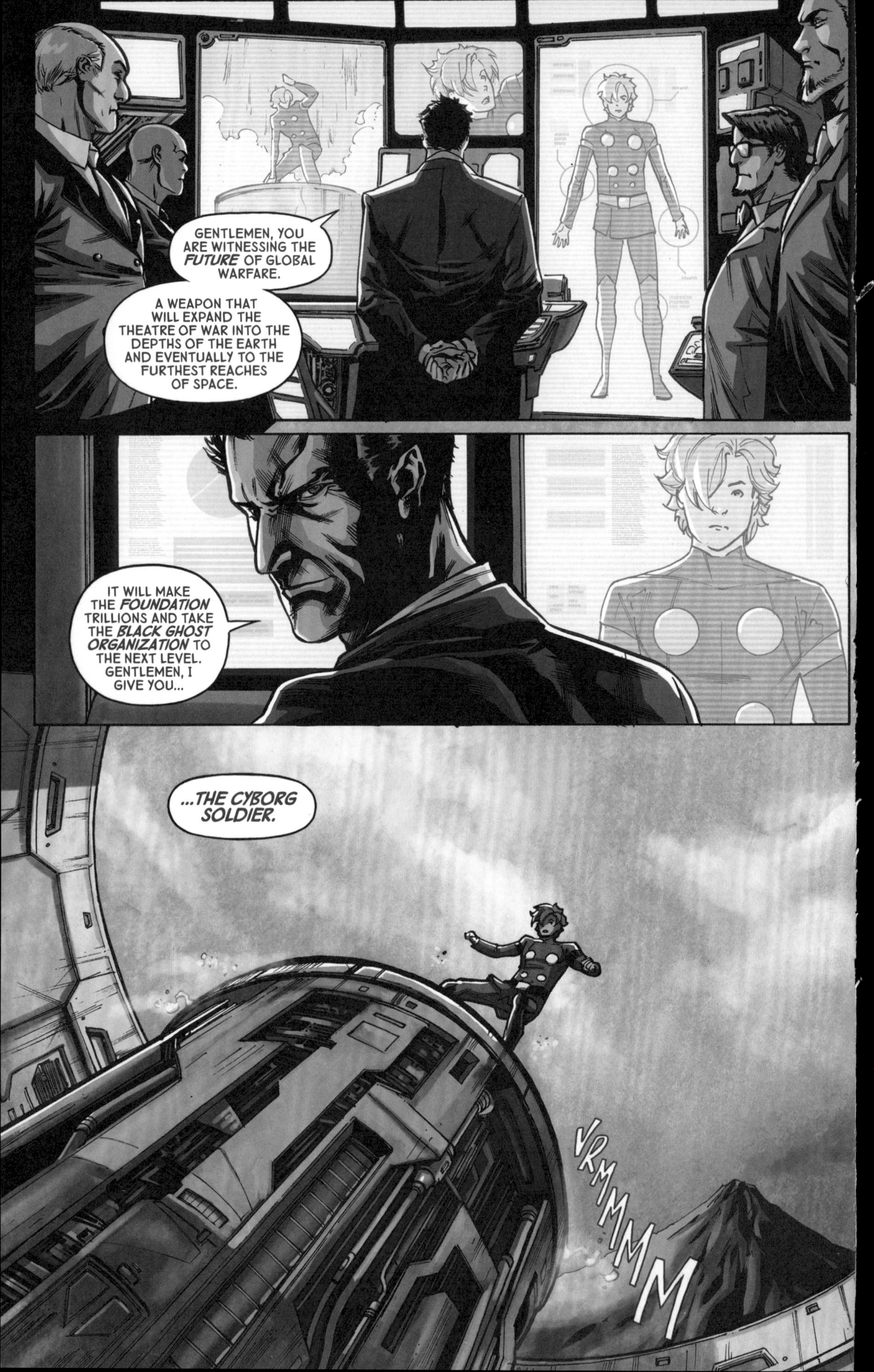
GENTLEMEN, YOU ARE WITNESSING THE *FUTURE* OF GLOBAL WARFARE.
A WEAPON THAT WILL EXPAND THE THEATRE OF WAR INTO THE DEPTHS OF THE EARTH AND EVENTUALLY TO THE FURTHEST REACHES OF SPACE.
IT WILL MAKE THE *FOUNDATION* TRILLIONS AND TAKE THE *BLACK GHOST ORGANIZATION* TO THE NEXT LEVEL. GENTLEMEN, I GIVE YOU...
...THE CYBORG SOLDIER.
VRMMMMM

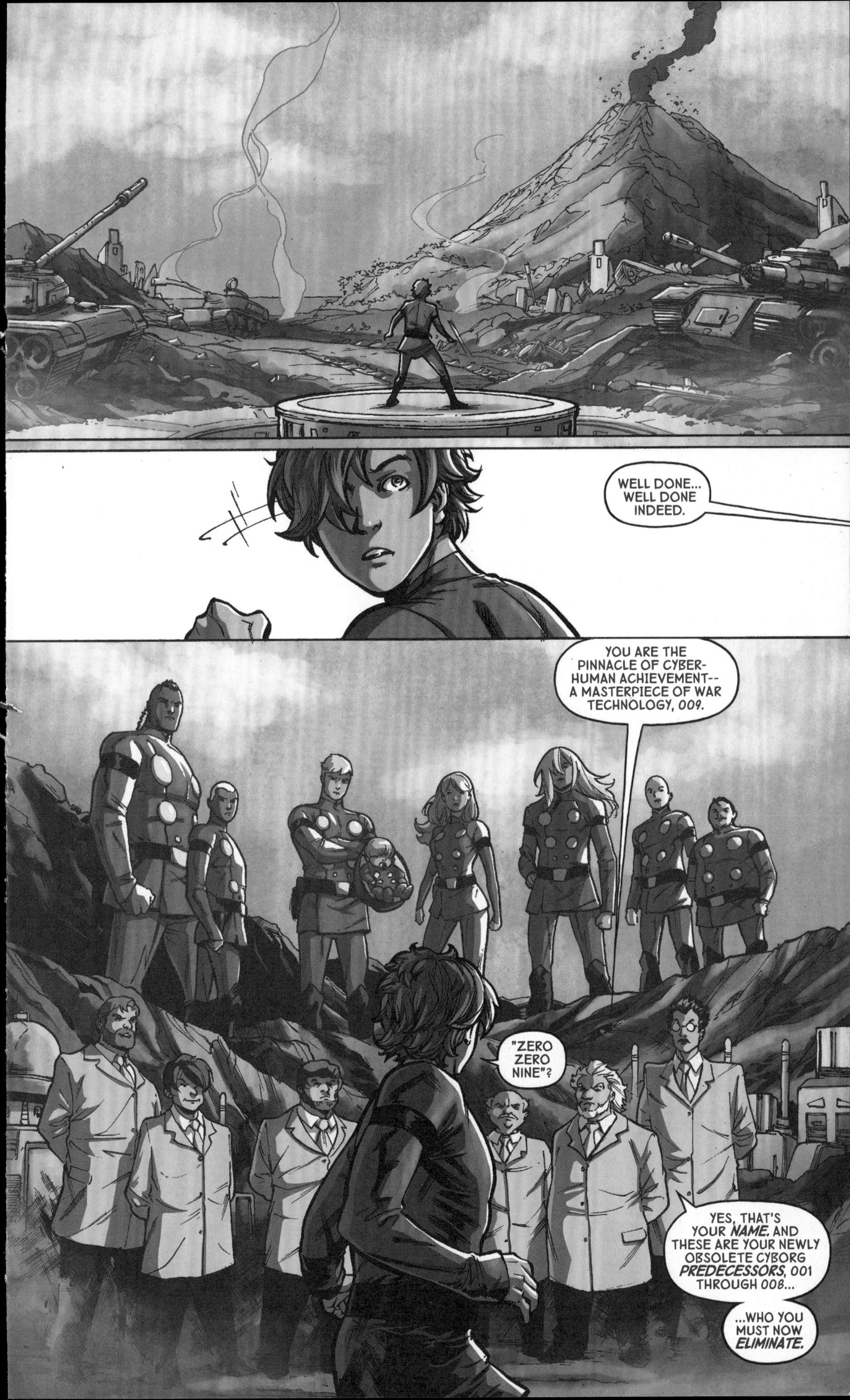
WELL DONE... WELL DONE INDEED.
YOU ARE THE PINNACLE OF CYBER-HUMAN ACHIEVEMENT--A MASTERPIECE OF WAR TECHNOLOGY, 009.
"ZERO ZERO NINE"?
YES, THAT'S YOUR *NAME.* AND THESE ARE YOUR NEWLY OBSOLETE CYBORG *PREDECESSORS,* 001 THROUGH 008...
...WHO YOU MUST NOW *ELIMINATE.*

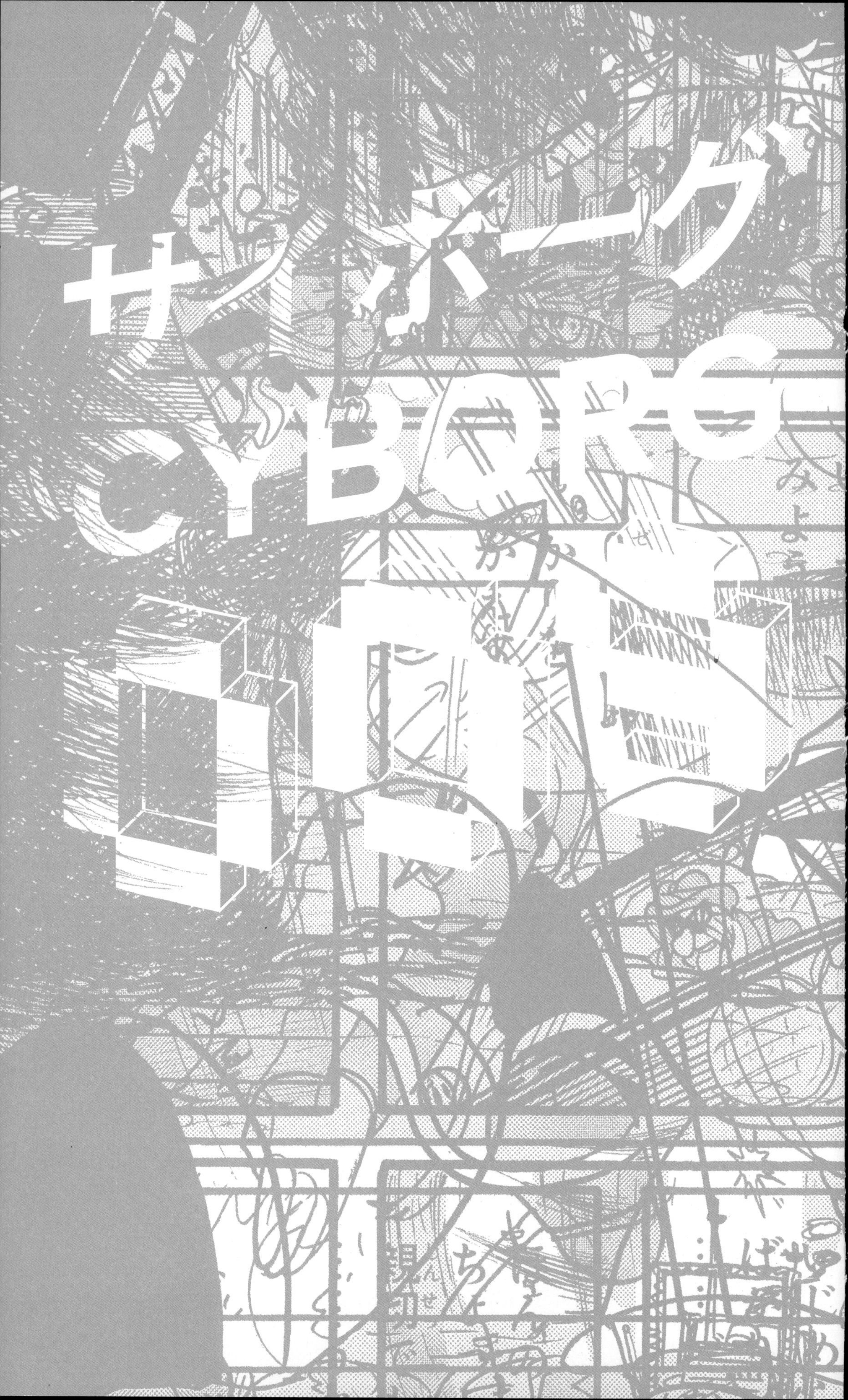
サイボーグ
CYBORG

AN ARCHAIA ENTERTAINMENT /// ISHIMORI PRODUCTION PRESENTATION

WRITTEN BY F.J. DeSANTO

AND BRADLEY CRAMP

ILLUSTRATED BY MARCUS TO

COLORED BY IAN HERRING

LETTERED BY DERON BENNETT

DESIGNED BY JON ADAMS

EDITED BY STEPHEN CHRISTY

CREATED BY SHOTARO ISHINOMORI

Archaia Entertainment LLC, Jack Cummins, President & COO, Mark Smylie, COO, Mike Kennedy, Publisher, Stephen Christy, Editor-in-Chief, Mel Caylo, Marketing Manager, Scott Newman, Production Manager. Published by Archaia. Archaia Entertainment LLC, 1680 Vine Street, Suite 1010, Los Angeles, California, 90028. Archaia.com. Cyborg 009 Original Graphic Novel, July 2013, FIRST PRINTING. 10 9 8 7 6 5 4 3 2 1. ISBN: 1-936393-94-8, ISBN-13: 978-1-936393-94-7. Cyborg 009 TM and © 2013 Ishinomori Production, Inc. Ishinomori Production. All Rights Reserved. Cyborg 009 mark and logo, characters, and elements are trademarks of Ishinomori Production. All Rights Reserved. Archaia™, Archaia™ "Black Label," and the Archaia Black Label Logo™ are TM 2013 Archaia Entertainment LLC. All Rights Reserved. No unauthorized reproductions permitted, except for review purposes. Any similarity to persons or Black Ghosts alive or dead is purely coincidental. Printed in China by GLOBAL PSD.

ISBN 978-1-936393-94-7
51995

9 781936 393947

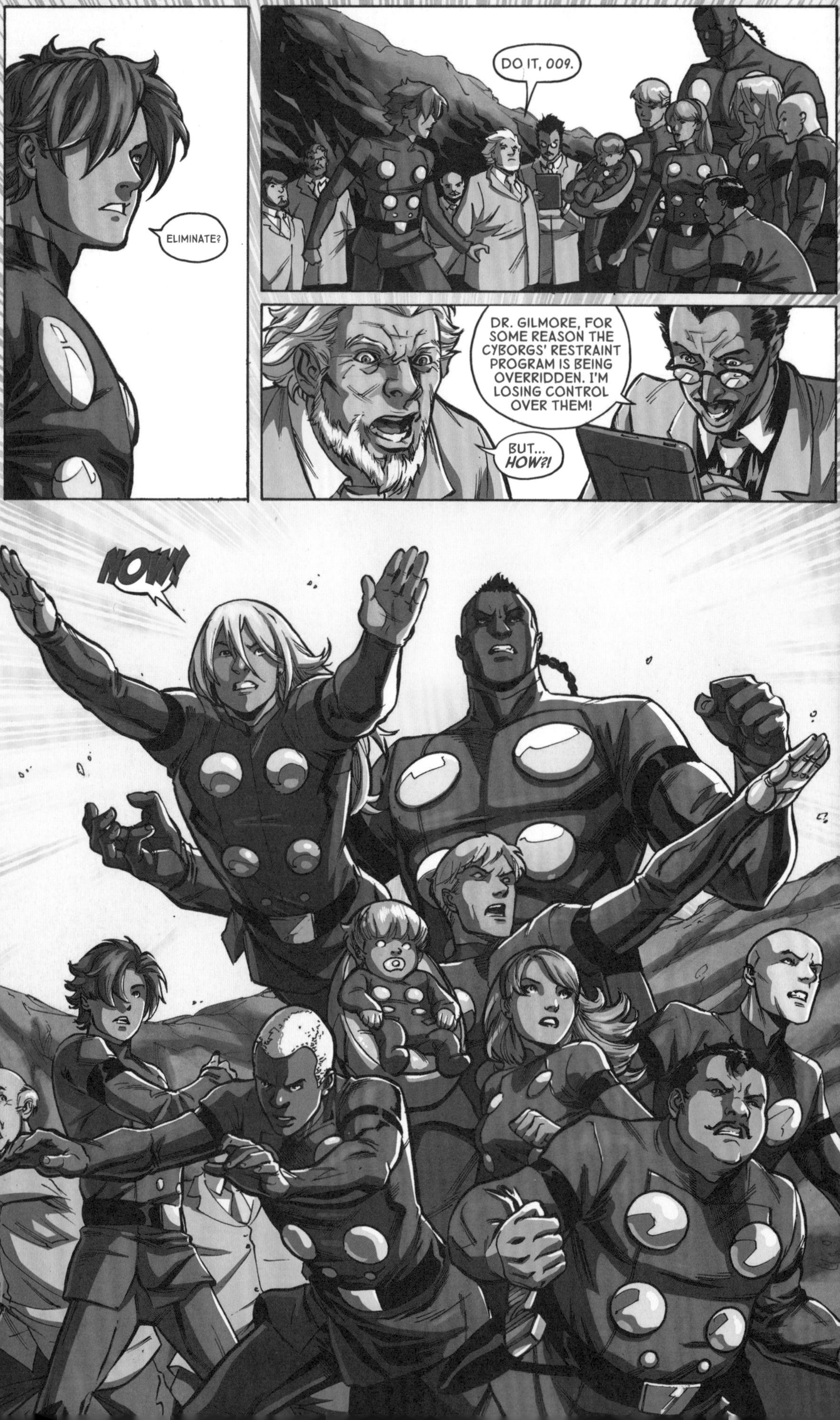
ELIMINATE?
DO IT, 009.
DR. GILMORE, FOR SOME REASON THE CYBORGS' RESTRAINT PROGRAM IS BEING OVERRIDDEN. I'M LOSING CONTROL OVER THEM!
BUT... HOW?!
NOW!

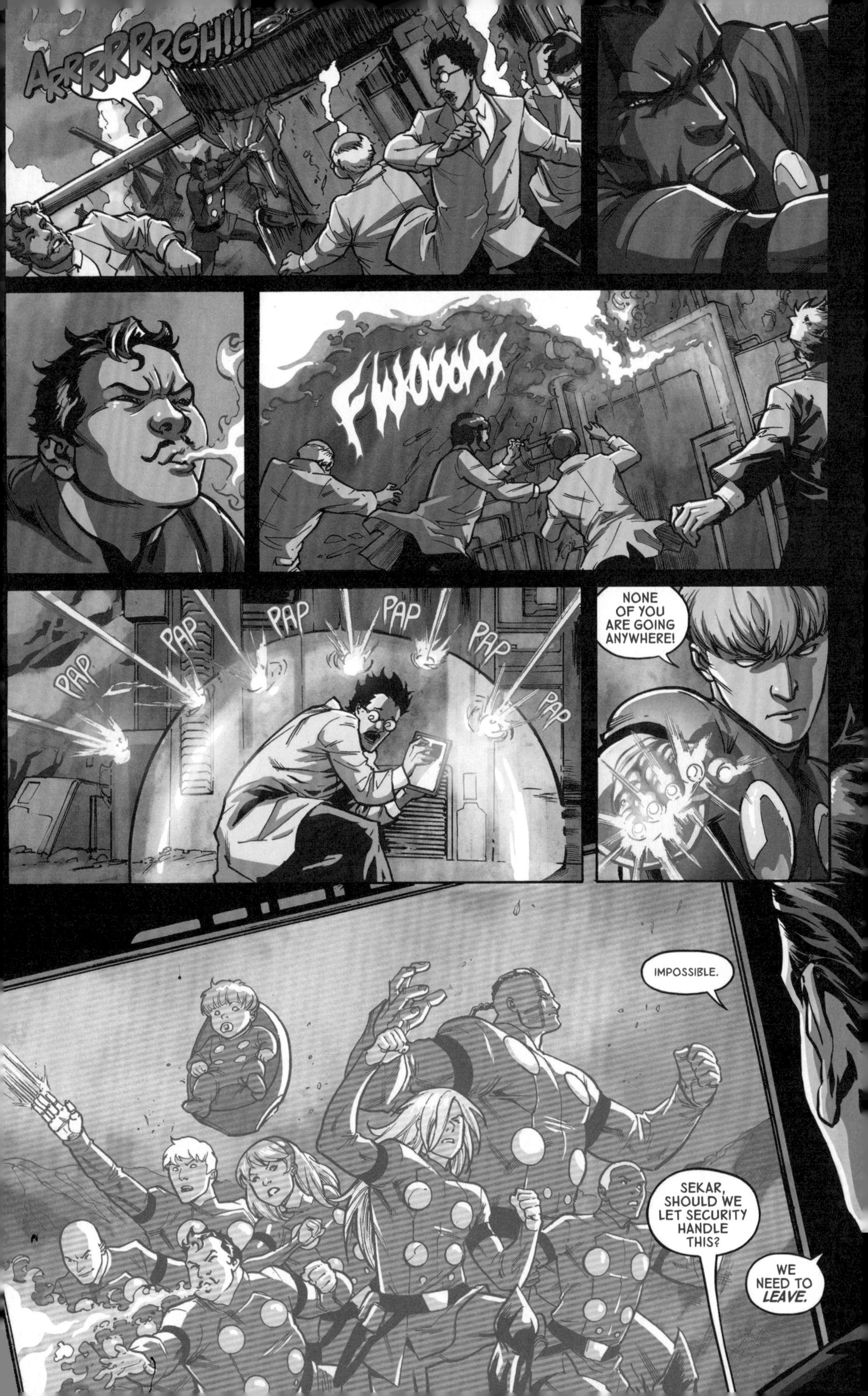
ARRRRRGH!!!
FWOOOM
PAP
PAP
PAP
PAP
PAP
PAP
NONE OF YOU ARE GOING ANYWHERE!
IMPOSSIBLE.
SEKAR, SHOULD WE LET SECURITY HANDLE THIS?
WE NEED TO *LEAVE.*

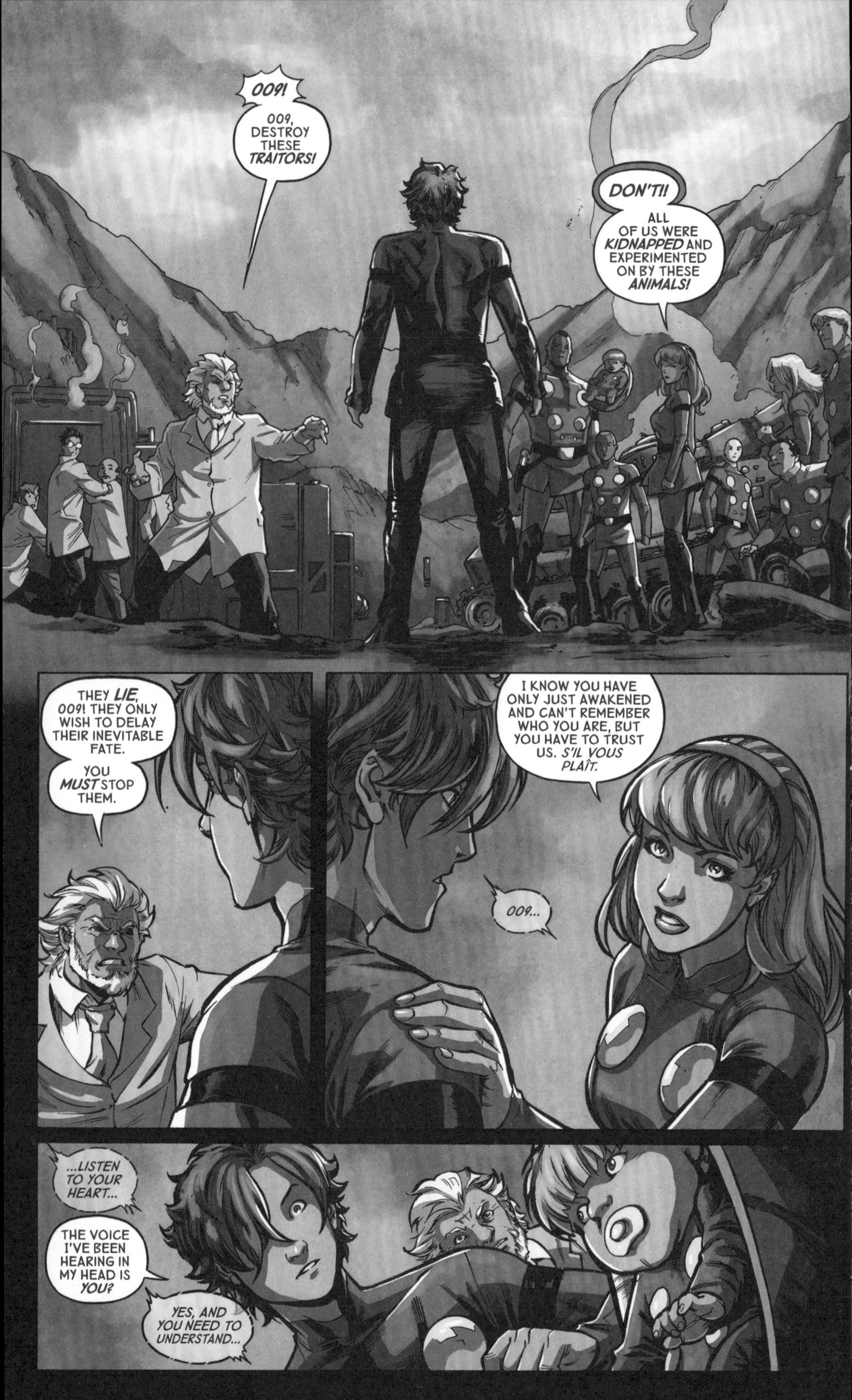
009!
009, DESTROY THESE *TRAITORS!*
DON'T!!
ALL OF US WERE *KIDNAPPED* AND EXPERIMENTED ON BY THESE *ANIMALS!*
THEY *LIE,* 009! THEY ONLY WISH TO DELAY THEIR INEVITABLE FATE.
YOU *MUST* STOP THEM.
I KNOW YOU HAVE ONLY JUST AWAKENED AND CAN'T REMEMBER WHO YOU ARE, BUT YOU HAVE TO TRUST US. *S'IL VOUS PLAÎT.*
009...
...LISTEN TO YOUR HEART...
THE VOICE I'VE BEEN HEARING IN MY HEAD IS *YOU?*
YES, AND YOU NEED TO UNDERSTAND...

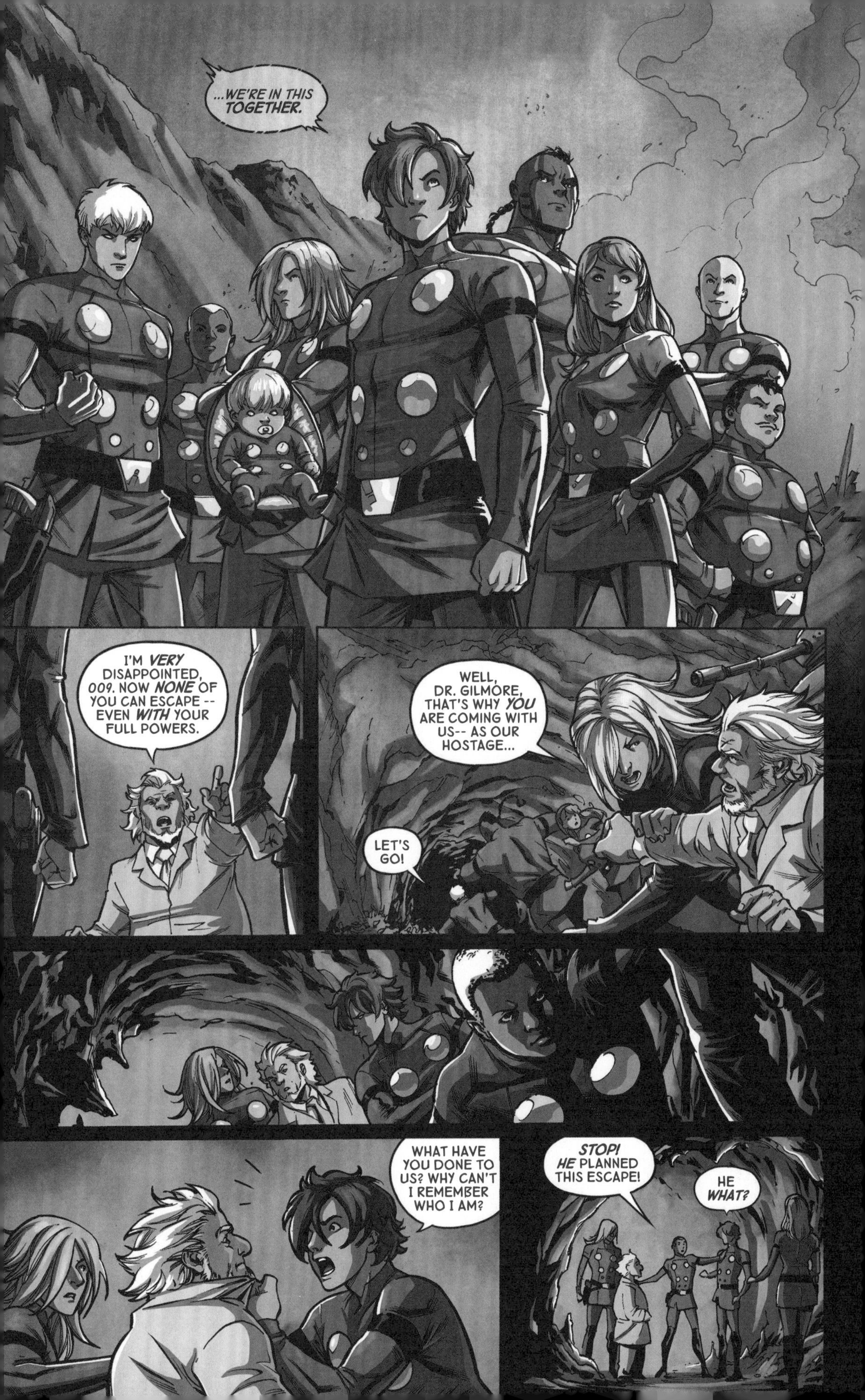

...WE'RE IN THIS TOGETHER.
I'M VERY DISAPPOINTED, 009. NOW NONE OF YOU CAN ESCAPE -- EVEN WITH YOUR FULL POWERS.
WELL, DR. GILMORE, THAT'S WHY YOU ARE COMING WITH US-- AS OUR HOSTAGE...
LET'S GO!
WHAT HAVE YOU DONE TO US? WHY CAN'T I REMEMBER WHO I AM?
STOP! HE PLANNED THIS ESCAPE!
HE WHAT?

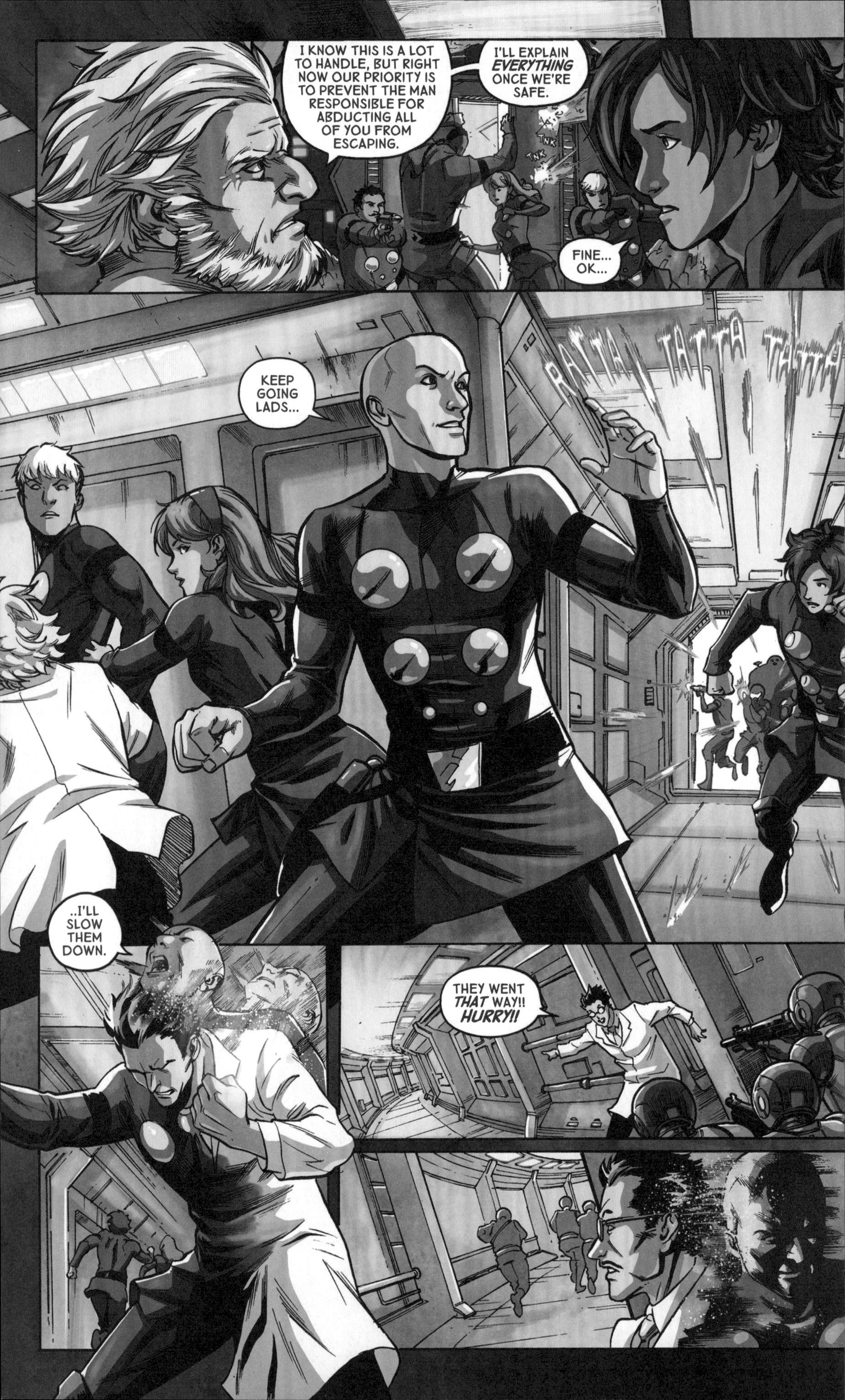
I KNOW THIS IS A LOT TO HANDLE, BUT RIGHT NOW OUR PRIORITY IS TO PREVENT THE MAN RESPONSIBLE FOR ABDUCTING ALL OF YOU FROM ESCAPING.
I'LL EXPLAIN *EVERYTHING* ONCE WE'RE SAFE.
TNK
TNK
FINE... OK...
KEEP GOING LADS...
RATTA TATTA TATTA
..I'LL SLOW THEM DOWN.
THEY WENT *THAT* WAY!! ***HURRY!!***

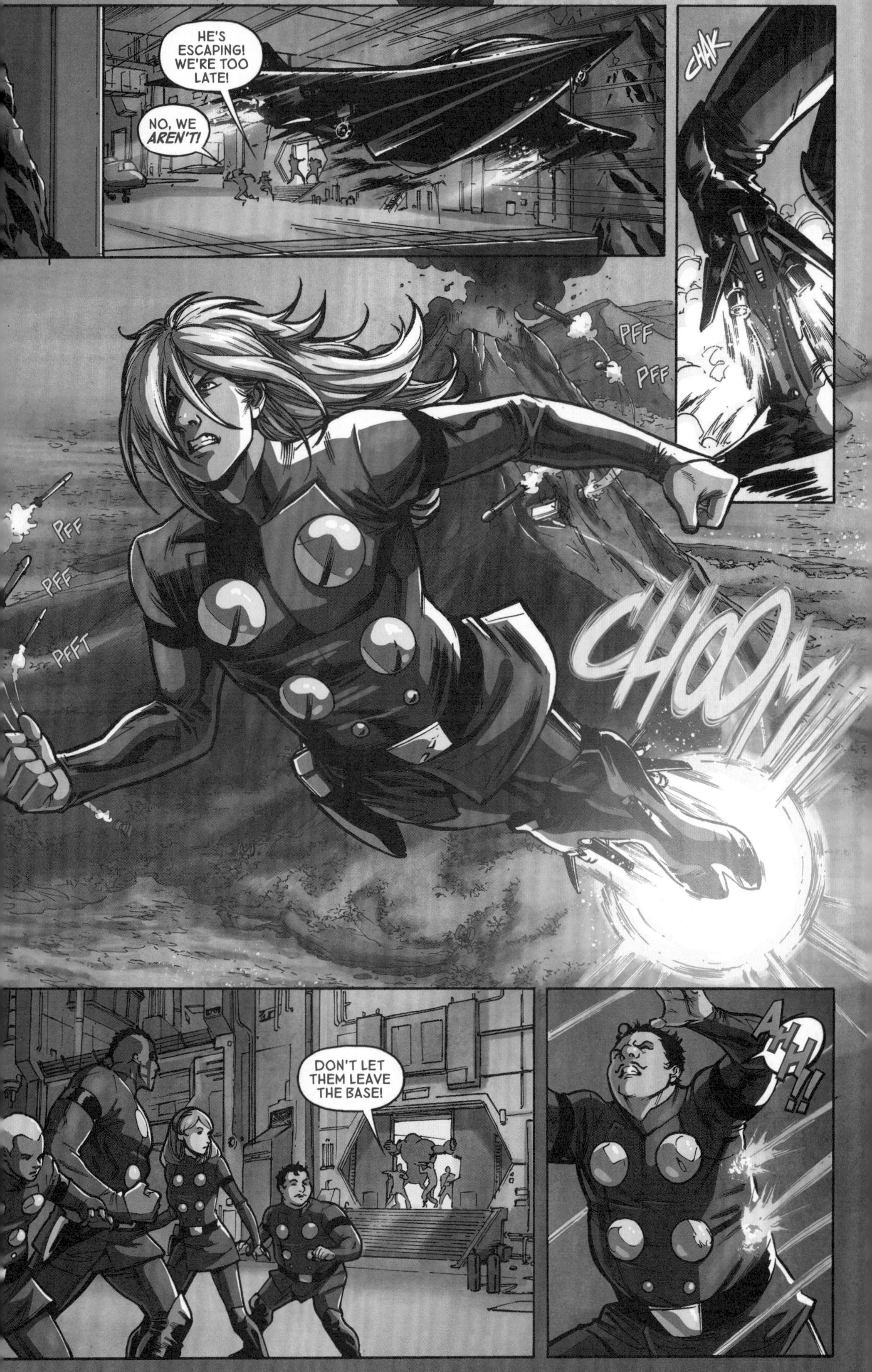

HE'S ESCAPING! WE'RE TOO LATE!
NO, WE *AREN'T!*
CHAK
PFF
PFF
PFF
PFF
PFFT
CHOOM
DON'T LET THEM LEAVE THE BASE!
AHH!!

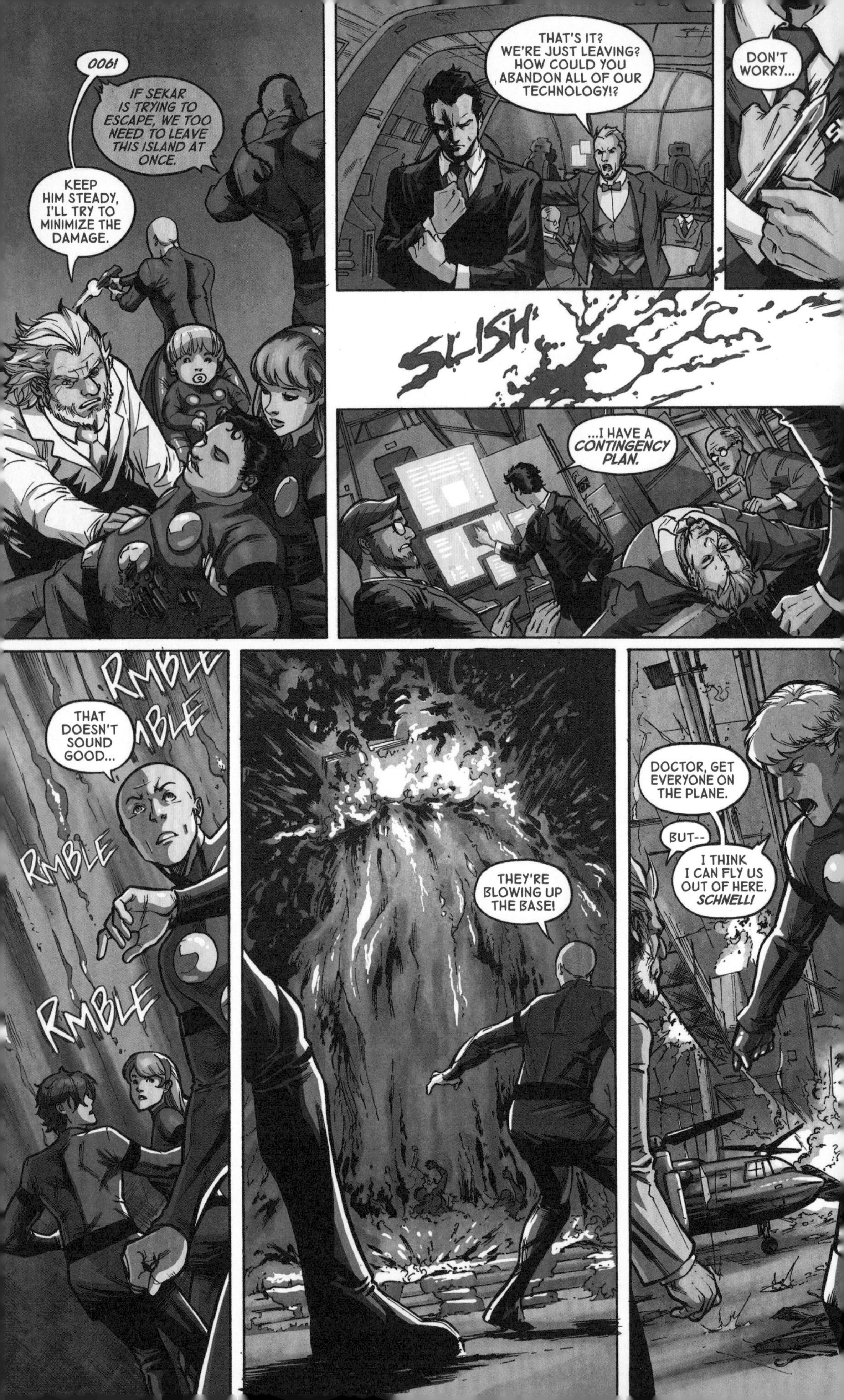
OOGI
IF SEKAR IS TRYING TO ESCAPE, WE TOO NEED TO LEAVE THIS ISLAND AT ONCE.
KEEP HIM STEADY, I'LL TRY TO MINIMIZE THE DAMAGE.
THAT'S IT? WE'RE JUST LEAVING? HOW COULD YOU ABANDON ALL OF OUR TECHNOLOGY!?
DON'T WORRY...
SLISH
...I HAVE A CONTINGENCY PLAN.
RMBLE
RMBLE
THAT DOESN'T SOUND GOOD...
RMBLE
RMBLE
THEY'RE BLOWING UP THE BASE!
DOCTOR, GET EVERYONE ON THE PLANE.
BUT--
I THINK I CAN FLY US OUT OF HERE. SCHNELL!

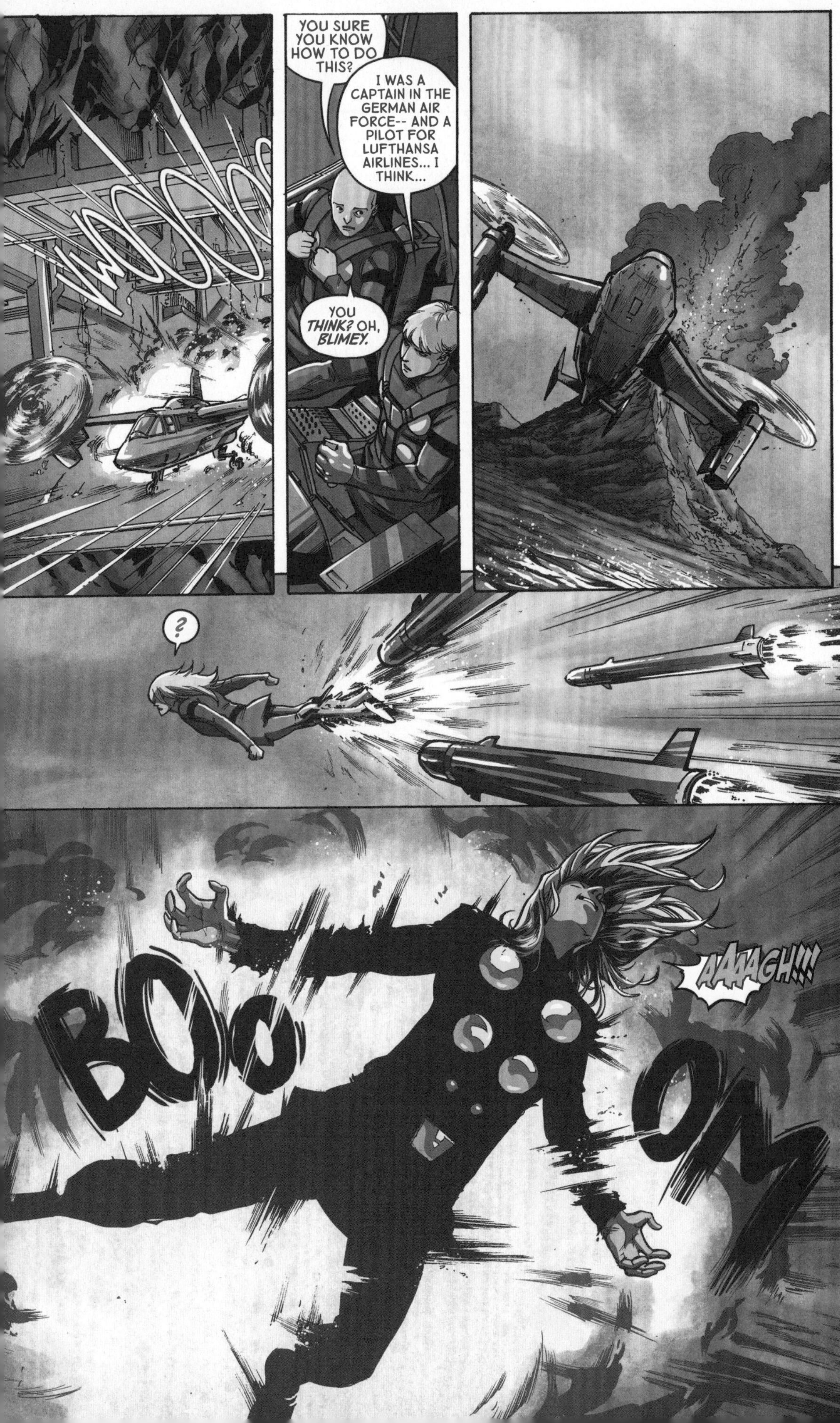
WOOOOO
YOU SURE YOU KNOW HOW TO DO THIS?
I WAS A CAPTAIN IN THE GERMAN AIR FORCE-- AND A PILOT FOR LUFTHANSA AIRLINES... I THINK...
YOU *THINK?* OH, *BLIMEY.*
?
BOOOOM
AAAAGH!!!

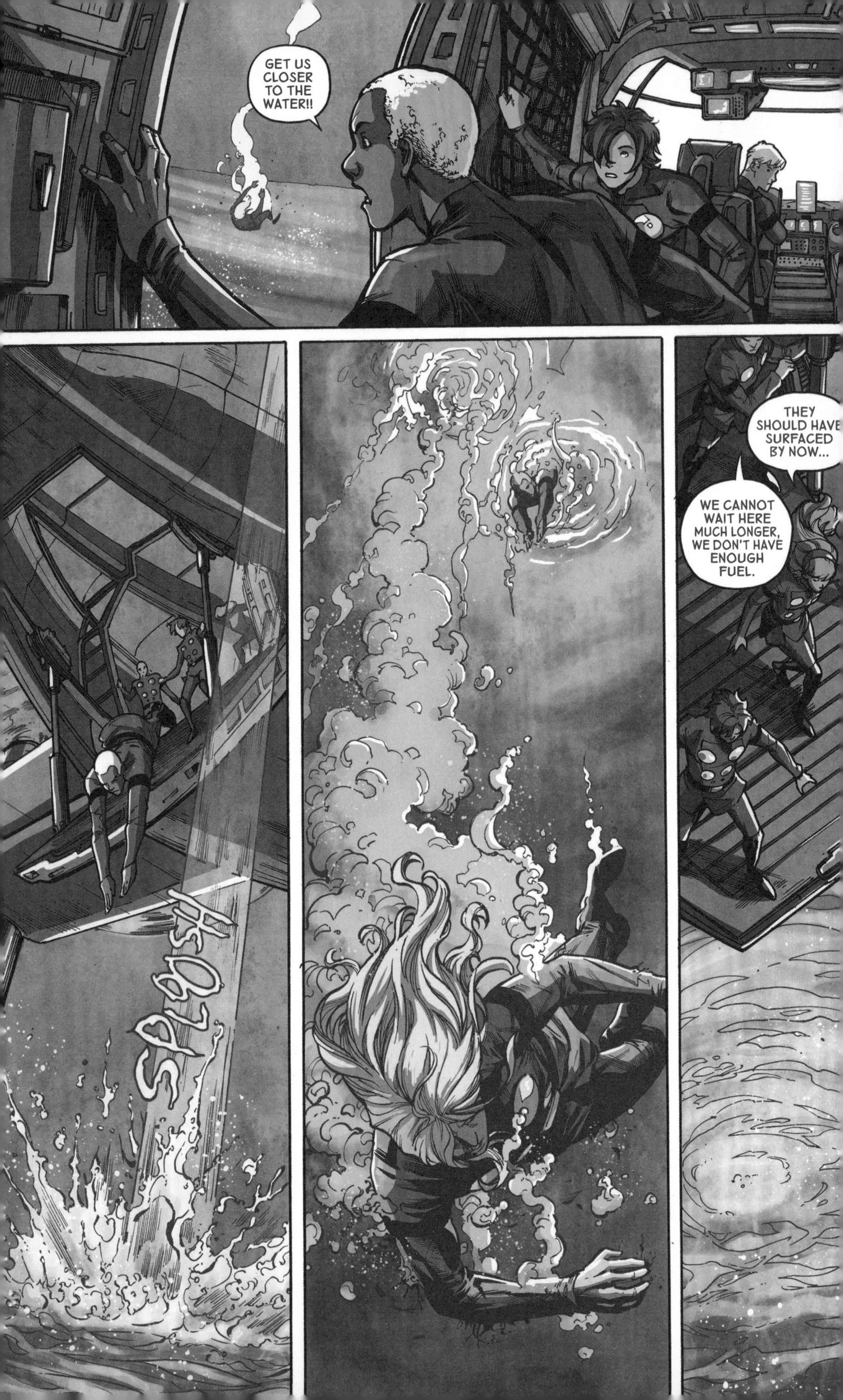
GET US CLOSER TO THE WATER!!
SPLASH
THEY SHOULD HAVE SURFACED BY NOW...
WE CANNOT WAIT HERE MUCH LONGER, WE DON'T HAVE ENOUGH FUEL.

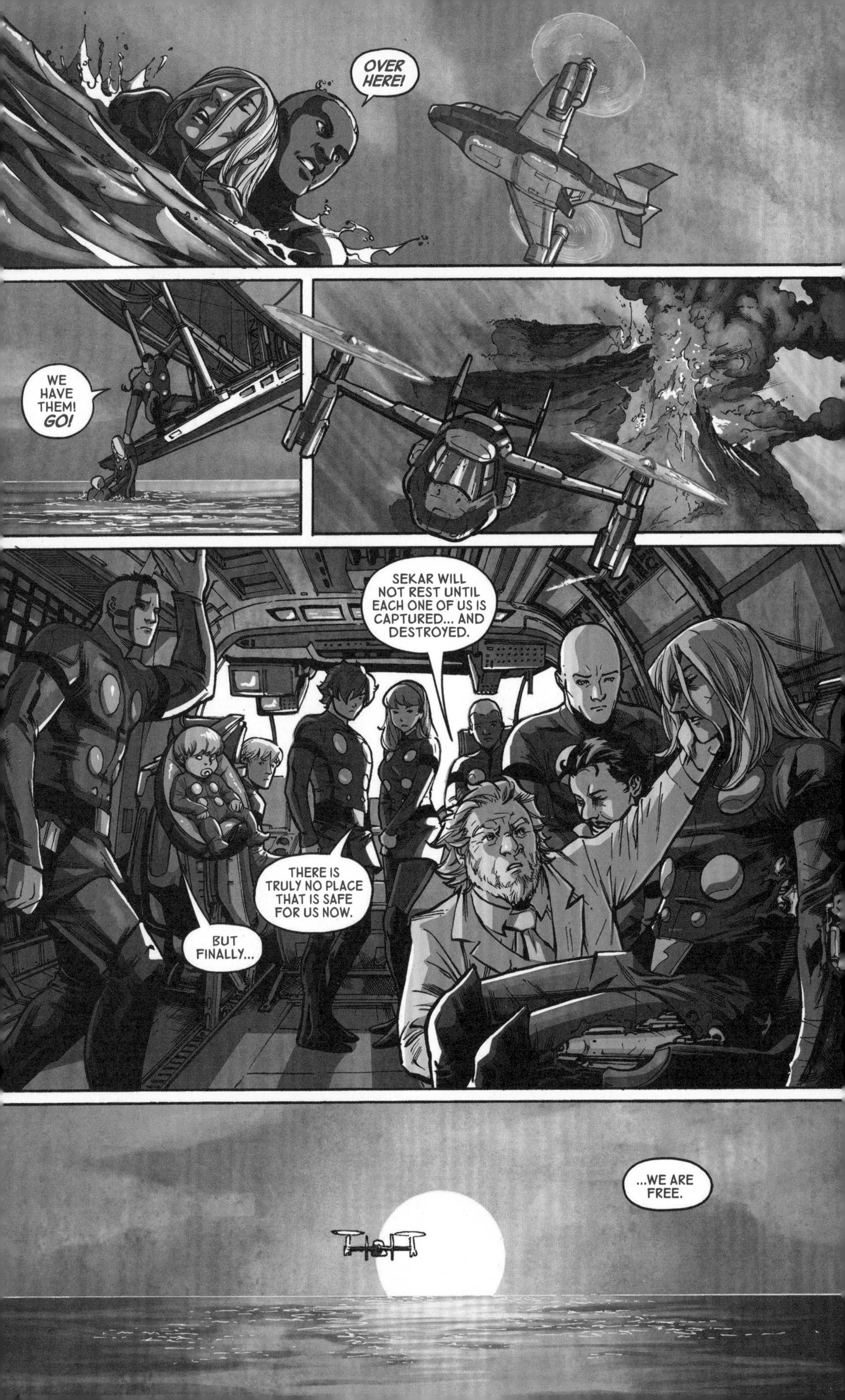
OVER HERE!
WE HAVE THEM! GO!
SEKAR WILL NOT REST UNTIL EACH ONE OF US IS CAPTURED... AND DESTROYED.
THERE IS TRULY NO PLACE THAT IS SAFE FOR US NOW.
BUT FINALLY...
...WE ARE FREE.

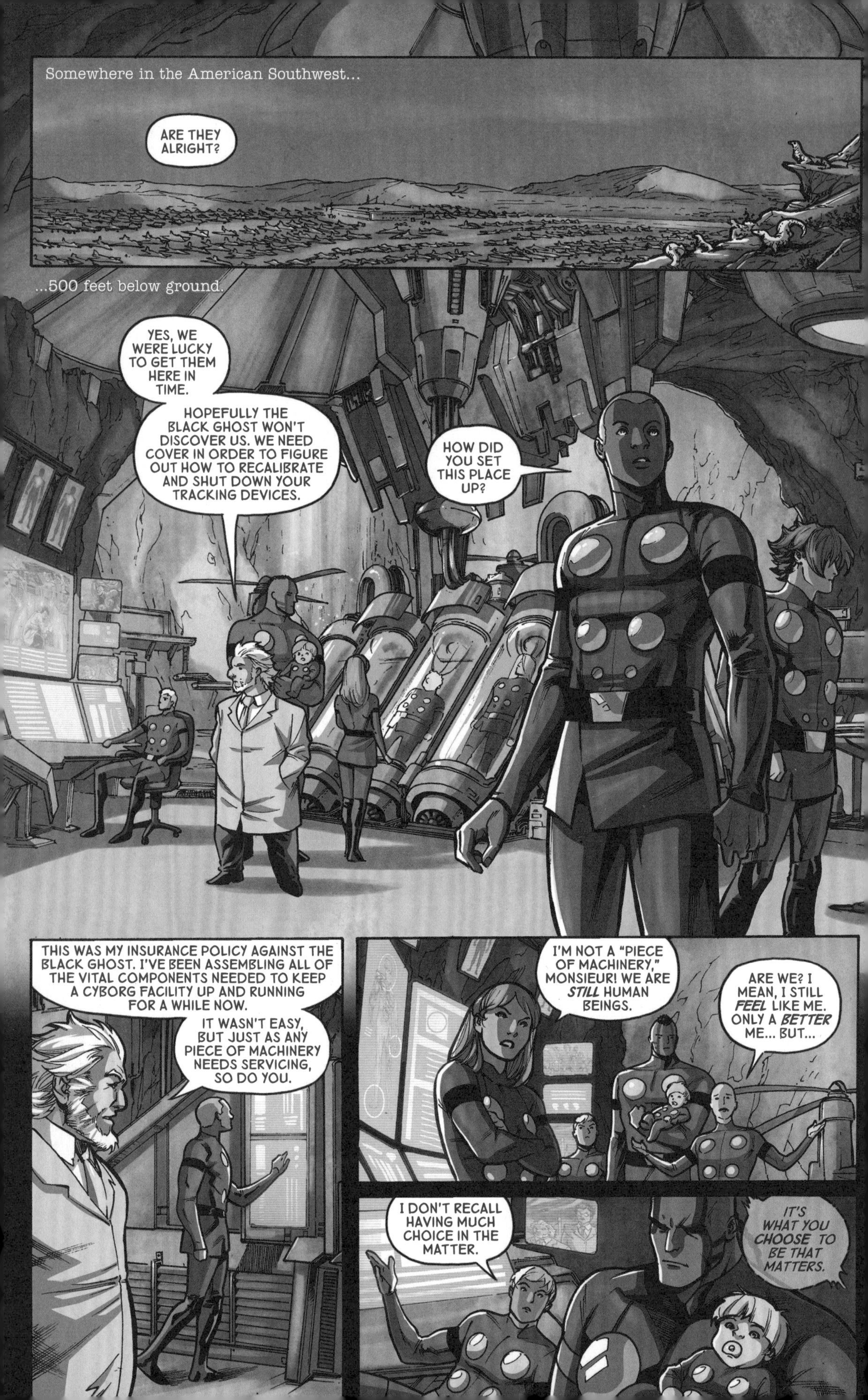
Somewhere in the American Southwest...
ARE THEY ALRIGHT?
...500 feet below ground.
YES, WE WERE LUCKY TO GET THEM HERE IN TIME.
HOPEFULLY THE BLACK GHOST WON'T DISCOVER US. WE NEED COVER IN ORDER TO FIGURE OUT HOW TO RECALIBRATE AND SHUT DOWN YOUR TRACKING DEVICES.
HOW DID YOU SET THIS PLACE UP?
THIS WAS MY INSURANCE POLICY AGAINST THE BLACK GHOST. I'VE BEEN ASSEMBLING ALL OF THE VITAL COMPONENTS NEEDED TO KEEP A CYBORG FACILITY UP AND RUNNING FOR A WHILE NOW.
IT WASN'T EASY, BUT JUST AS ANY PIECE OF MACHINERY NEEDS SERVICING, SO DO YOU.
I'M NOT A "PIECE OF MACHINERY," MONSIEUR! WE ARE *STILL* HUMAN BEINGS.
ARE WE? I MEAN, I STILL *FEEL* LIKE ME. ONLY A *BETTER* ME... BUT...
I DON'T RECALL HAVING MUCH CHOICE IN THE MATTER.
IT'S WHAT YOU CHOOSE TO BE THAT MATTERS.

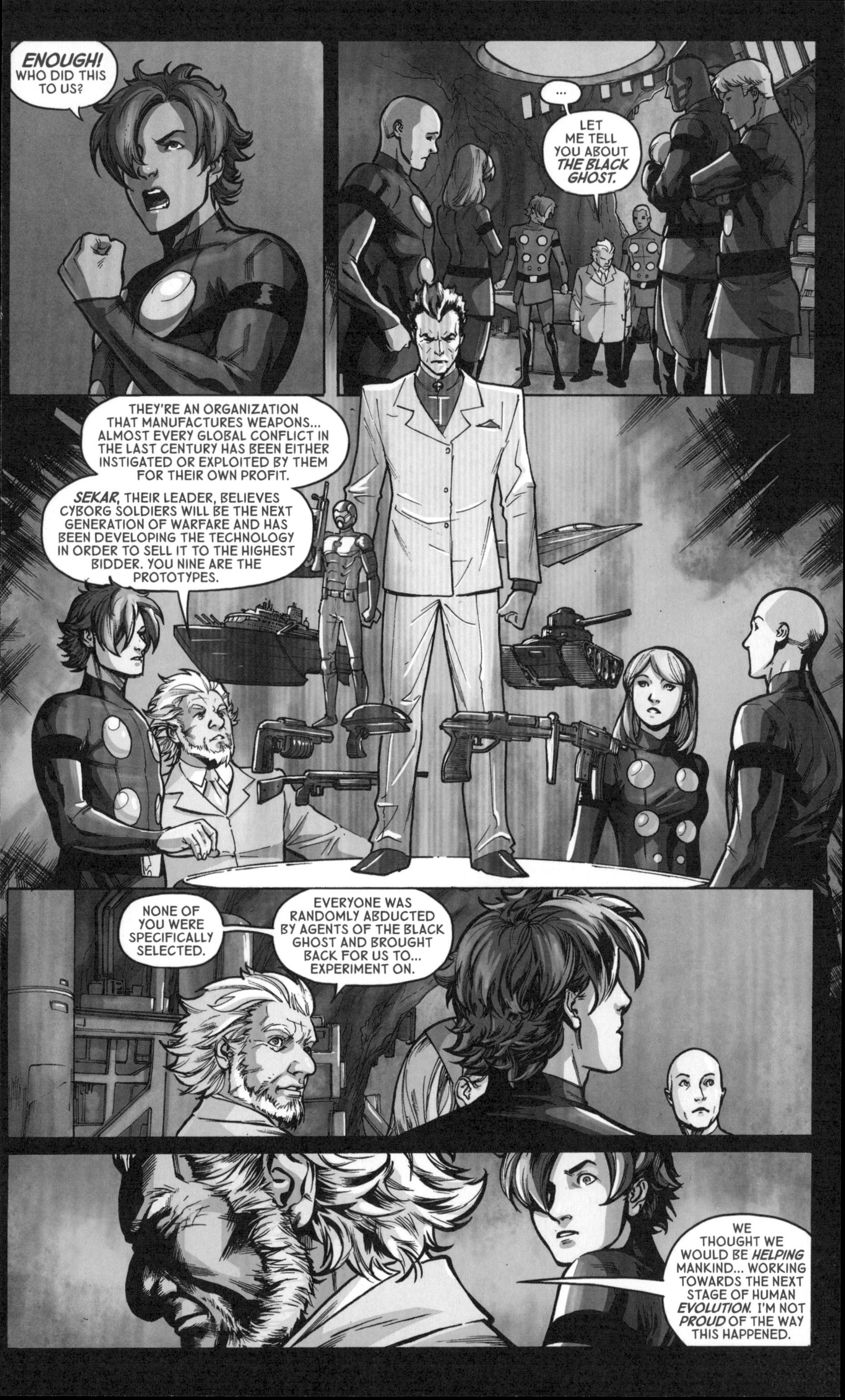
ENOUGH! WHO DID THIS TO US?
...
LET ME TELL YOU ABOUT THE BLACK GHOST.
THEY'RE AN ORGANIZATION THAT MANUFACTURES WEAPONS... ALMOST EVERY GLOBAL CONFLICT IN THE LAST CENTURY HAS BEEN EITHER INSTIGATED OR EXPLOITED BY THEM FOR THEIR OWN PROFIT.
SEKAR, THEIR LEADER, BELIEVES CYBORG SOLDIERS WILL BE THE NEXT GENERATION OF WARFARE AND HAS BEEN DEVELOPING THE TECHNOLOGY IN ORDER TO SELL IT TO THE HIGHEST BIDDER. YOU NINE ARE THE PROTOTYPES.
NONE OF YOU WERE SPECIFICALLY SELECTED.
EVERYONE WAS RANDOMLY ABDUCTED BY AGENTS OF THE BLACK GHOST AND BROUGHT BACK FOR US TO... EXPERIMENT ON.
WE THOUGHT WE WOULD BE HELPING MANKIND... WORKING TOWARDS THE NEXT STAGE OF HUMAN EVOLUTION. I'M NOT PROUD OF THE WAY THIS HAPPENED.

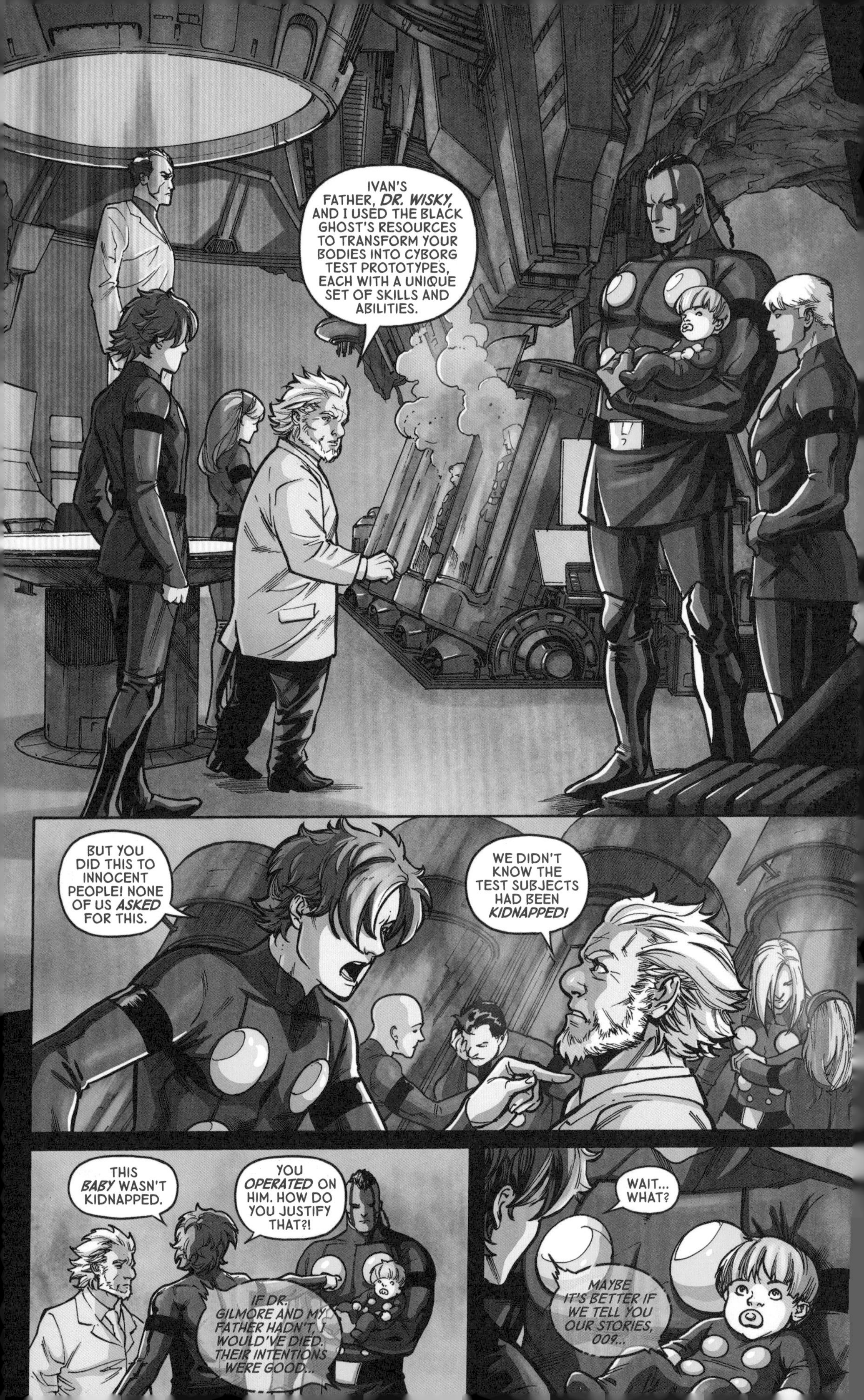
IVAN'S FATHER, DR. WISKY, AND I USED THE BLACK GHOST'S RESOURCES TO TRANSFORM YOUR BODIES INTO CYBORG TEST PROTOTYPES, EACH WITH A UNIQUE SET OF SKILLS AND ABILITIES.
BUT YOU DID THIS TO INNOCENT PEOPLE! NONE OF US ASKED FOR THIS.
WE DIDN'T KNOW THE TEST SUBJECTS HAD BEEN KIDNAPPED!
THIS BABY WASN'T KIDNAPPED.
YOU OPERATED ON HIM. HOW DO YOU JUSTIFY THAT?!
IF DR. GILMORE AND MY FATHER HADN'T, I WOULD'VE DIED. THEIR INTENTIONS WERE GOOD...
WAIT... WHAT?
MAYBE IT'S BETTER IF WE TELL YOU OUR STORIES, 009...

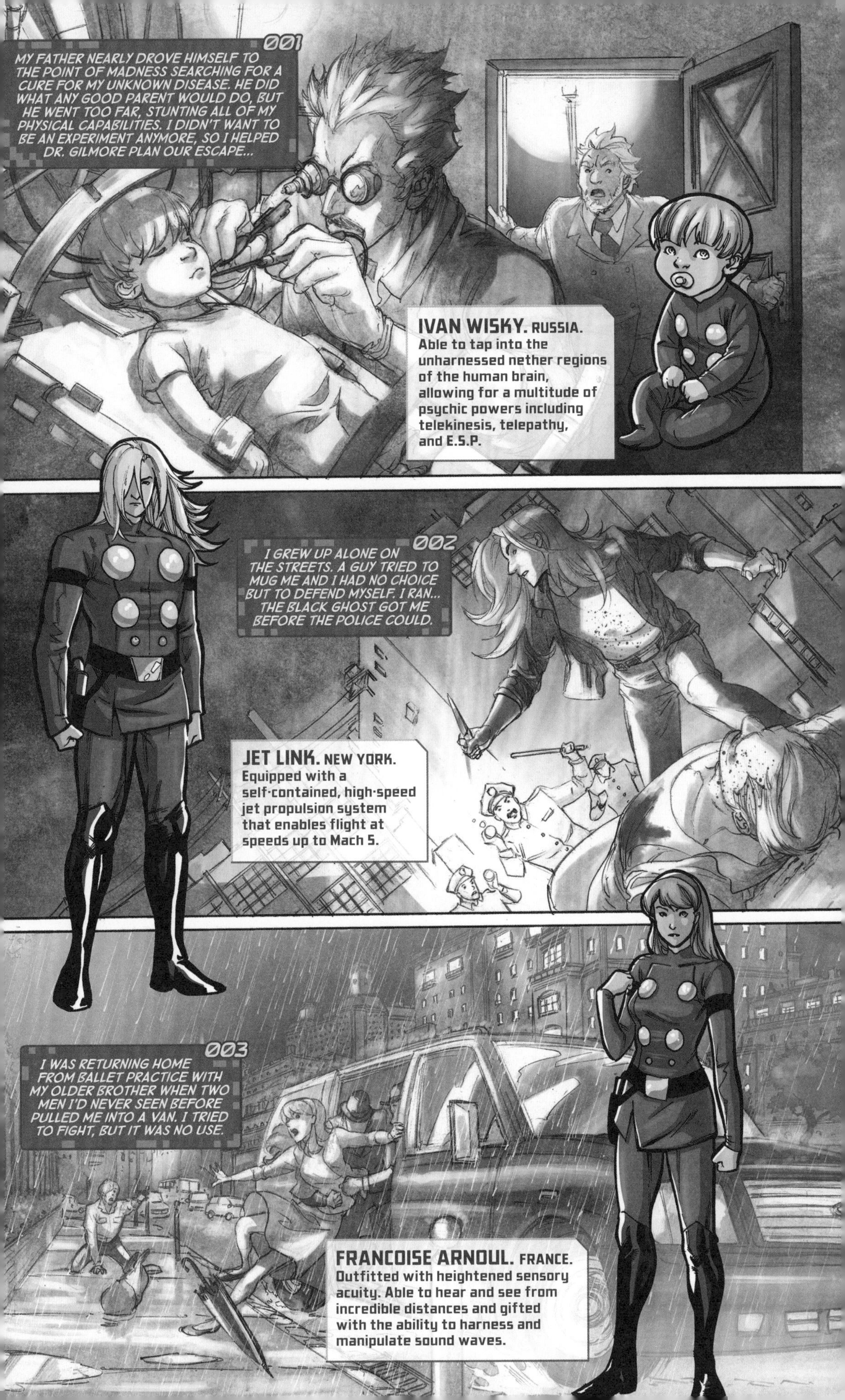
001
MY FATHER NEARLY DROVE HIMSELF TO THE POINT OF MADNESS SEARCHING FOR A CURE FOR MY UNKNOWN DISEASE. HE DID WHAT ANY GOOD PARENT WOULD DO, BUT HE WENT TOO FAR, STUNTING ALL OF MY PHYSICAL CAPABILITIES. I DIDN'T WANT TO BE AN EXPERIMENT ANYMORE, SO I HELPED DR. GILMORE PLAN OUR ESCAPE...
IVAN WISKY. RUSSIA.
Able to tap into the unharnessed nether regions of the human brain, allowing for a multitude of psychic powers including telekinesis, telepathy, and E.S.P.
002
I GREW UP ALONE ON THE STREETS. A GUY TRIED TO MUG ME AND I HAD NO CHOICE BUT TO DEFEND MYSELF. I RAN... THE BLACK GHOST GOT ME BEFORE THE POLICE COULD.
JET LINK. NEW YORK.
Equipped with a self-contained, high-speed jet propulsion system that enables flight at speeds up to Mach 5.
003
I WAS RETURNING HOME FROM BALLET PRACTICE WITH MY OLDER BROTHER WHEN TWO MEN I'D NEVER SEEN BEFORE PULLED ME INTO A VAN. I TRIED TO FIGHT, BUT IT WAS NO USE.
FRANCOISE ARNOUL. FRANCE.
Outfitted with heightened sensory acuity. Able to hear and see from incredible distances and gifted with the ability to harness and manipulate sound waves.

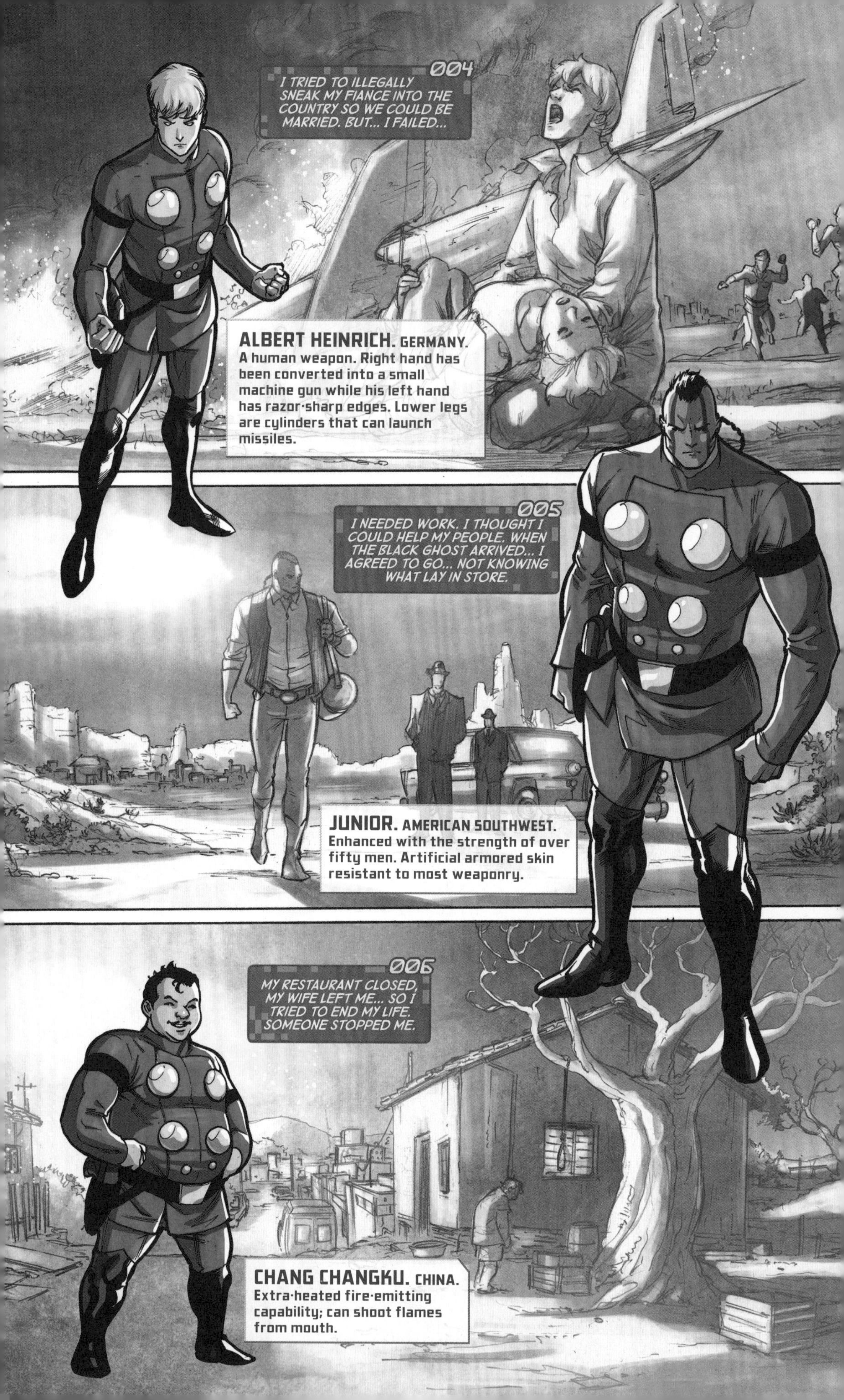
004
I TRIED TO ILLEGALLY SNEAK MY FIANCE INTO THE COUNTRY SO WE COULD BE MARRIED. BUT... I FAILED...
ALBERT HEINRICH. GERMANY.
A human weapon. Right hand has been converted into a small machine gun while his left hand has razor-sharp edges. Lower legs are cylinders that can launch missiles.
005
I NEEDED WORK. I THOUGHT I COULD HELP MY PEOPLE. WHEN THE BLACK GHOST ARRIVED... I AGREED TO GO... NOT KNOWING WHAT LAY IN STORE.
JUNIOR. AMERICAN SOUTHWEST.
Enhanced with the strength of over fifty men. Artificial armored skin resistant to most weaponry.
006
MY RESTAURANT CLOSED, MY WIFE LEFT ME... SO I TRIED TO END MY LIFE. SOMEONE STOPPED ME.
CHANG CHANGKU. CHINA.
Extra-heated fire-emitting capability; can shoot flames from mouth.

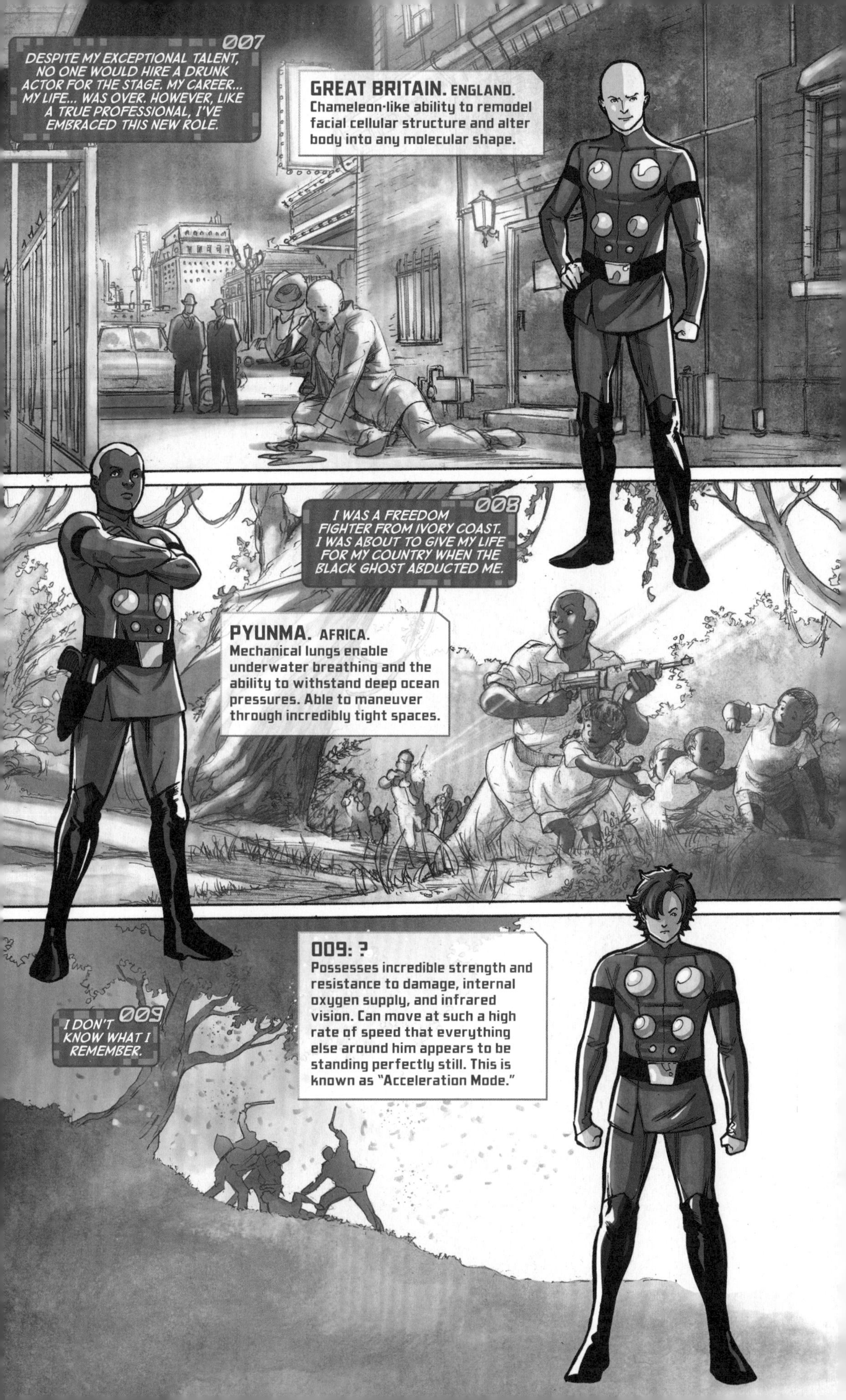
007
DESPITE MY EXCEPTIONAL TALENT, NO ONE WOULD HIRE A DRUNK ACTOR FOR THE STAGE. MY CAREER... MY LIFE... WAS OVER. HOWEVER, LIKE A TRUE PROFESSIONAL, I'VE EMBRACED THIS NEW ROLE.
GREAT BRITAIN. ENGLAND.
Chameleon-like ability to remodel facial cellular structure and alter body into any molecular shape.
008
I WAS A FREEDOM FIGHTER FROM IVORY COAST. I WAS ABOUT TO GIVE MY LIFE FOR MY COUNTRY WHEN THE BLACK GHOST ABDUCTED ME.
PYUNMA. AFRICA.
Mechanical lungs enable underwater breathing and the ability to withstand deep ocean pressures. Able to maneuver through incredibly tight spaces.
009
I DON'T KNOW WHAT I REMEMBER.
009: ?
Possesses incredible strength and resistance to damage, internal oxygen supply, and infrared vision. Can move at such a high rate of speed that everything else around him appears to be standing perfectly still. This is known as "Acceleration Mode."

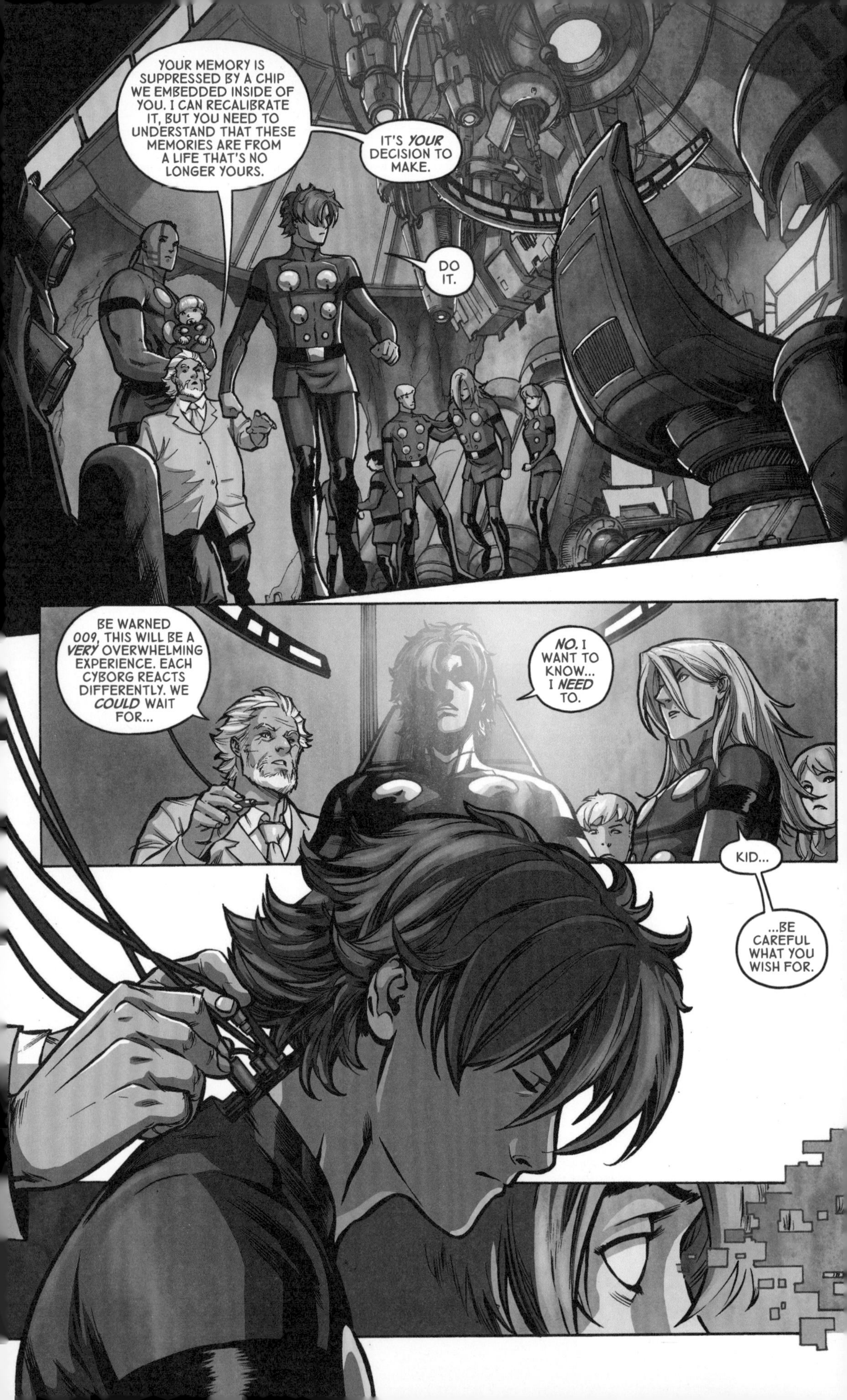
YOUR MEMORY IS SUPPRESSED BY A CHIP WE EMBEDDED INSIDE OF YOU. I CAN RECALIBRATE IT, BUT YOU NEED TO UNDERSTAND THAT THESE MEMORIES ARE FROM A LIFE THAT'S NO LONGER YOURS.
IT'S *YOUR* DECISION TO MAKE.
DO IT.
BE WARNED 009, THIS WILL BE A *VERY* OVERWHELMING EXPERIENCE. EACH CYBORG REACTS DIFFERENTLY. WE *COULD* WAIT FOR...
NO. I WANT TO KNOW... I *NEED* TO.
KID...
...BE CAREFUL WHAT YOU WISH FOR.

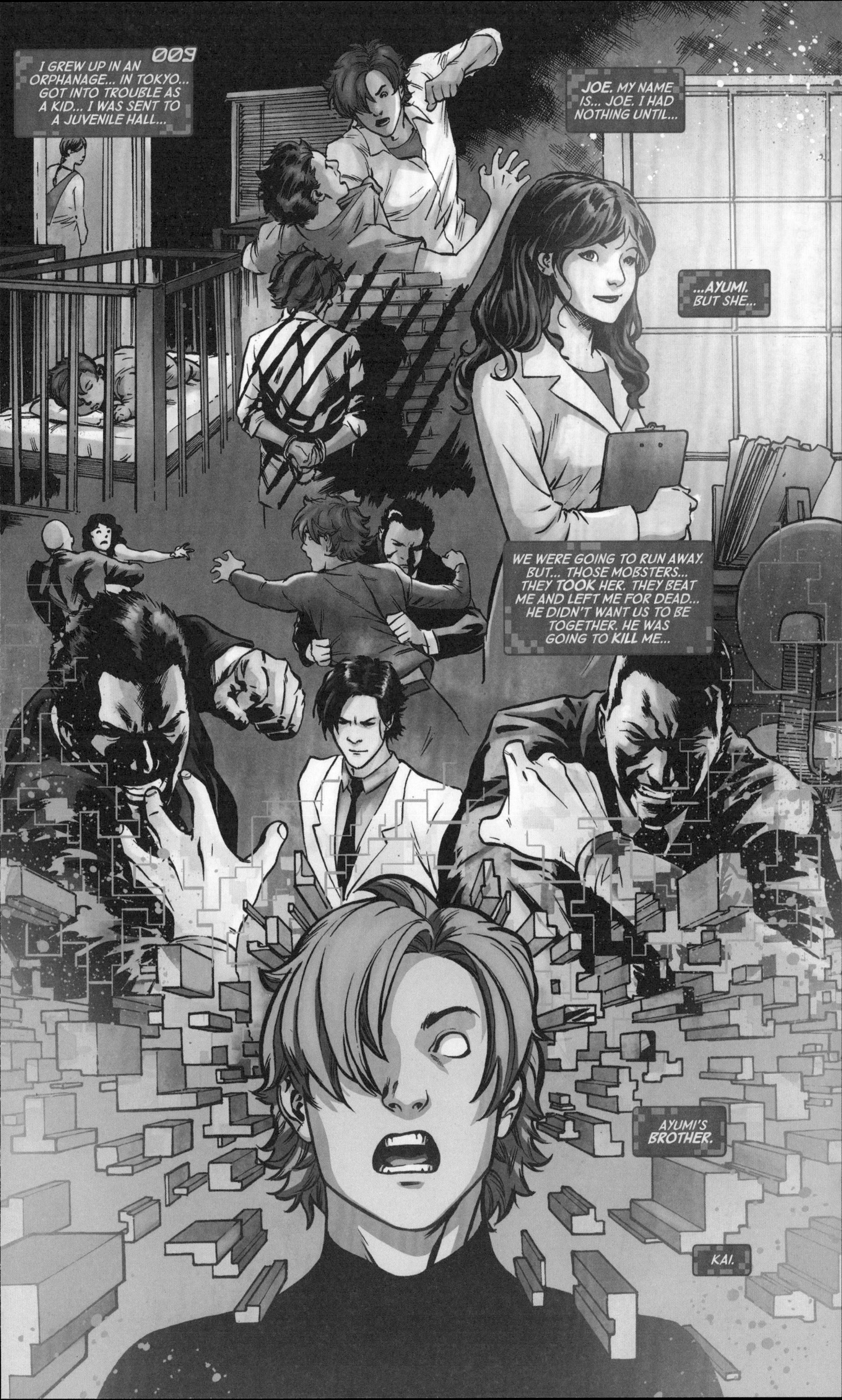

009
I GREW UP IN AN ORPHANAGE... IN TOKYO... GOT INTO TROUBLE AS A KID... I WAS SENT TO A JUVENILE HALL...
JOE. MY NAME IS... JOE. I HAD NOTHING UNTIL...
...AYUMI. BUT SHE...
WE WERE GOING TO RUN AWAY. BUT... THOSE MOBSTERS... THEY TOOK HER. THEY BEAT ME AND LEFT ME FOR DEAD... HE DIDN'T WANT US TO BE TOGETHER. HE WAS GOING TO KILL ME...
AYUMI'S BROTHER.
KAI.

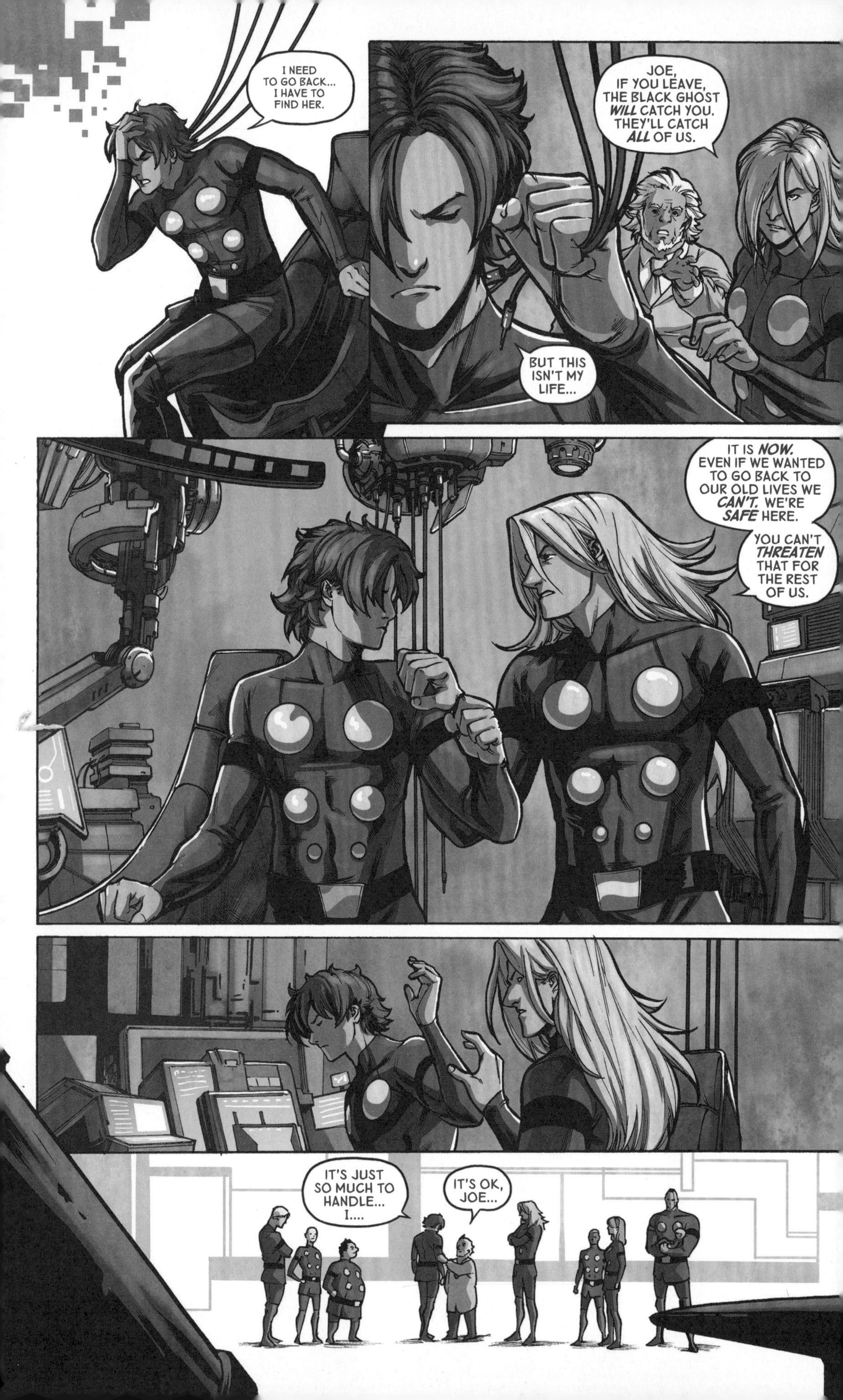
I NEED TO GO BACK... I HAVE TO FIND HER.
JOE, IF YOU LEAVE, THE BLACK GHOST WILL CATCH YOU. THEY'LL CATCH ALL OF US.
BUT THIS ISN'T MY LIFE...
IT IS NOW. EVEN IF WE WANTED TO GO BACK TO OUR OLD LIVES WE CAN'T. WE'RE SAFE HERE.
YOU CAN'T THREATEN THAT FOR THE REST OF US.
IT'S JUST SO MUCH TO HANDLE... I....
IT'S OK, JOE...

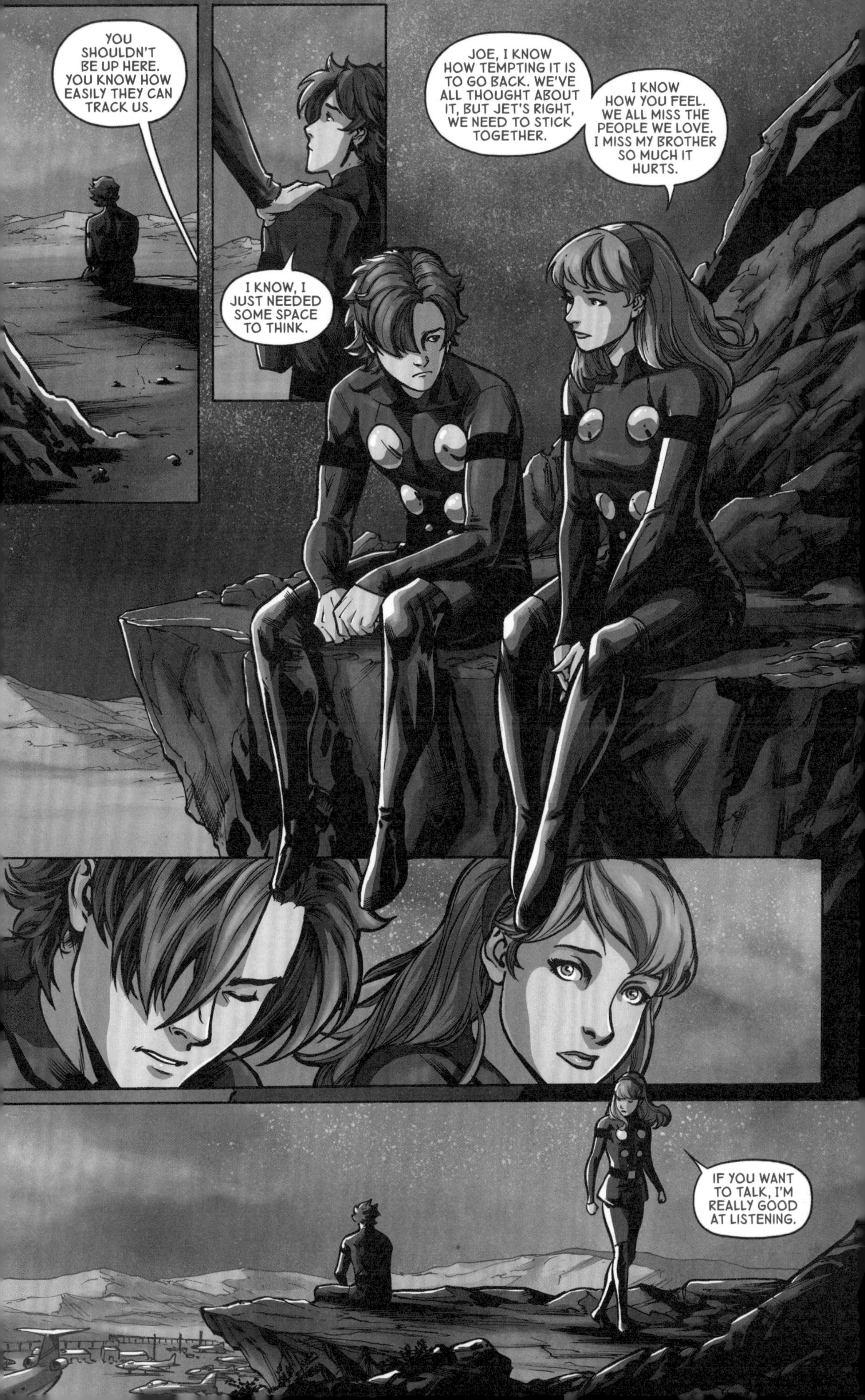
YOU SHOULDN'T BE UP HERE. YOU KNOW HOW EASILY THEY CAN TRACK US.
I KNOW, I JUST NEEDED SOME SPACE TO THINK.
JOE, I KNOW HOW TEMPTING IT IS TO GO BACK. WE'VE ALL THOUGHT ABOUT IT, BUT JET'S RIGHT, WE NEED TO STICK TOGETHER.
I KNOW HOW YOU FEEL. WE ALL MISS THE PEOPLE WE LOVE. I MISS MY BROTHER SO MUCH IT HURTS.
IF YOU WANT TO TALK, I'M REALLY GOOD AT LISTENING.

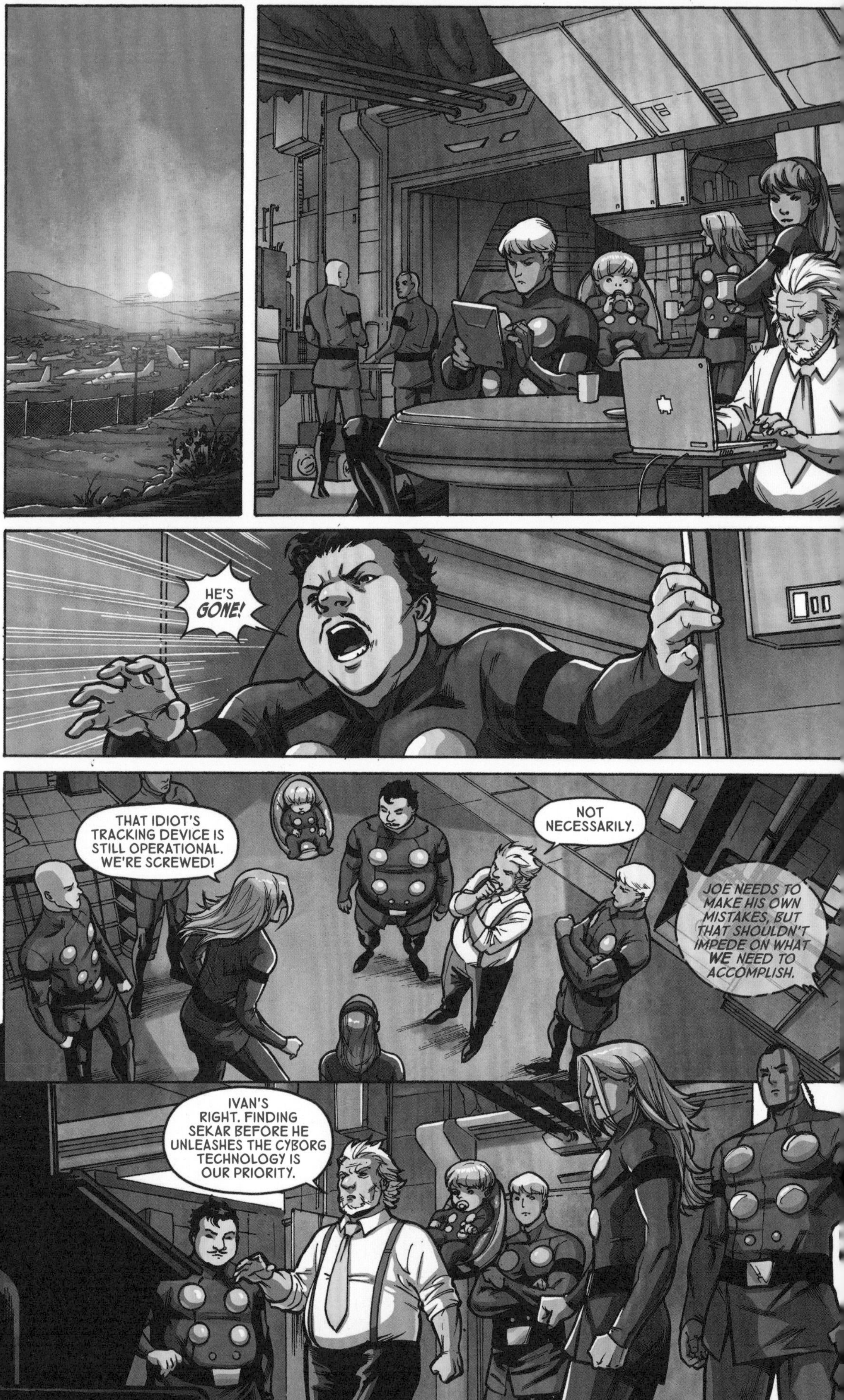
HE'S GONE!
THAT IDIOT'S TRACKING DEVICE IS STILL OPERATIONAL. WE'RE SCREWED!
NOT NECESSARILY.
JOE NEEDS TO MAKE HIS OWN MISTAKES, BUT THAT SHOULDN'T IMPEDE ON WHAT WE NEED TO ACCOMPLISH.
IVAN'S RIGHT. FINDING SEKAR BEFORE HE UNLEASHES THE CYBORG TECHNOLOGY IS OUR PRIORITY.

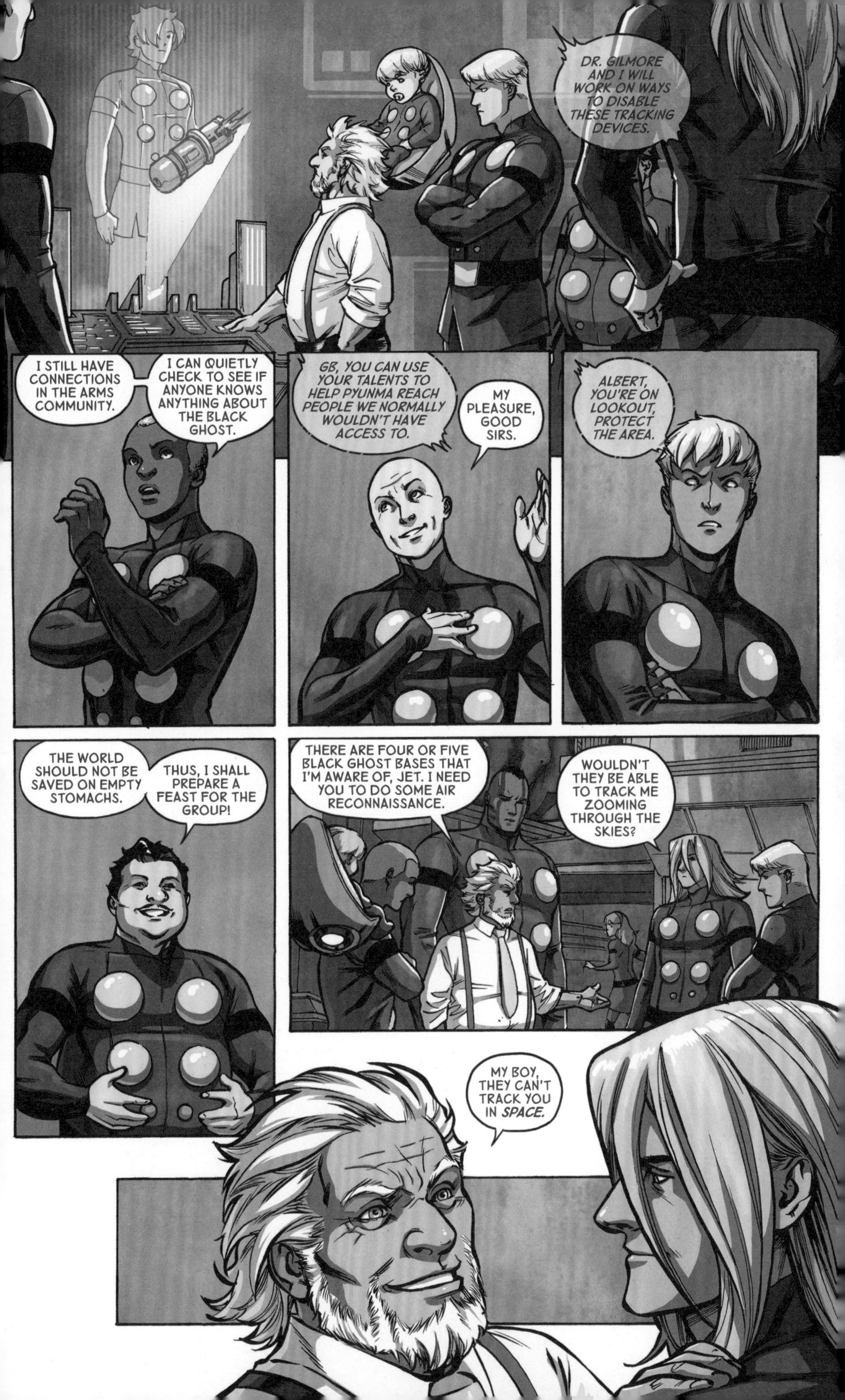
DR. GILMORE AND I WILL WORK ON WAYS TO DISABLE THESE TRACKING DEVICES.
I STILL HAVE CONNECTIONS IN THE ARMS COMMUNITY.
I CAN QUIETLY CHECK TO SEE IF ANYONE KNOWS ANYTHING ABOUT THE BLACK GHOST.
GB, YOU CAN USE YOUR TALENTS TO HELP PYUNMA REACH PEOPLE WE NORMALLY WOULDN'T HAVE ACCESS TO.
MY PLEASURE, GOOD SIRS.
ALBERT, YOU'RE ON LOOKOUT, PROTECT THE AREA.
THE WORLD SHOULD NOT BE SAVED ON EMPTY STOMACHS.
THUS, I SHALL PREPARE A FEAST FOR THE GROUP!
THERE ARE FOUR OR FIVE BLACK GHOST BASES THAT I'M AWARE OF, JET. I NEED YOU TO DO SOME AIR RECONNAISSANCE.
WOULDN'T THEY BE ABLE TO TRACK ME ZOOMING THROUGH THE SKIES?
MY BOY, THEY CAN'T TRACK YOU IN *SPACE.*

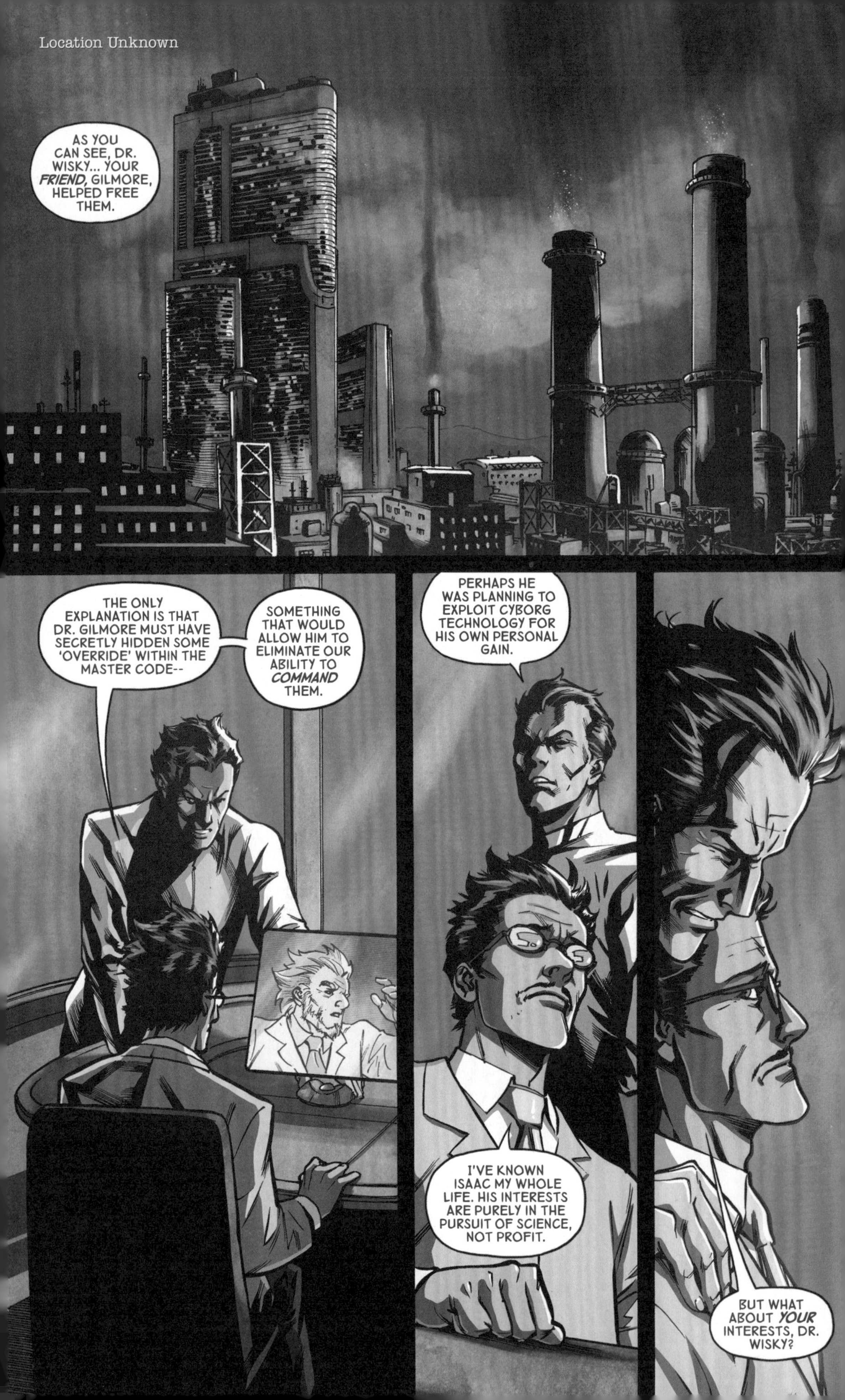
Location Unknown
AS YOU CAN SEE, DR. WISKY... YOUR FRIEND, GILMORE, HELPED FREE THEM.
THE ONLY EXPLANATION IS THAT DR. GILMORE MUST HAVE SECRETLY HIDDEN SOME 'OVERRIDE' WITHIN THE MASTER CODE--
SOMETHING THAT WOULD ALLOW HIM TO ELIMINATE OUR ABILITY TO COMMAND THEM.
PERHAPS HE WAS PLANNING TO EXPLOIT CYBORG TECHNOLOGY FOR HIS OWN PERSONAL GAIN.
I'VE KNOWN ISAAC MY WHOLE LIFE. HIS INTERESTS ARE PURELY IN THE PURSUIT OF SCIENCE, NOT PROFIT.
BUT WHAT ABOUT YOUR INTERESTS, DR. WISKY?

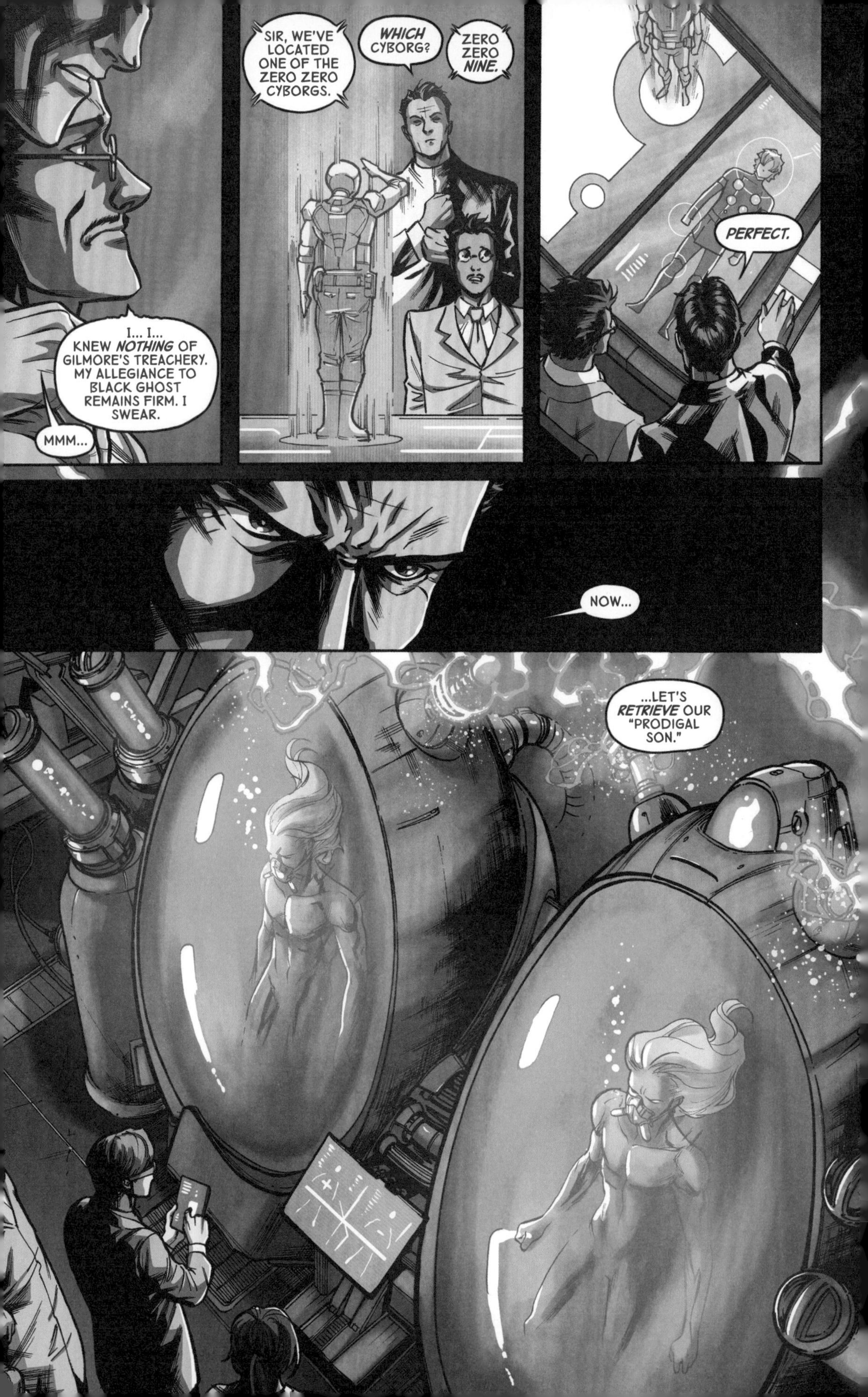
I... I... KNEW *NOTHING* OF GILMORE'S TREACHERY. MY ALLEGIANCE TO BLACK GHOST REMAINS FIRM. I SWEAR.
MMM...
SIR, WE'VE LOCATED ONE OF THE ZERO ZERO CYBORGS.
WHICH CYBORG?
ZERO ZERO *NINE.*
PERFECT.
NOW...
...LET'S *RETRIEVE* OUR "PRODIGAL SON."

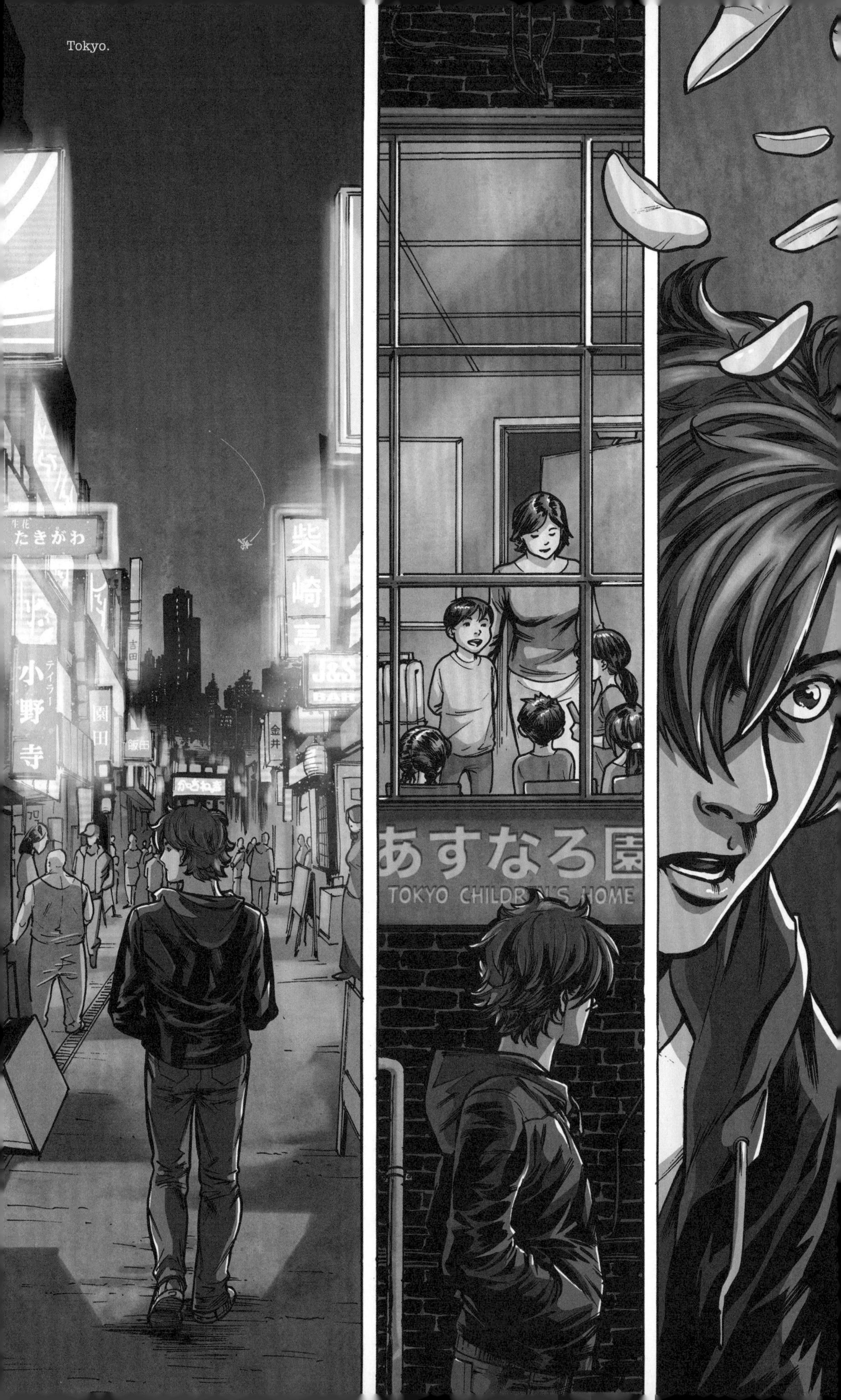
Tokyo.
たきがわ
柴崎亭
テイラー
小野寺
あすなろ園

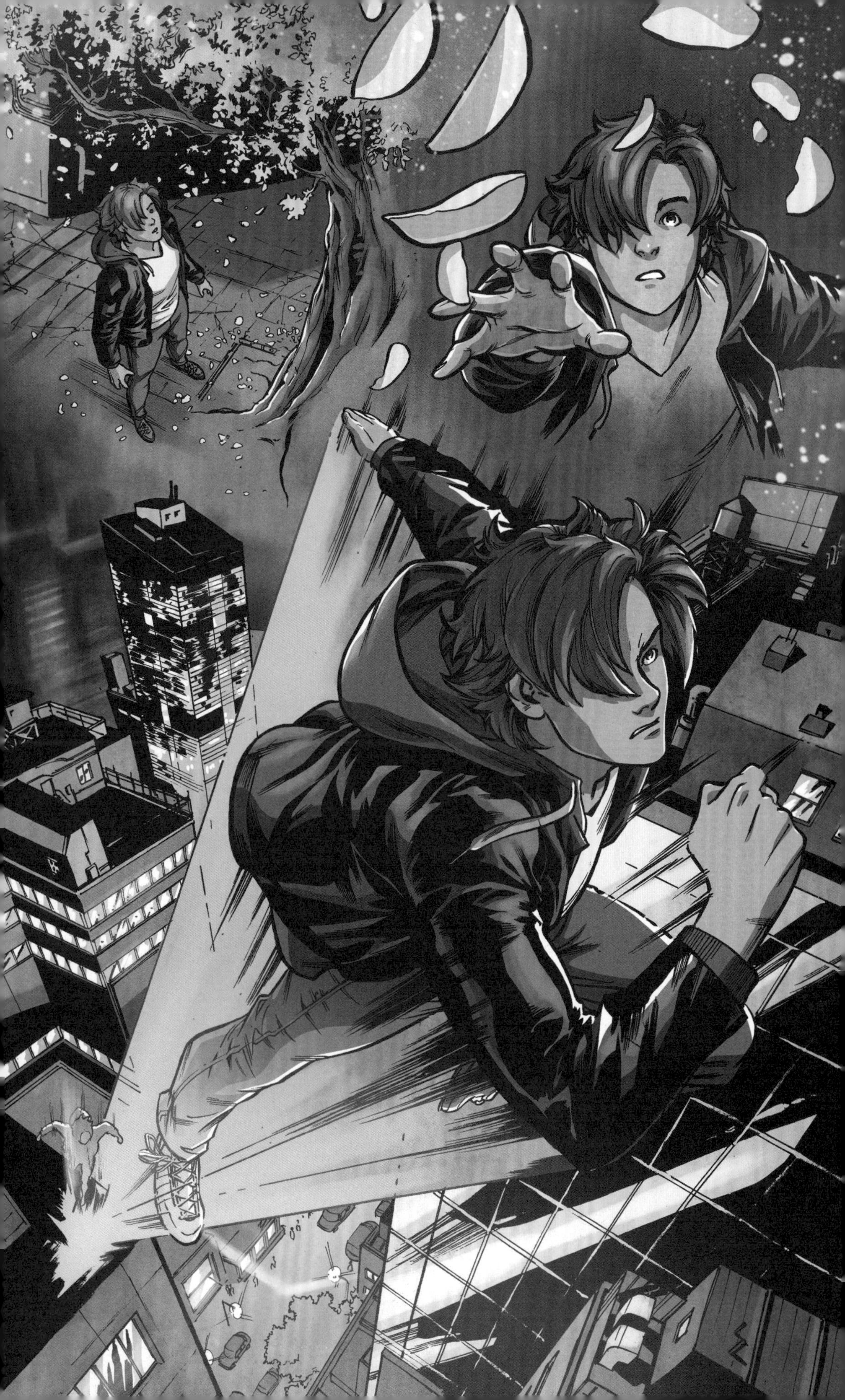

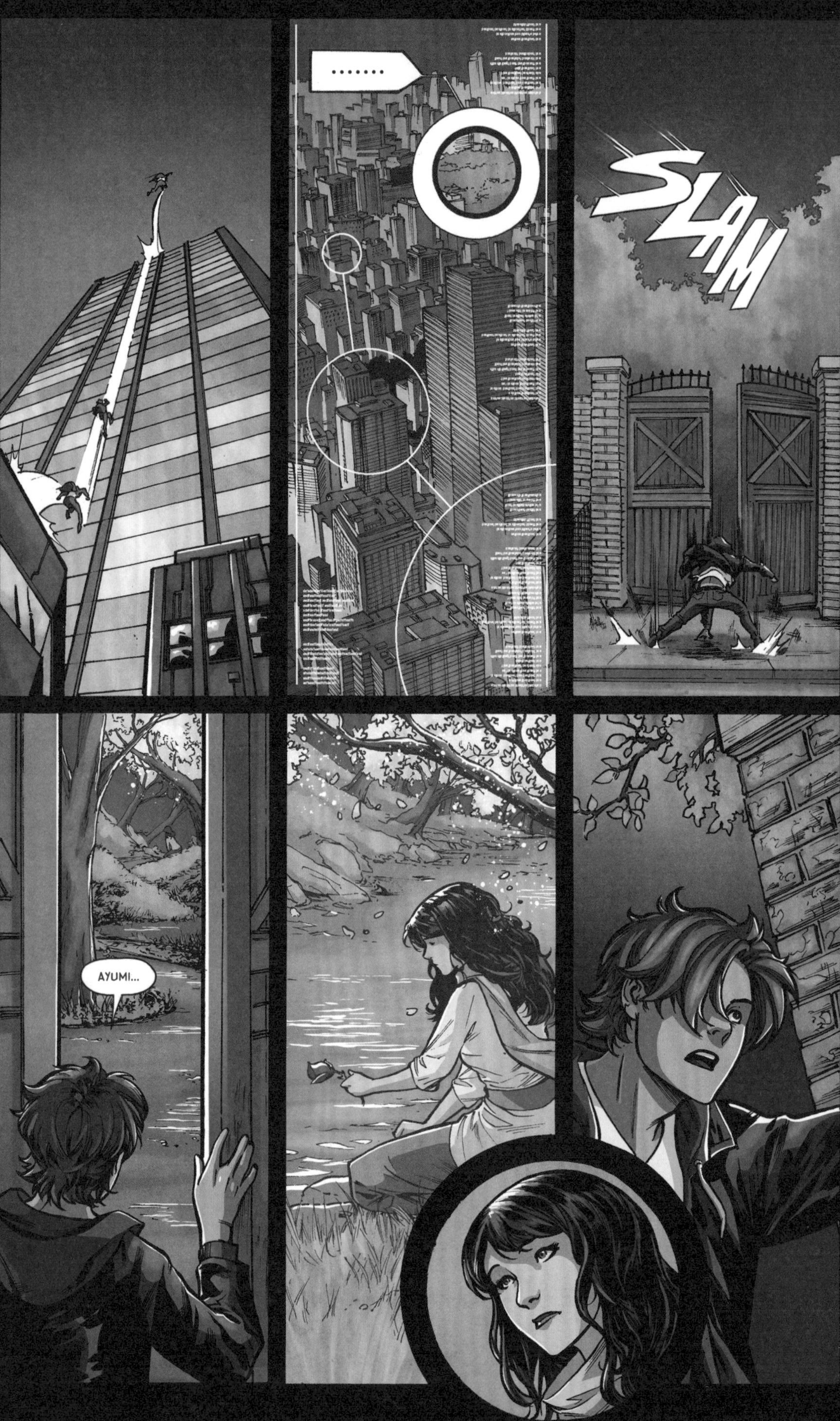
....
SLAM
AYUMI...

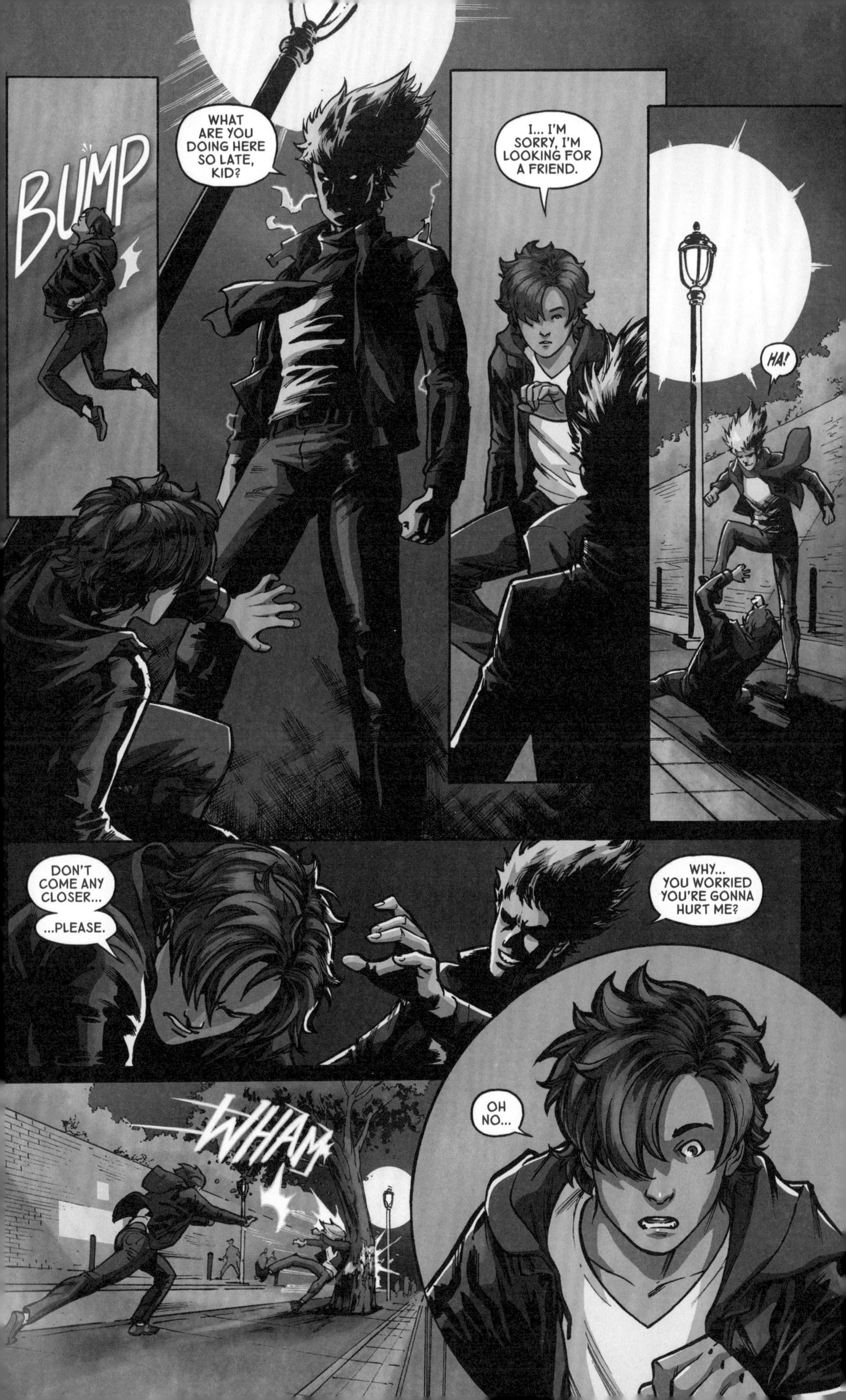
BUMP
WHAT ARE YOU DOING HERE SO LATE, KID?
I... I'M SORRY, I'M LOOKING FOR A FRIEND.
HA!
DON'T COME ANY CLOSER...
...PLEASE.
WHY... YOU WORRIED YOU'RE GONNA HURT ME?
WHAM
OH NO...

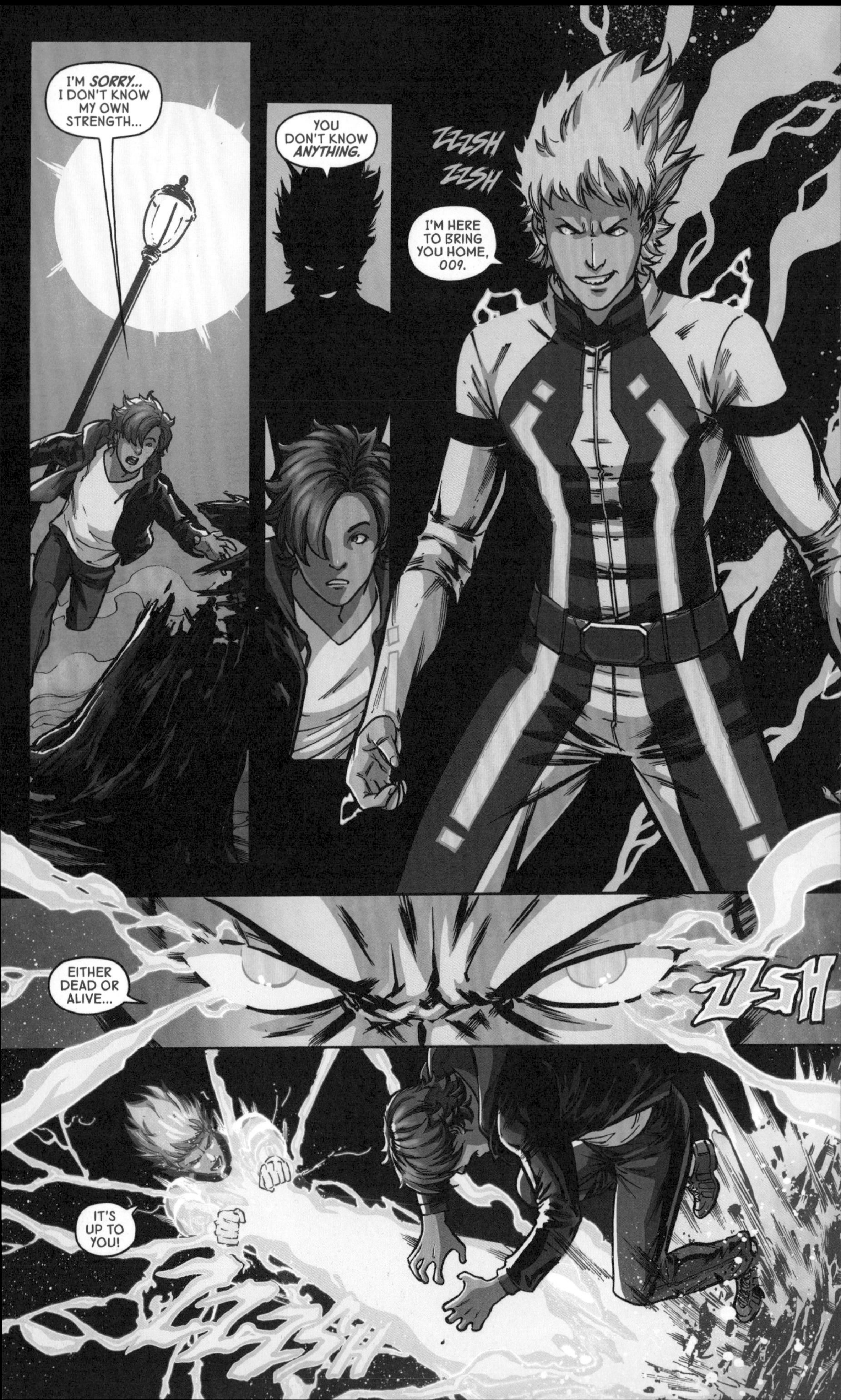
I'M *SORRY...* I DON'T KNOW MY OWN STRENGTH...
YOU DON'T KNOW *ANYTHING.*
ZZZSH
ZZSH
I'M HERE TO BRING YOU HOME, 009.
EITHER DEAD OR ALIVE...
ZZSH
IT'S UP TO YOU!
ZZZSH

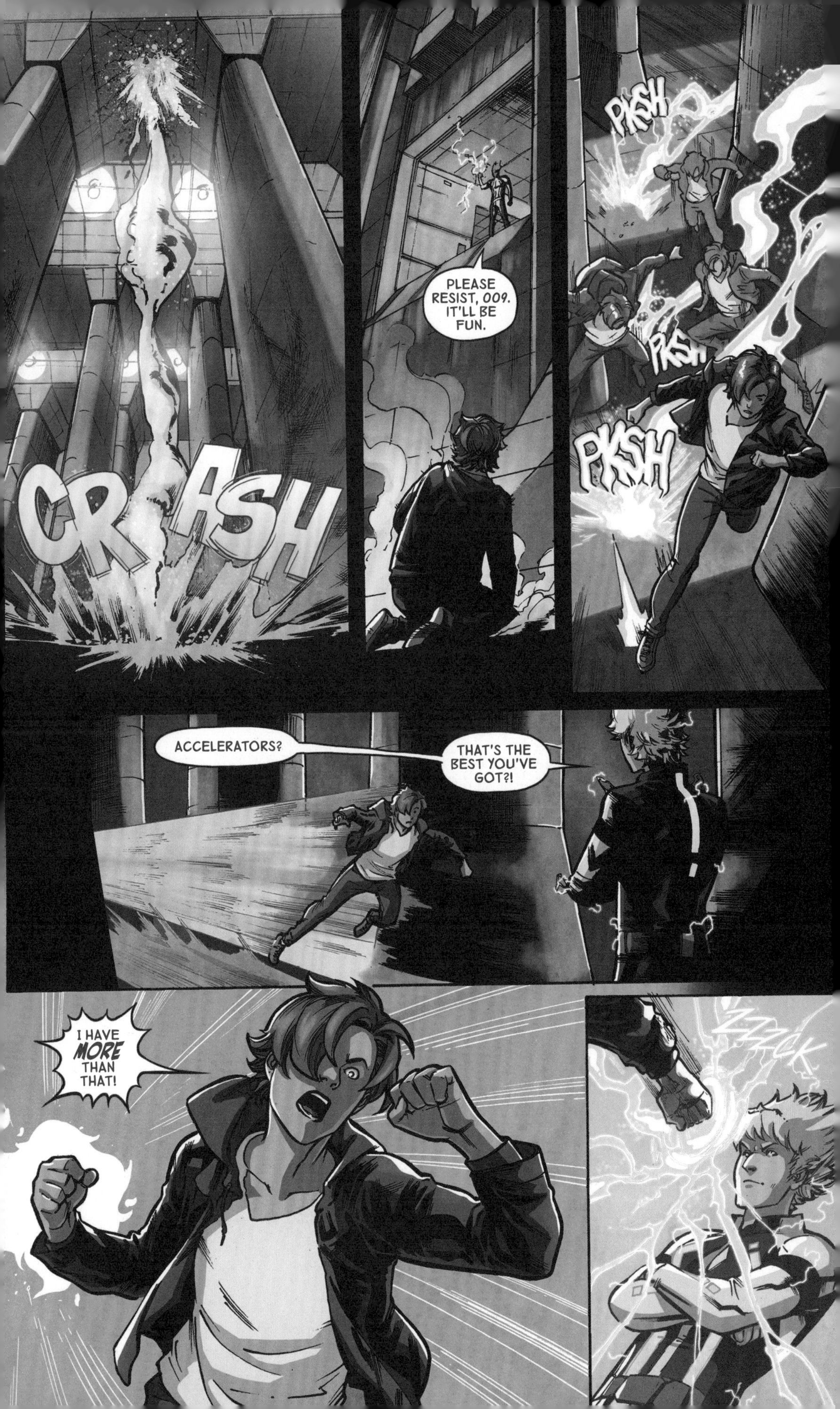
CRASH
PLEASE RESIST, 009. IT'LL BE FUN.
PKSH
PKSH
PKSH
ACCELERATORS?
THAT'S THE BEST YOU'VE GOT?!
I HAVE *MORE* THAN THAT!

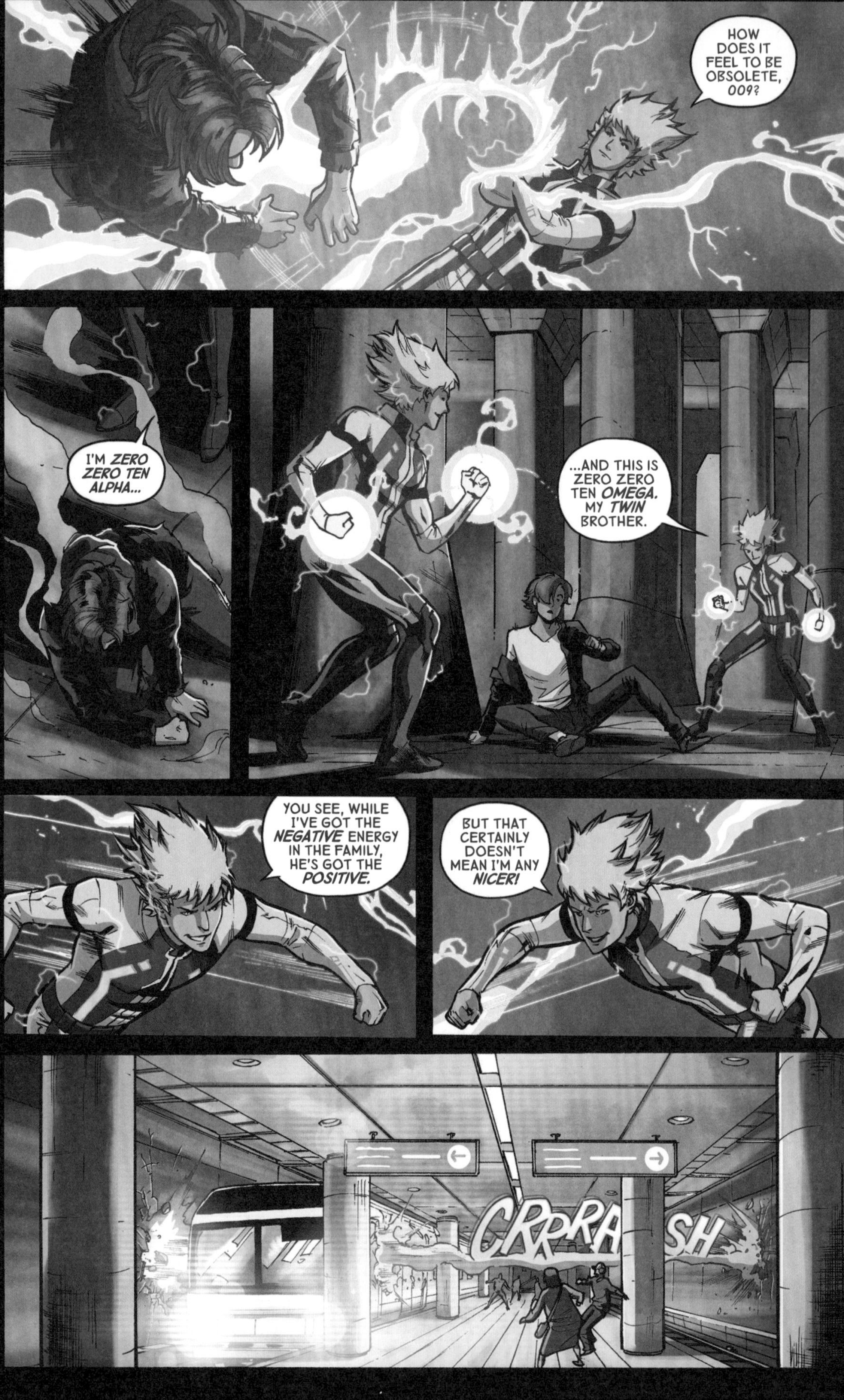
HOW DOES IT FEEL TO BE OBSOLETE, 009?
I'M ZERO ZERO TEN ALPHA...
...AND THIS IS ZERO ZERO TEN OMEGA. MY TWIN BROTHER.
YOU SEE, WHILE I'VE GOT THE NEGATIVE ENERGY IN THE FAMILY, HE'S GOT THE POSITIVE.
BUT THAT CERTAINLY DOESN'T MEAN I'M ANY NICER!
CRRRAASH

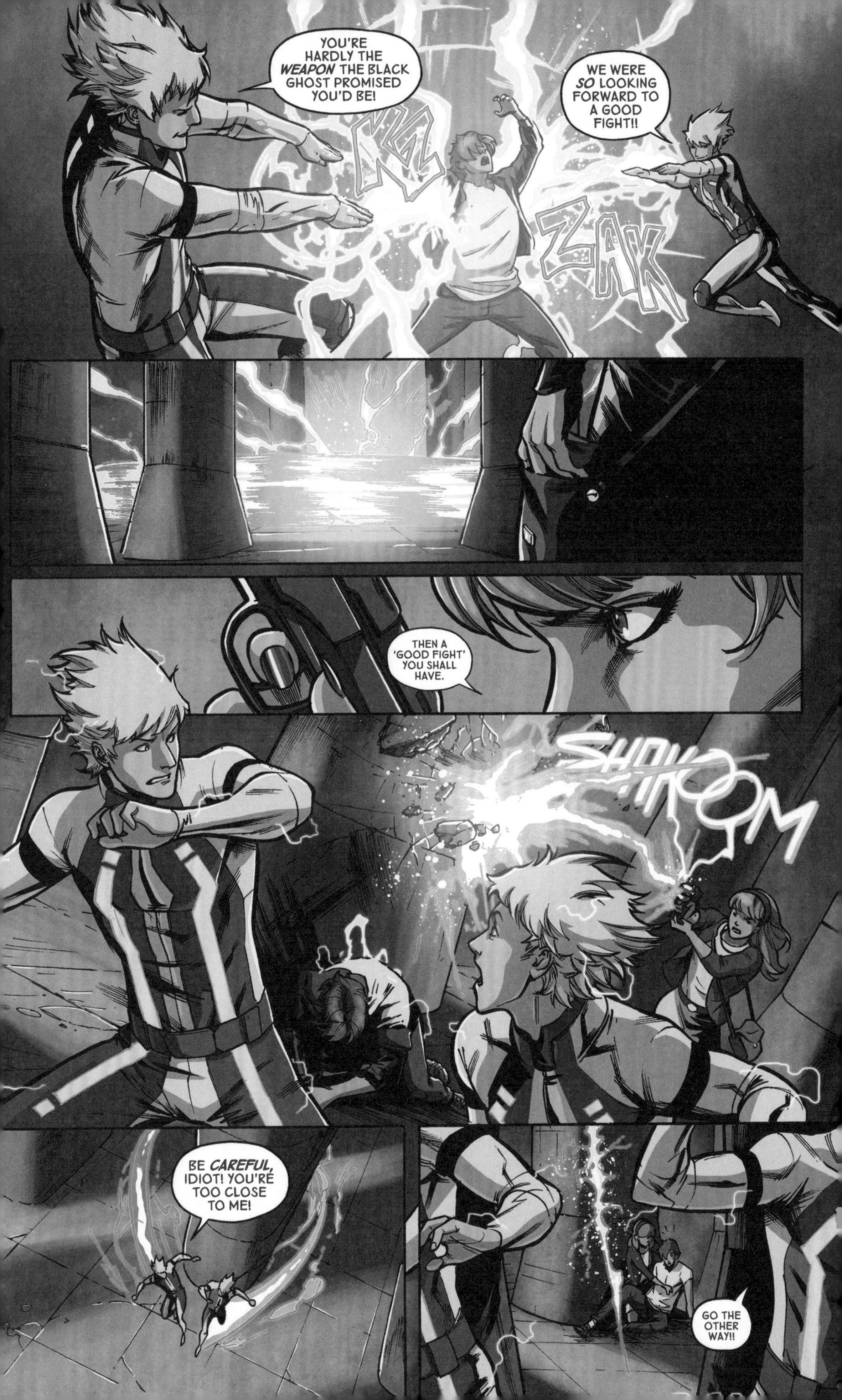
YOU'RE HARDLY THE *WEAPON* THE BLACK GHOST PROMISED YOU'D BE!
WE WERE *SO* LOOKING FORWARD TO A GOOD FIGHT!!
ZAK
THEN A 'GOOD FIGHT' YOU SHALL HAVE.
SHAKOOM
BE *CAREFUL*, IDIOT! YOU'RE TOO CLOSE TO ME!
GO THE OTHER WAY!!

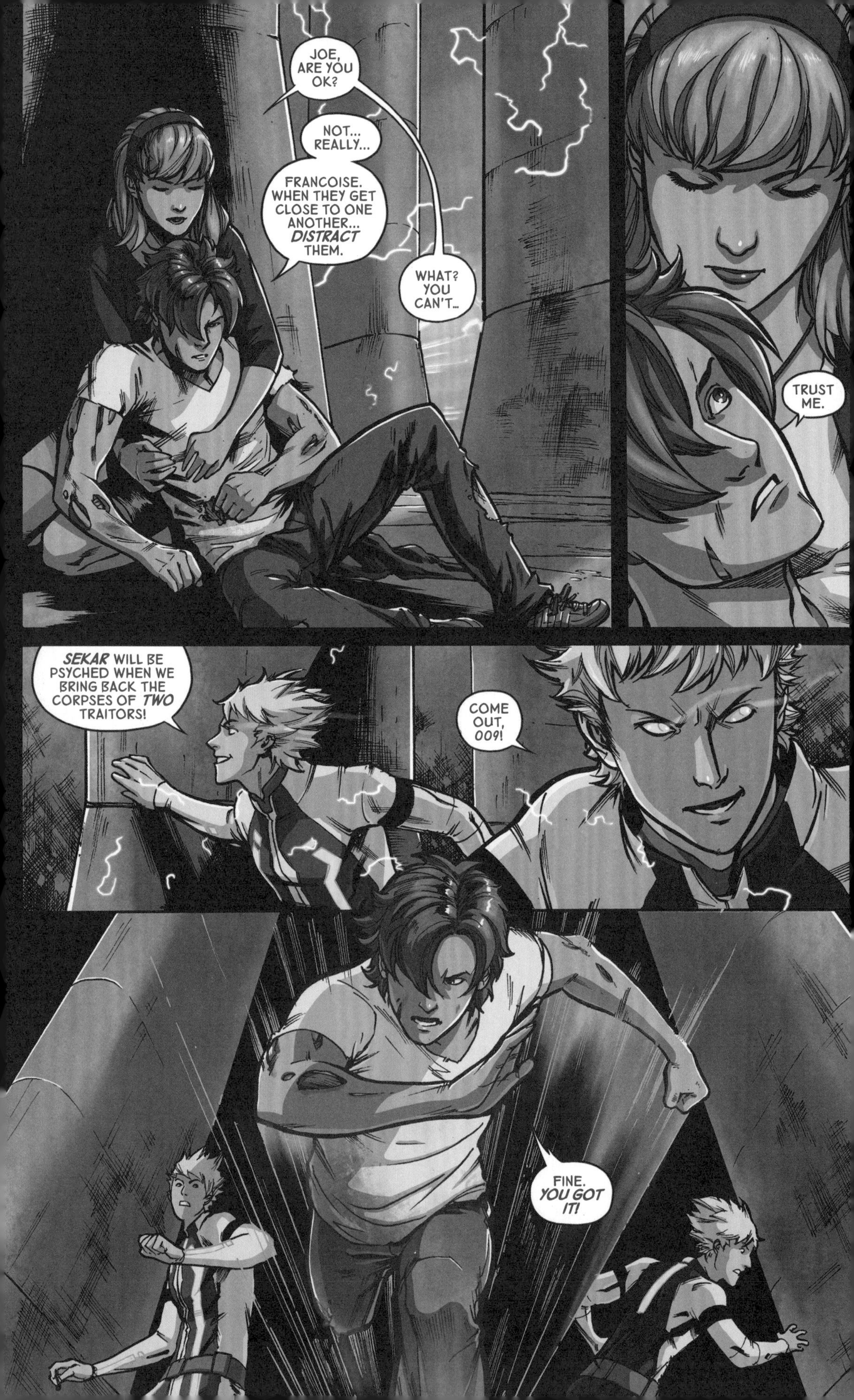
JOE, ARE YOU OK?
NOT... REALLY...
FRANCOISE. WHEN THEY GET CLOSE TO ONE ANOTHER... *DISTRACT* THEM.
WHAT? YOU CAN'T...
TRUST ME.
SEKAR WILL BE PSYCHED WHEN WE BRING BACK THE CORPSES OF *TWO* TRAITORS!
COME OUT, 009!
FINE. *YOU GOT IT!*

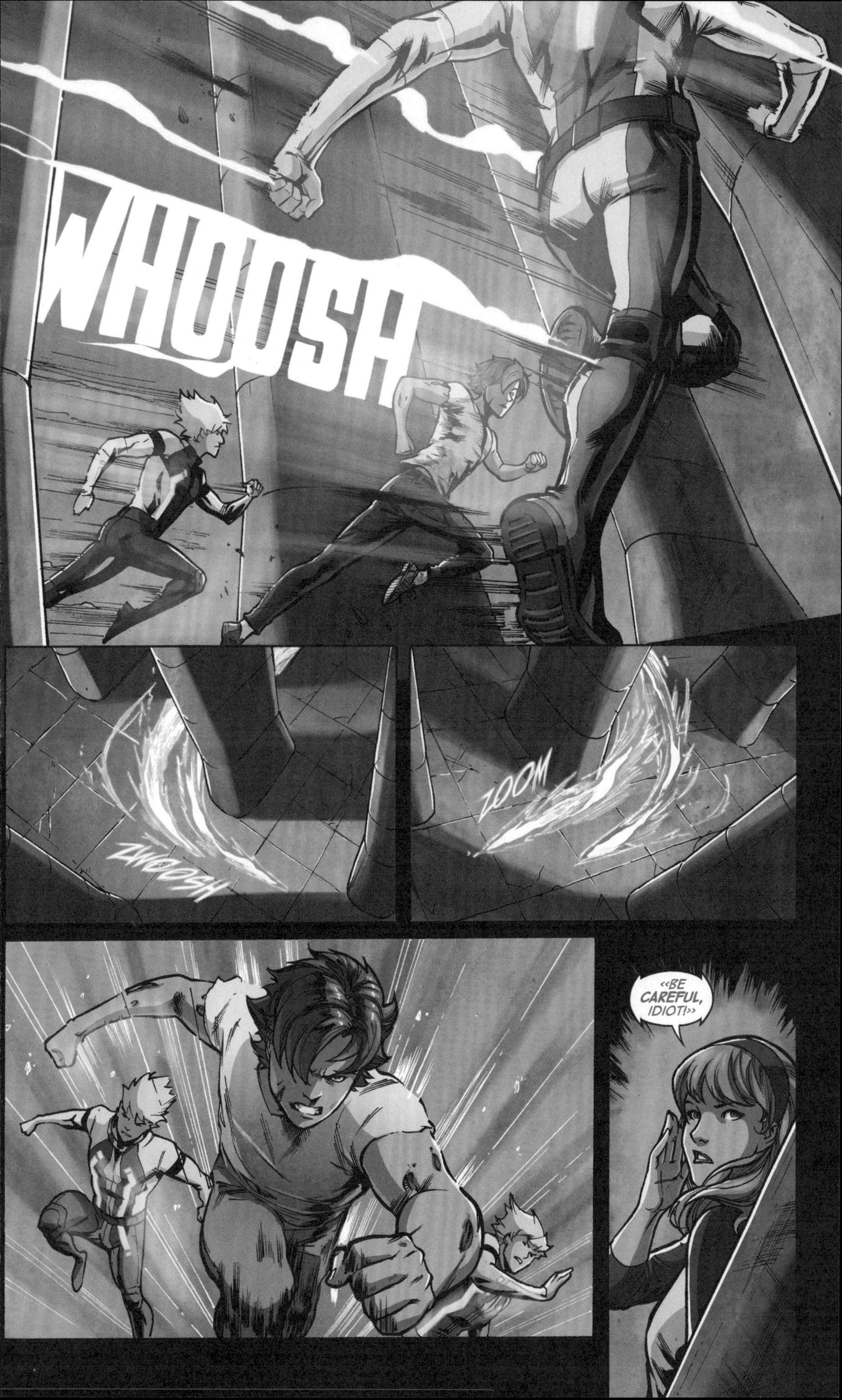
WHOOSH
ZWOOSH
ZOOM
<<BE CAREFUL, IDIOT!>>

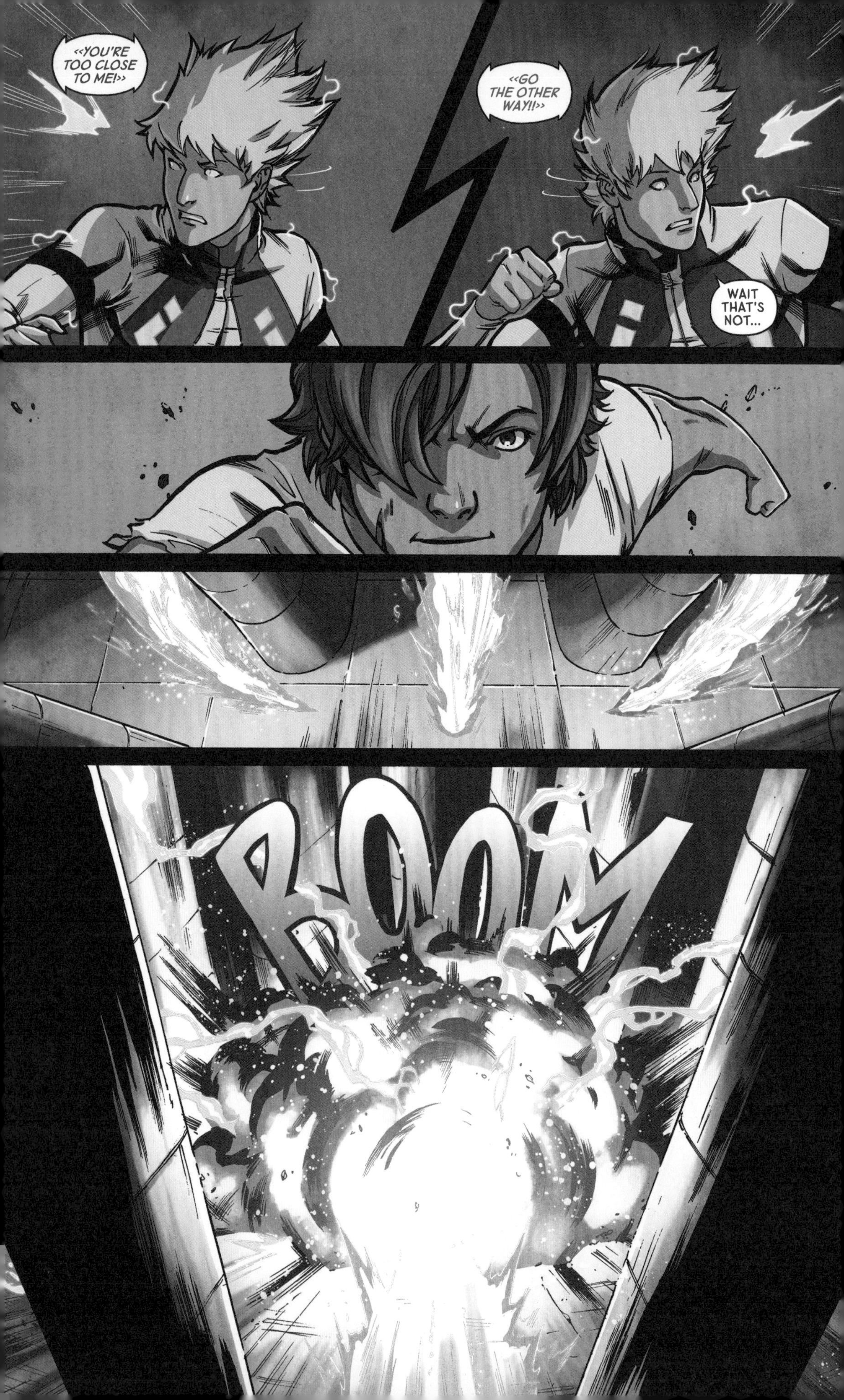
<<YOU'RE TOO CLOSE TO ME!>>
<<GO THE OTHER WAY!!>>
WAIT THAT'S NOT...
BOOM

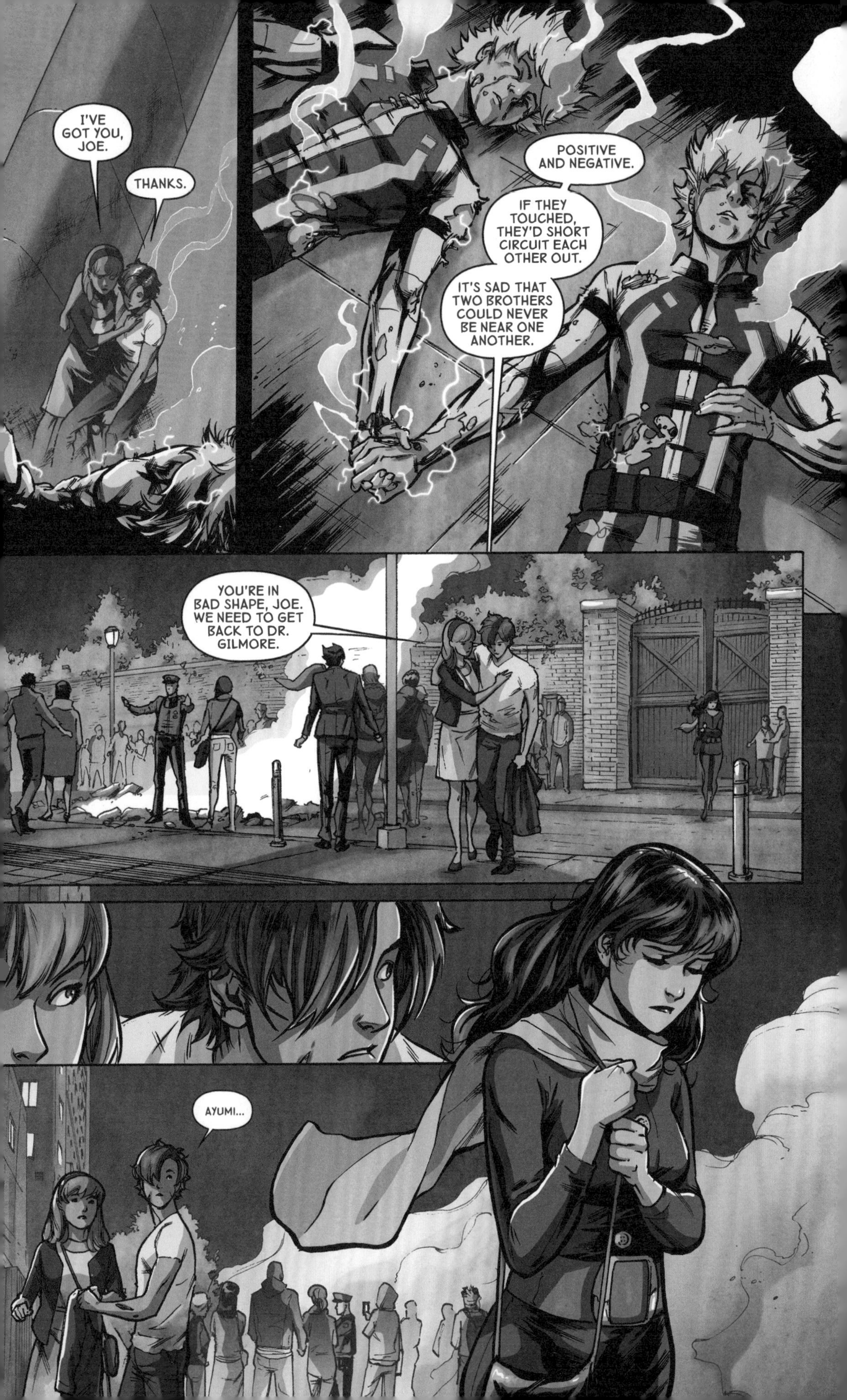
I'VE GOT YOU, JOE.
THANKS.
POSITIVE AND NEGATIVE.
IF THEY TOUCHED, THEY'D SHORT CIRCUIT EACH OTHER OUT.
IT'S SAD THAT TWO BROTHERS COULD NEVER BE NEAR ONE ANOTHER.
YOU'RE IN BAD SHAPE, JOE. WE NEED TO GET BACK TO DR. GILMORE.
AYUMI...

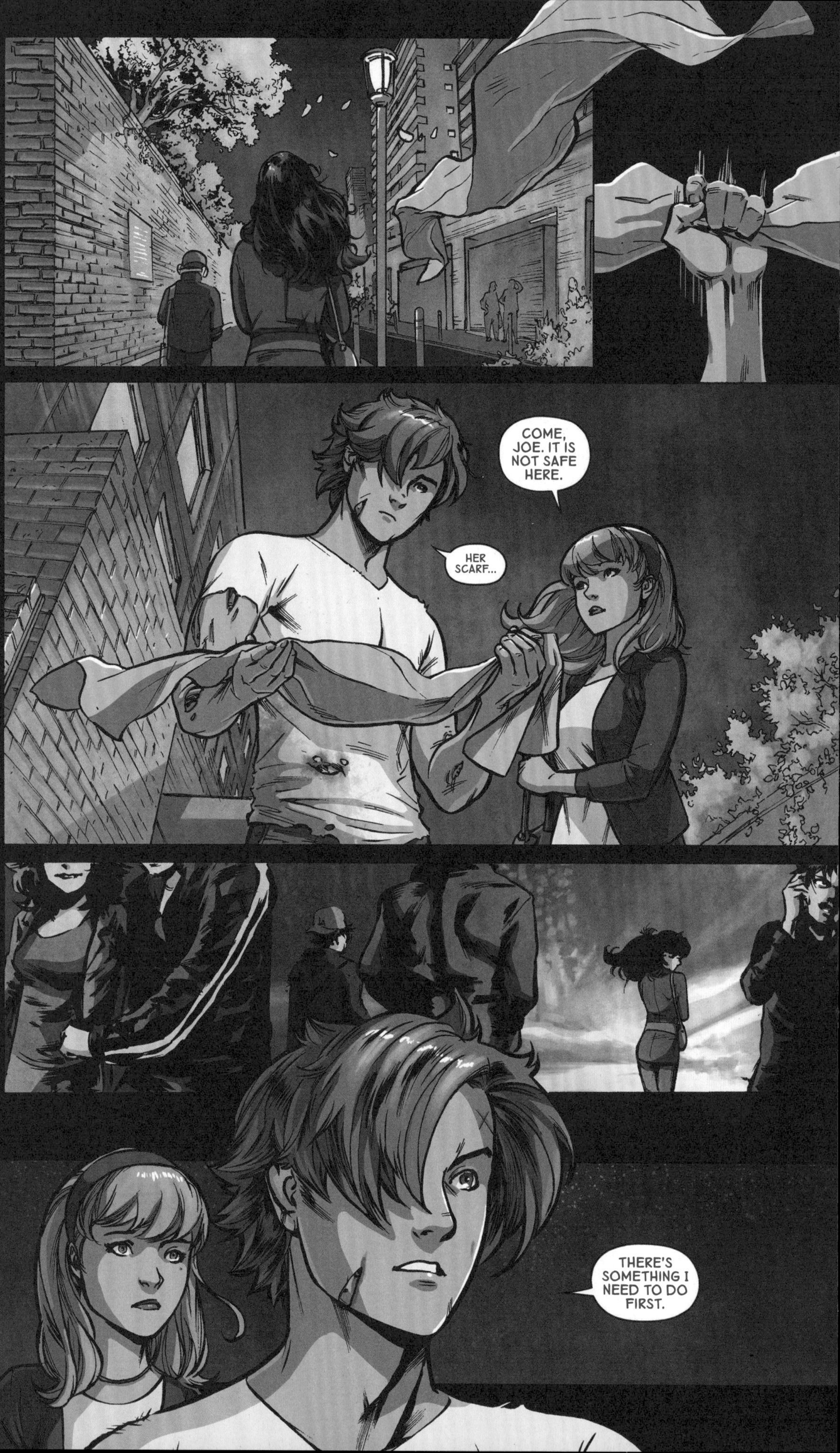
COME, JOE. IT IS NOT SAFE HERE.
HER SCARF...
THERE'S SOMETHING I NEED TO DO FIRST.

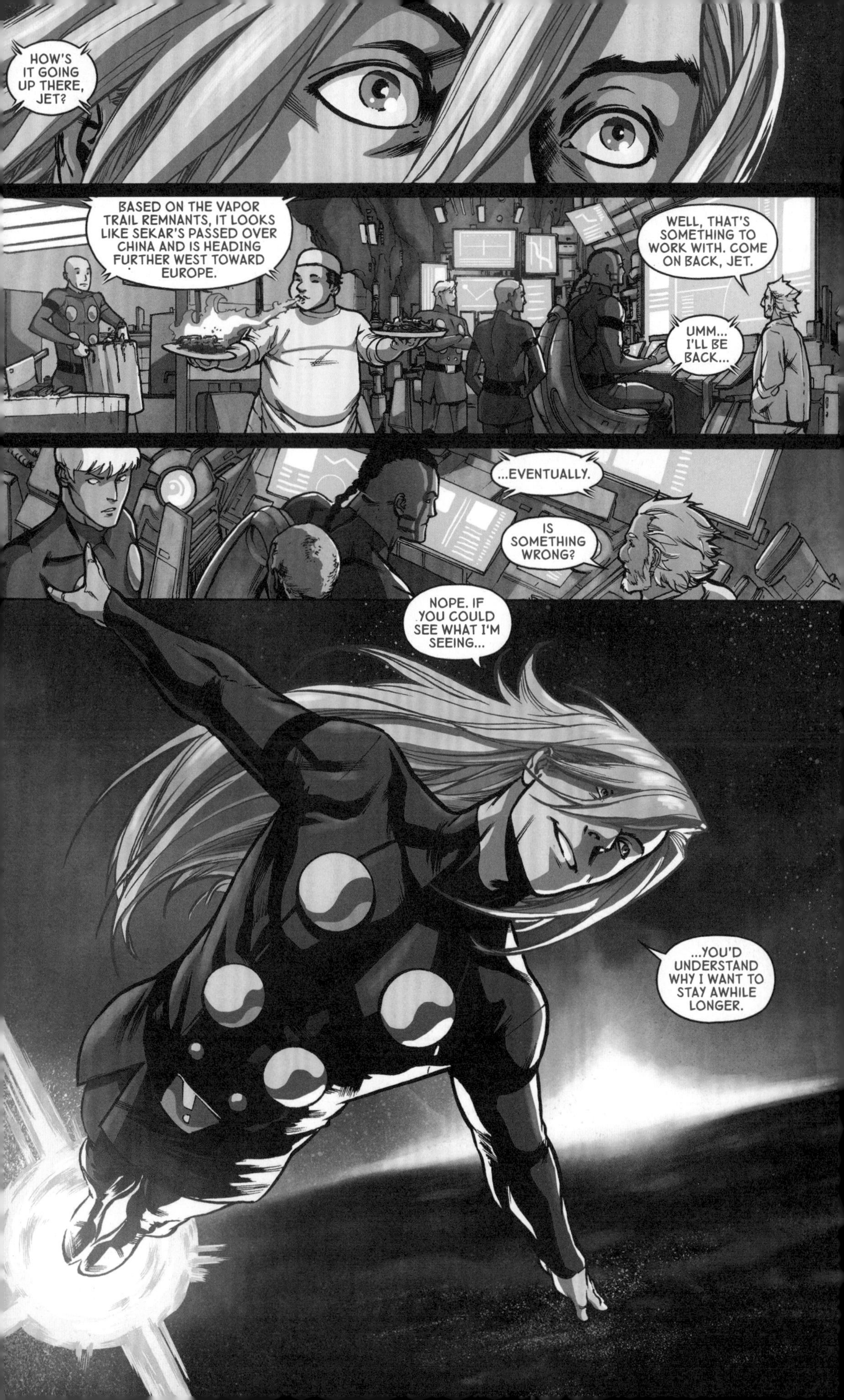
HOW'S IT GOING UP THERE, JET?
BASED ON THE VAPOR TRAIL REMNANTS, IT LOOKS LIKE SEKAR'S PASSED OVER CHINA AND IS HEADING FURTHER WEST TOWARD EUROPE.
WELL, THAT'S SOMETHING TO WORK WITH. COME ON BACK, JET.
UMM... I'LL BE BACK...
...EVENTUALLY.
IS SOMETHING WRONG?
NOPE. IF YOU COULD SEE WHAT I'M SEEING...
...YOU'D UNDERSTAND WHY I WANT TO STAY AWHILE LONGER.

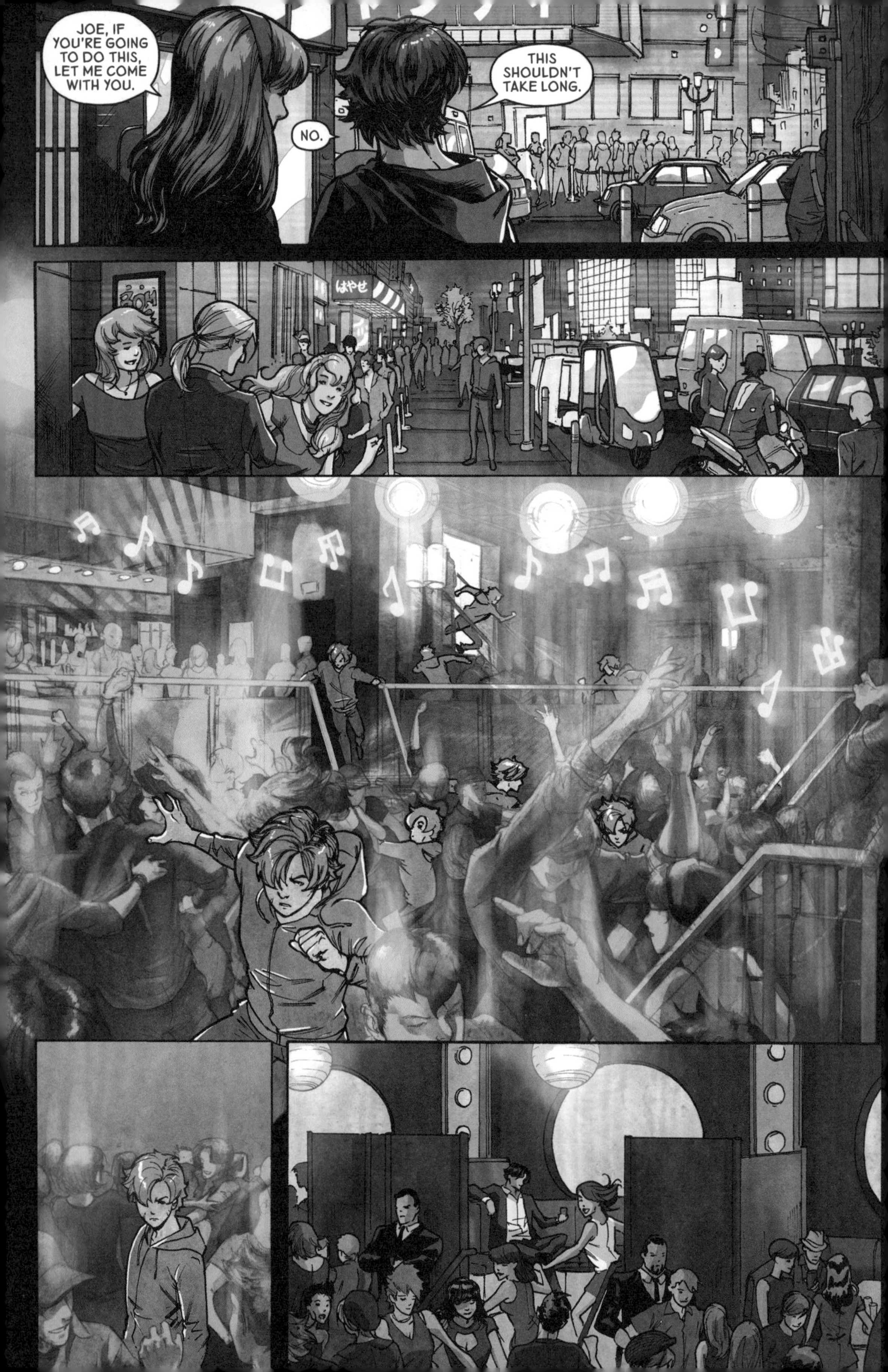
JOE, IF YOU'RE GOING TO DO THIS, LET ME COME WITH YOU.
NO.
THIS SHOULDN'T TAKE LONG.
はやせ

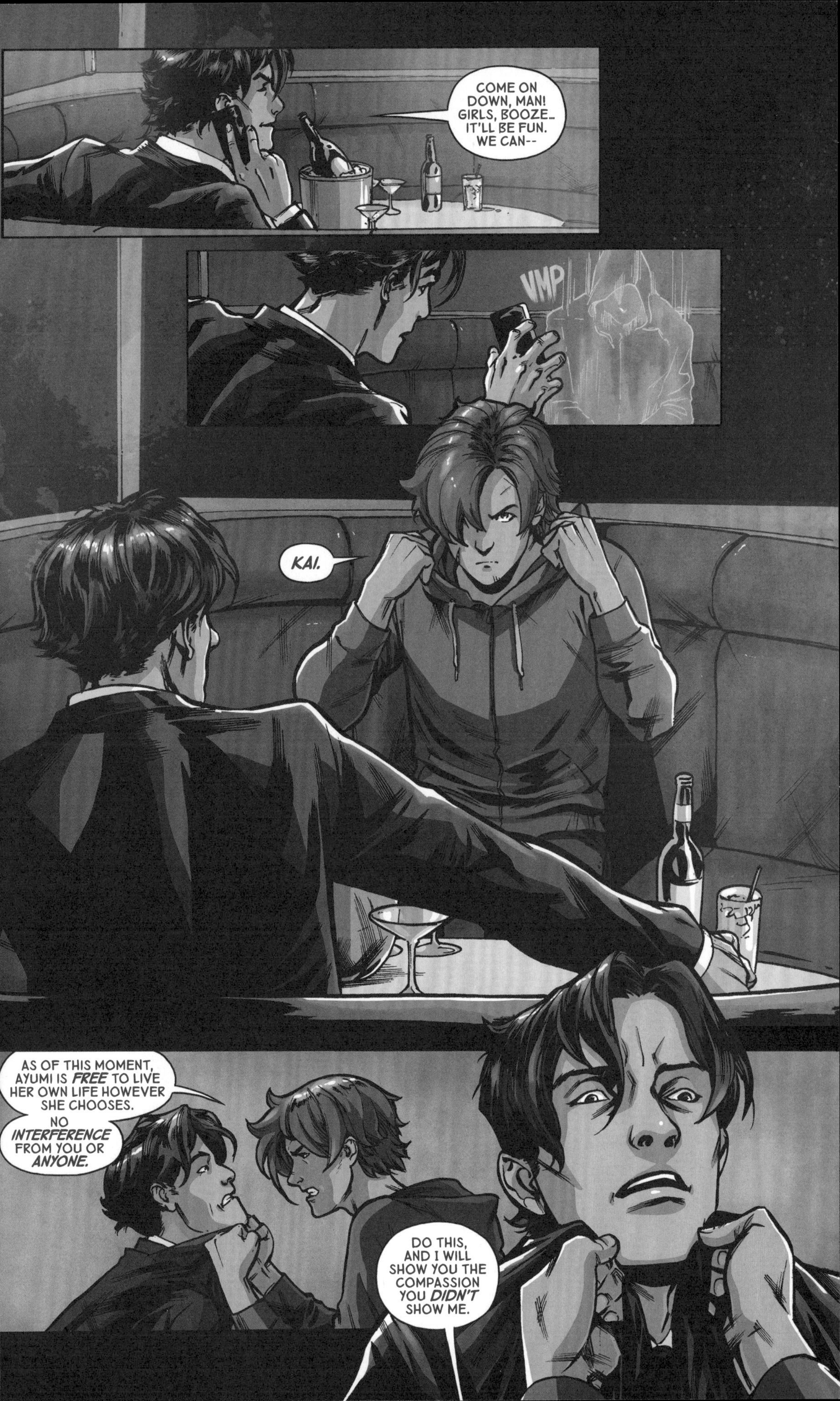
COME ON DOWN, MAN! GIRLS, BOOZE... IT'LL BE FUN. WE CAN--
VMP
KAI.
AS OF THIS MOMENT, AYUMI IS *FREE* TO LIVE HER OWN LIFE HOWEVER SHE CHOOSES.
NO *INTERFERENCE* FROM YOU OR *ANYONE.*
DO THIS, AND I WILL SHOW YOU THE COMPASSION YOU *DIDN'T* SHOW ME.

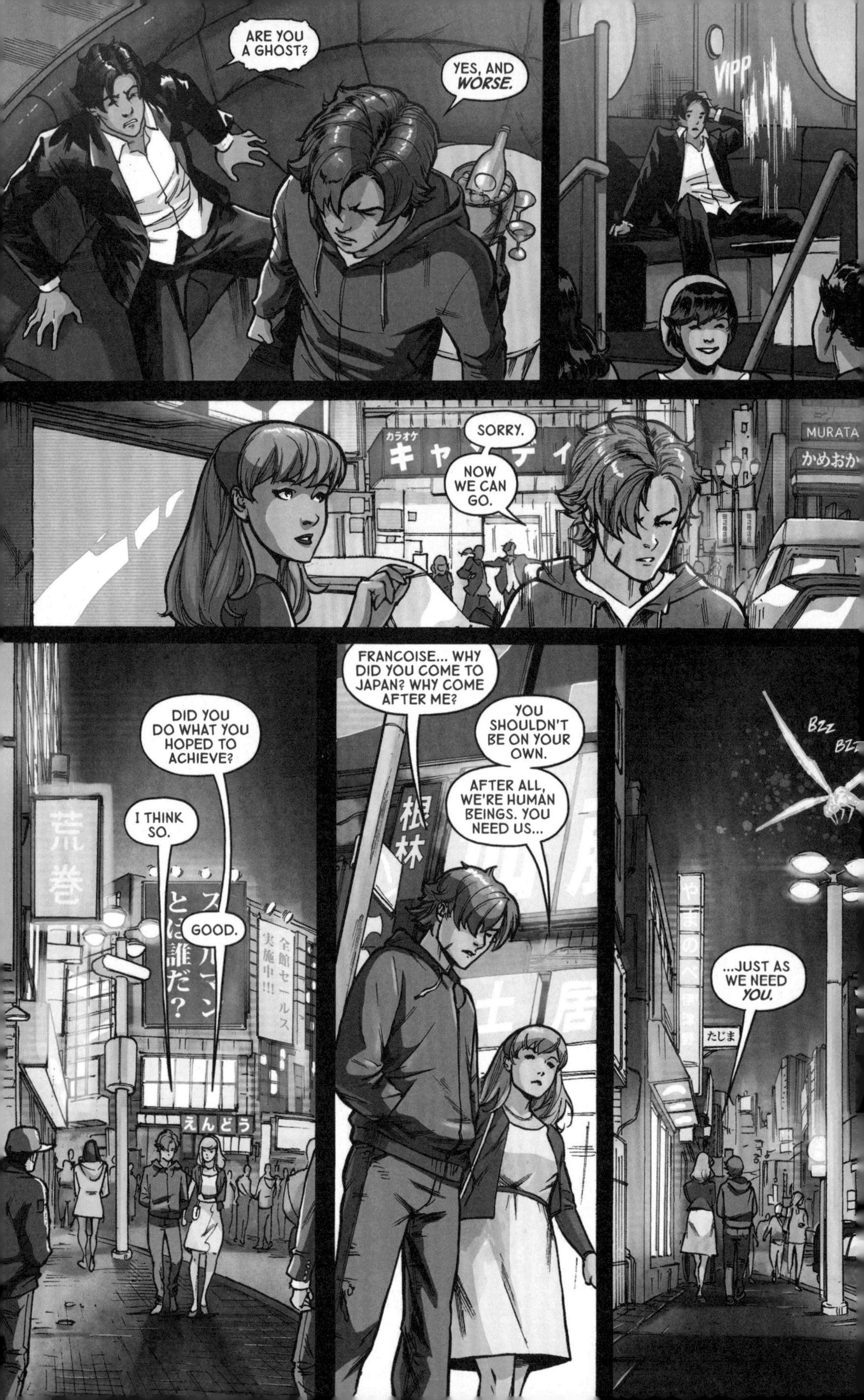
ARE YOU A GHOST?
YES, AND *WORSE.*
VIPP
SORRY.
NOW WE CAN GO.
MURATA
DID YOU DO WHAT YOU HOPED TO ACHIEVE?
I THINK SO.
GOOD.
FRANCOISE... WHY DID YOU COME TO JAPAN? WHY COME AFTER ME?
YOU SHOULDN'T BE ON YOUR OWN.
AFTER ALL, WE'RE HUMAN BEINGS. YOU NEED US...
BZZ
...JUST AS WE NEED *YOU.*

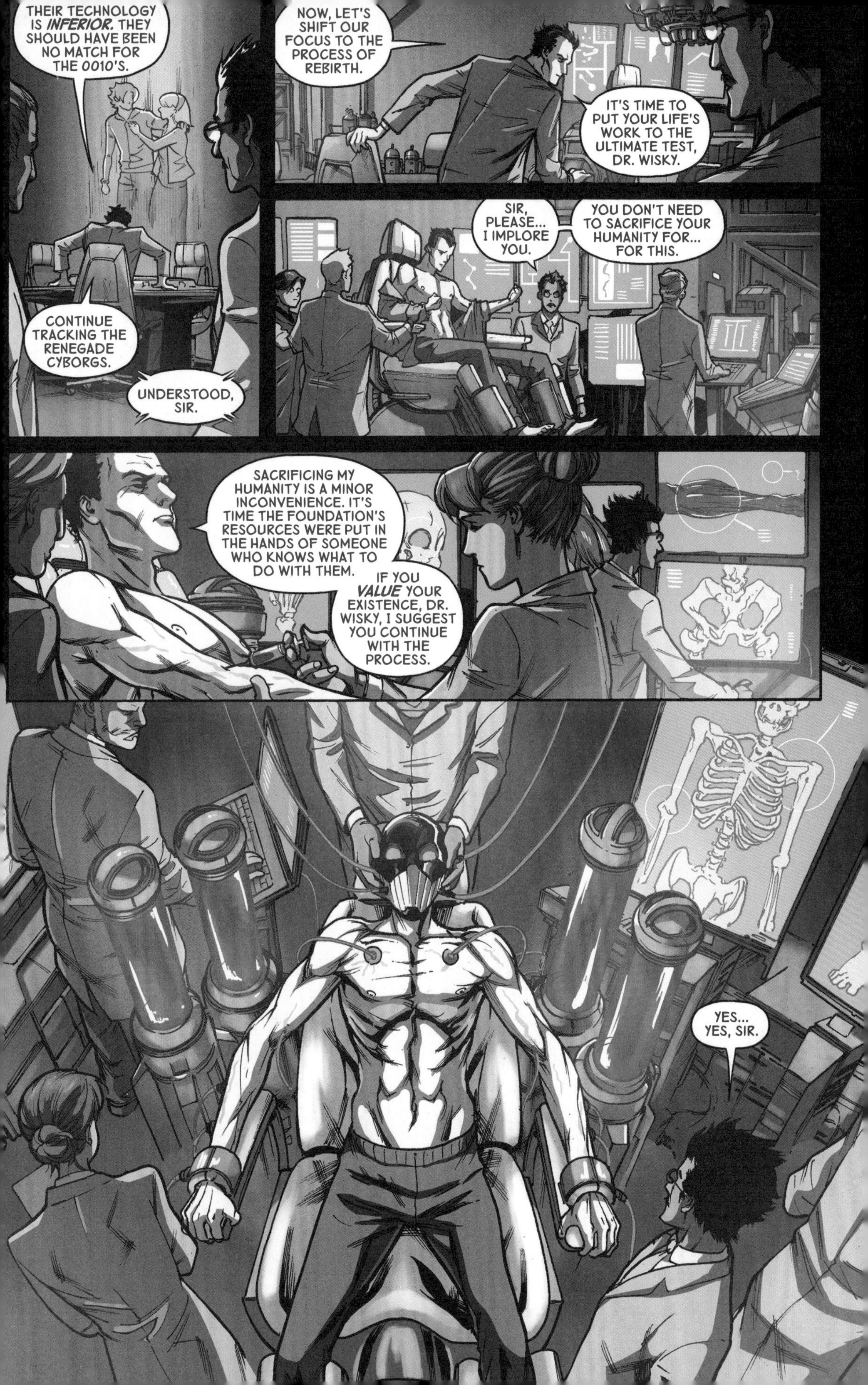
THEIR TECHNOLOGY IS *INFERIOR.* THEY SHOULD HAVE BEEN NO MATCH FOR THE 0010'S.
CONTINUE TRACKING THE RENEGADE CYBORGS.
UNDERSTOOD, SIR.
NOW, LET'S SHIFT OUR FOCUS TO THE PROCESS OF REBIRTH.
IT'S TIME TO PUT YOUR LIFE'S WORK TO THE ULTIMATE TEST, DR. WISKY.
SIR, PLEASE... I IMPLORE YOU.
YOU DON'T NEED TO SACRIFICE YOUR HUMANITY FOR... FOR THIS.
SACRIFICING MY HUMANITY IS A MINOR INCONVENIENCE. IT'S TIME THE FOUNDATION'S RESOURCES WERE PUT IN THE HANDS OF SOMEONE WHO KNOWS WHAT TO DO WITH THEM.
IF YOU *VALUE* YOUR EXISTENCE, DR. WISKY, I SUGGEST YOU CONTINUE WITH THE PROCESS.
YES... YES, SIR.

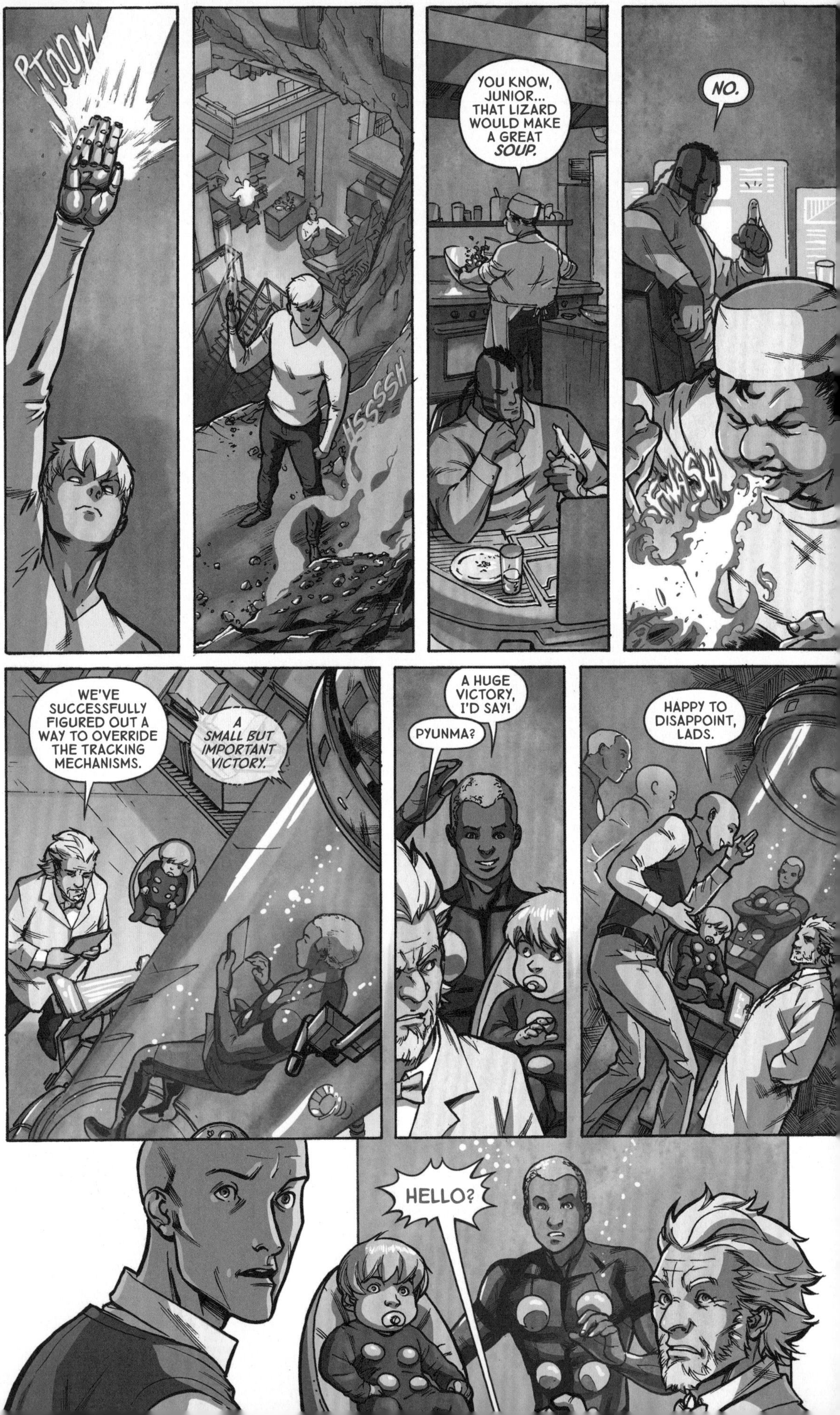
PTOOM
HSSSSH
YOU KNOW, JUNIOR... THAT LIZARD WOULD MAKE A GREAT SOUP.
NO.
FWASH
WE'VE SUCCESSFULLY FIGURED OUT A WAY TO OVERRIDE THE TRACKING MECHANISMS.
A SMALL BUT IMPORTANT VICTORY.
A HUGE VICTORY, I'D SAY!
PYUNMA?
HAPPY TO DISAPPOINT, LADS.
HELLO?

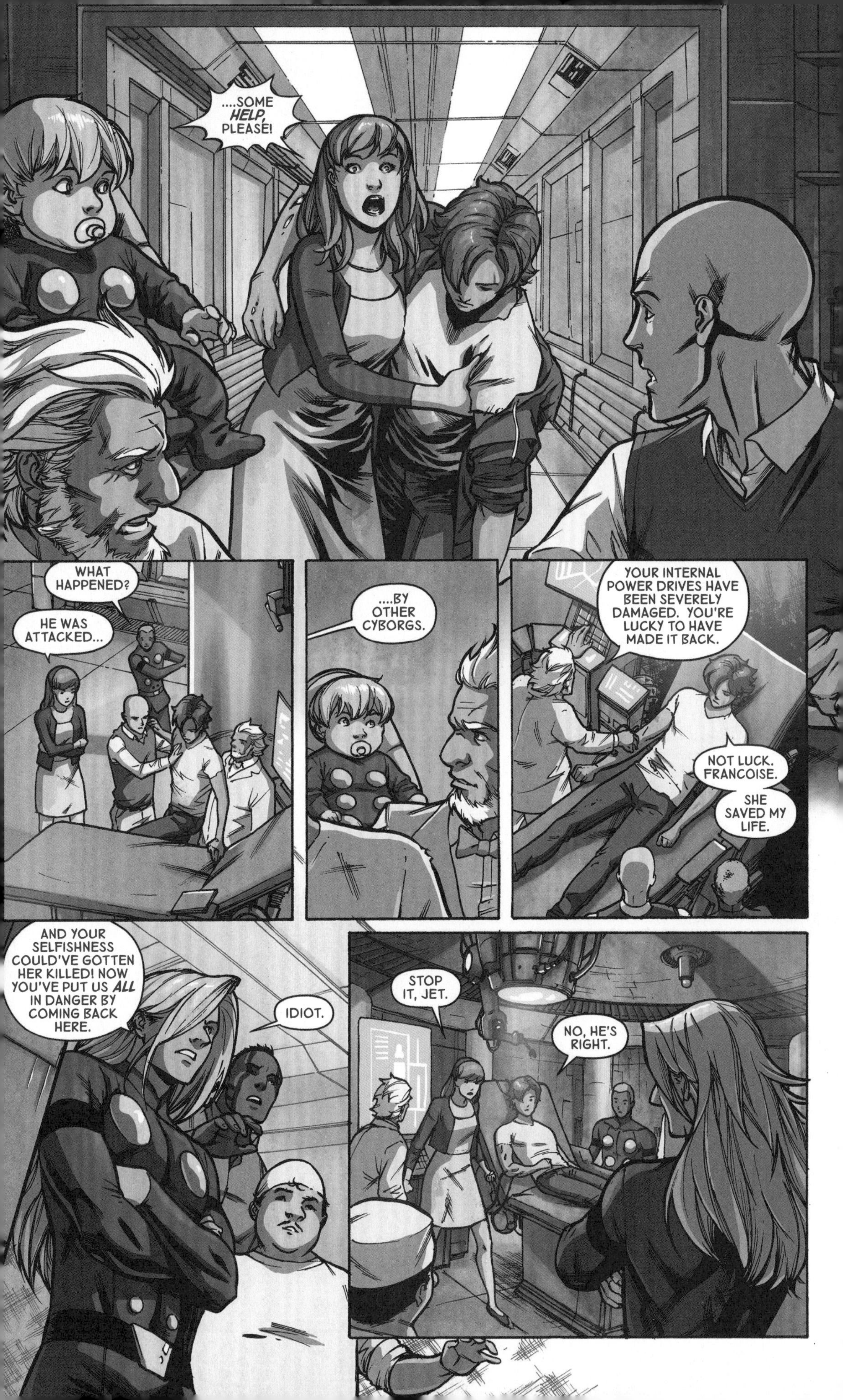
....SOME *HELP*, PLEASE!
WHAT HAPPENED?
HE WAS ATTACKED...
....BY OTHER CYBORGS.
YOUR INTERNAL POWER DRIVES HAVE BEEN SEVERELY DAMAGED. YOU'RE LUCKY TO HAVE MADE IT BACK.
NOT LUCK. FRANCOISE.
SHE SAVED MY LIFE.
AND YOUR SELFISHNESS COULD'VE GOTTEN HER KILLED! NOW YOU'VE PUT US *ALL* IN DANGER BY COMING BACK HERE.
IDIOT.
STOP IT, JET.
NO, HE'S RIGHT.

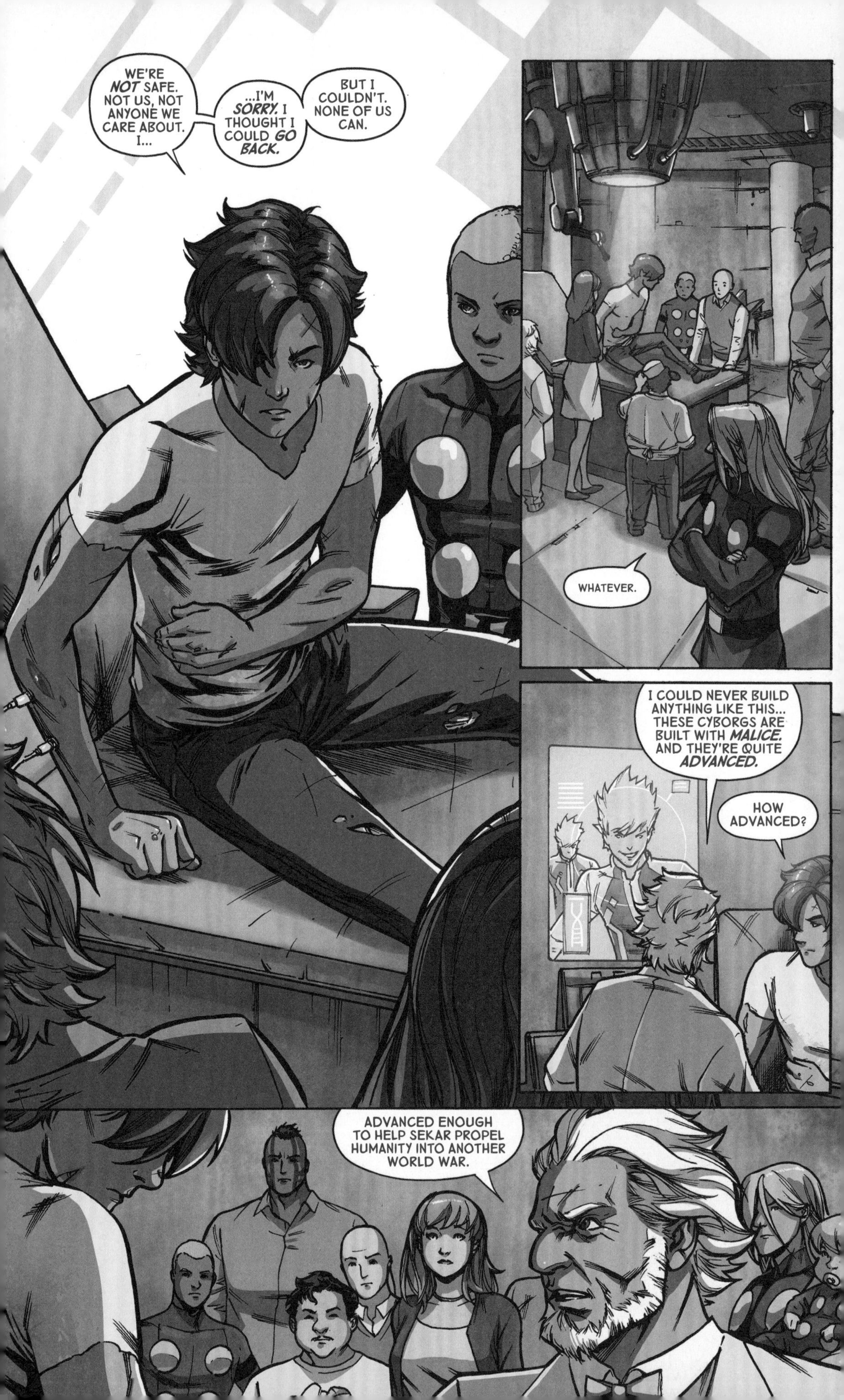
WE'RE *NOT* SAFE. NOT US, NOT ANYONE WE CARE ABOUT. I...
...I'M *SORRY.* I THOUGHT I COULD *GO BACK.*
BUT I COULDN'T. NONE OF US CAN.
WHATEVER.
I COULD NEVER BUILD ANYTHING LIKE THIS... THESE CYBORGS ARE BUILT WITH *MALICE.* AND THEY'RE QUITE *ADVANCED.*
HOW ADVANCED?
ADVANCED ENOUGH TO HELP SEKAR PROPEL HUMANITY INTO ANOTHER WORLD WAR.

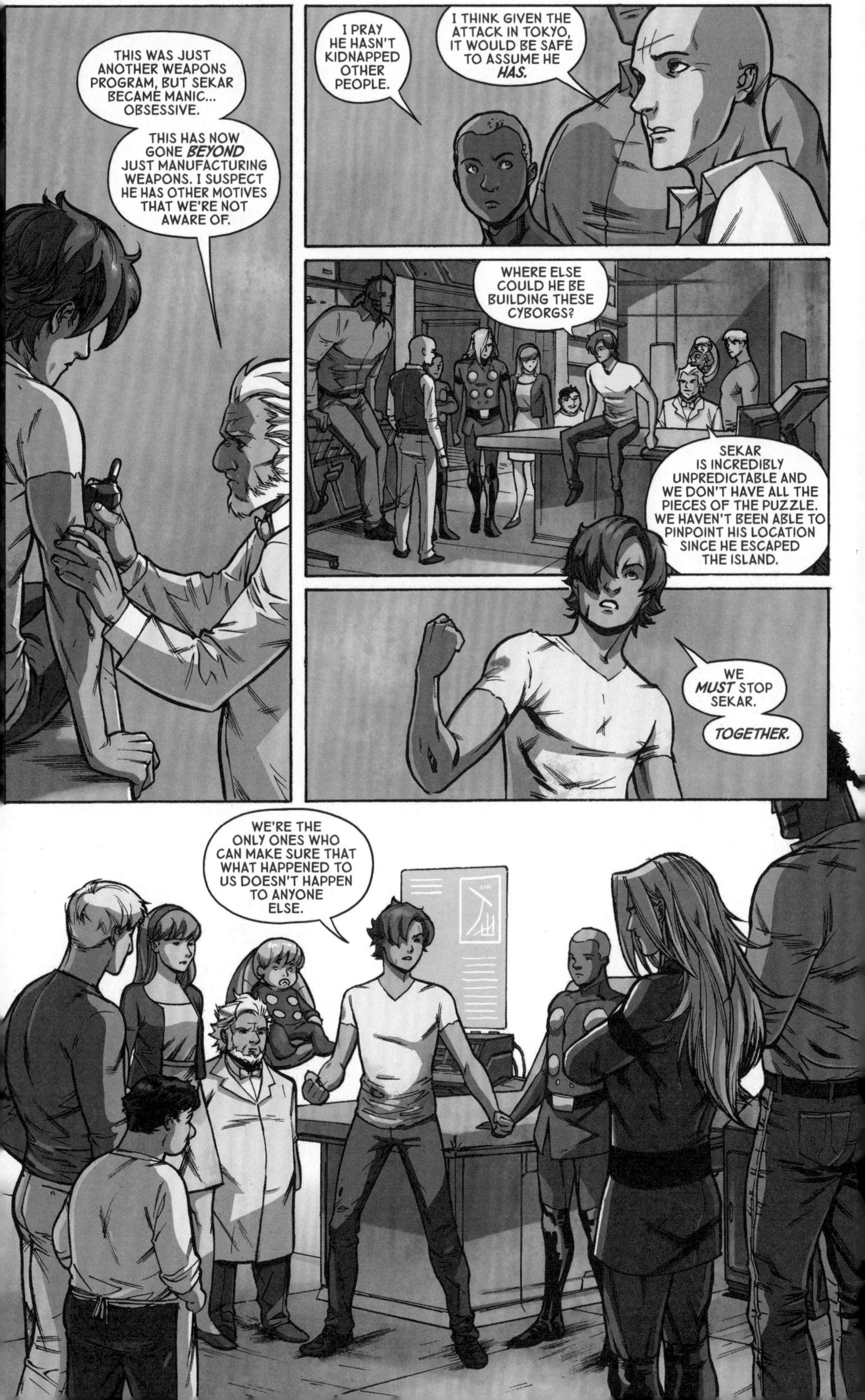
THIS WAS JUST ANOTHER WEAPONS PROGRAM, BUT SEKAR BECAME MANIC... OBSESSIVE.
THIS HAS NOW GONE *BEYOND* JUST MANUFACTURING WEAPONS. I SUSPECT HE HAS OTHER MOTIVES THAT WE'RE NOT AWARE OF.
I PRAY HE HASN'T KIDNAPPED OTHER PEOPLE.
I THINK GIVEN THE ATTACK IN TOKYO, IT WOULD BE SAFE TO ASSUME HE *HAS.*
WHERE ELSE COULD HE BE BUILDING THESE CYBORGS?
SEKAR IS INCREDIBLY UNPREDICTABLE AND WE DON'T HAVE ALL THE PIECES OF THE PUZZLE. WE HAVEN'T BEEN ABLE TO PINPOINT HIS LOCATION SINCE HE ESCAPED THE ISLAND.
WE *MUST* STOP SEKAR.
TOGETHER.
WE'RE THE ONLY ONES WHO CAN MAKE SURE THAT WHAT HAPPENED TO US DOESN'T HAPPEN TO ANYONE ELSE.

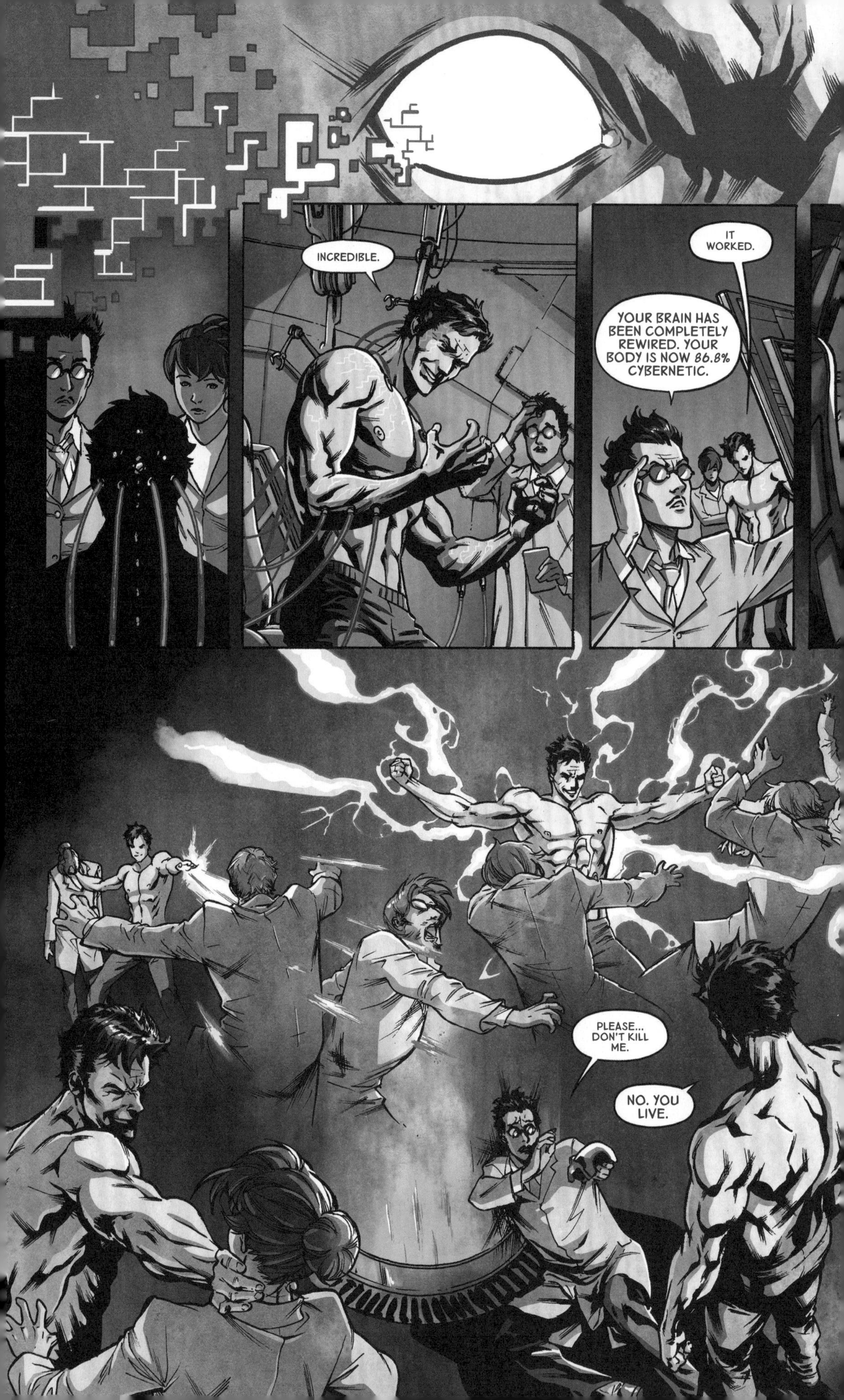
INCREDIBLE.
IT WORKED.
YOUR BRAIN HAS BEEN COMPLETELY REWIRED. YOUR BODY IS NOW 86.8% CYBERNETIC.
PLEASE... DON'T KILL ME.
NO. YOU LIVE.

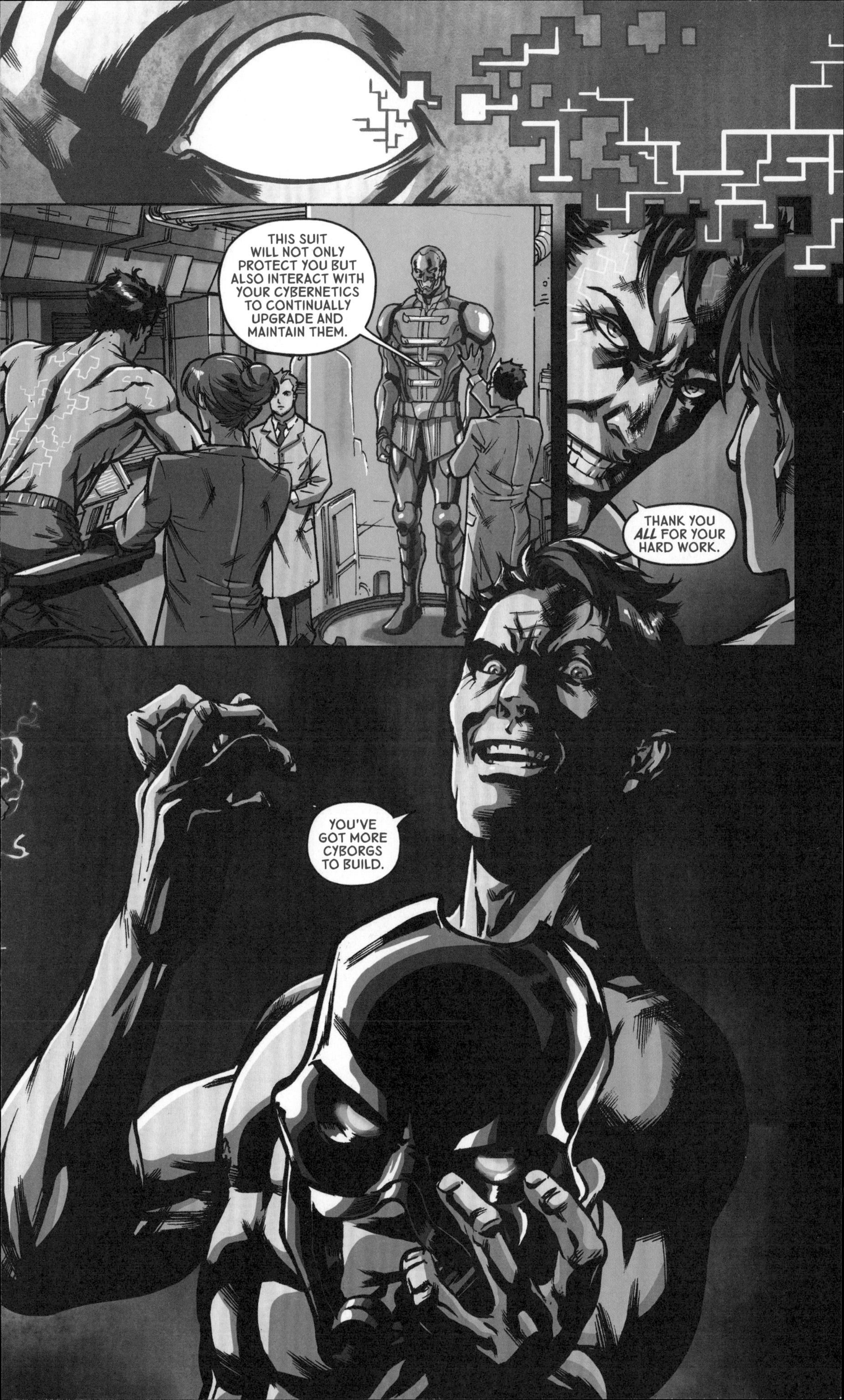
THIS SUIT WILL NOT ONLY PROTECT YOU BUT ALSO INTERACT WITH YOUR CYBERNETICS TO CONTINUALLY UPGRADE AND MAINTAIN THEM.
THANK YOU *ALL* FOR YOUR HARD WORK.
YOU'VE GOT MORE CYBORGS TO BUILD.

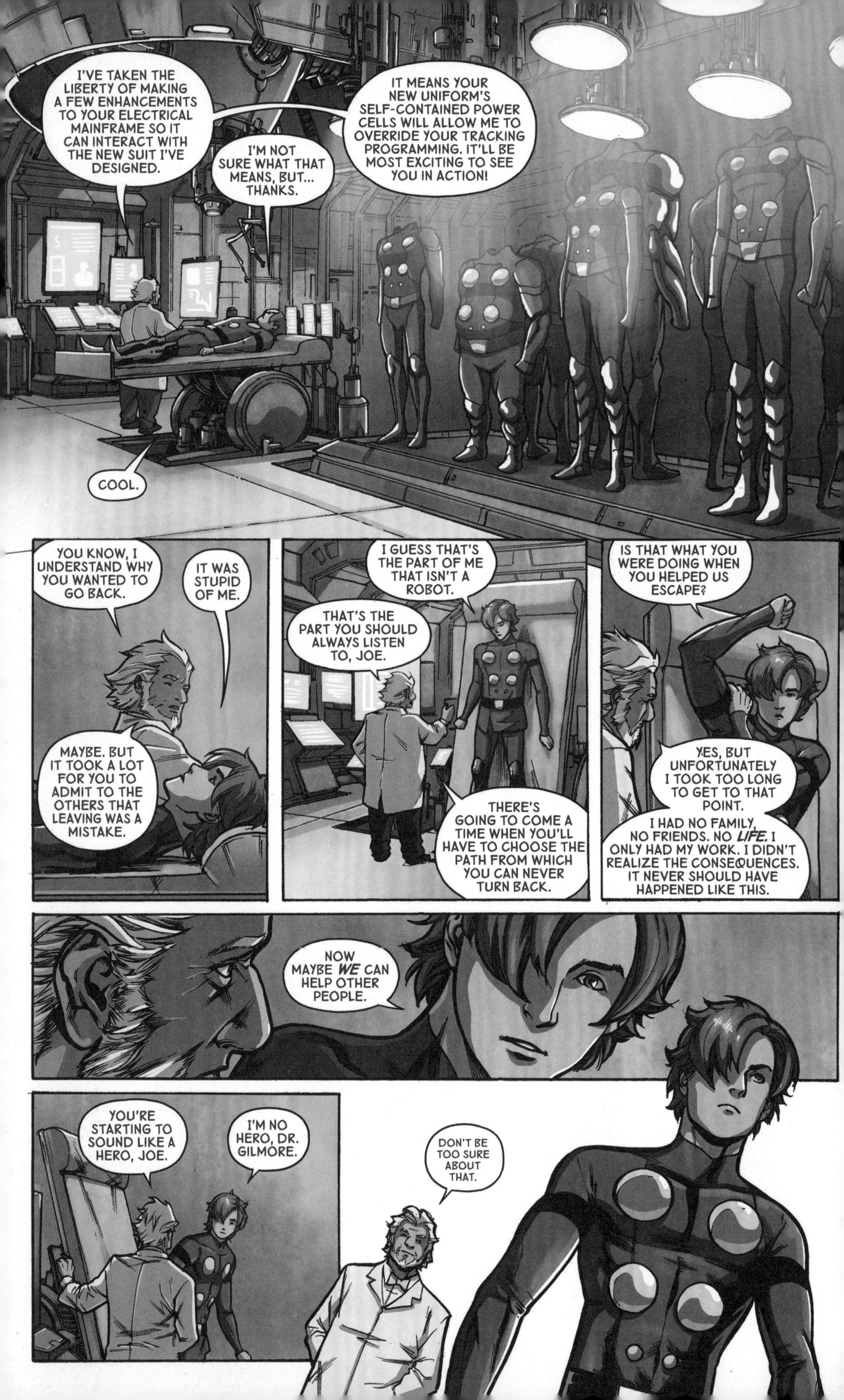

I'VE TAKEN THE LIBERTY OF MAKING A FEW ENHANCEMENTS TO YOUR ELECTRICAL MAINFRAME SO IT CAN INTERACT WITH THE NEW SUIT I'VE DESIGNED.
I'M NOT SURE WHAT THAT MEANS, BUT... THANKS.
IT MEANS YOUR NEW UNIFORM'S SELF-CONTAINED POWER CELLS WILL ALLOW ME TO OVERRIDE YOUR TRACKING PROGRAMMING. IT'LL BE MOST EXCITING TO SEE YOU IN ACTION!
COOL.
YOU KNOW, I UNDERSTAND WHY YOU WANTED TO GO BACK.
IT WAS STUPID OF ME.
MAYBE. BUT IT TOOK A LOT FOR YOU TO ADMIT TO THE OTHERS THAT LEAVING WAS A MISTAKE.
I GUESS THAT'S THE PART OF ME THAT ISN'T A ROBOT.
THAT'S THE PART YOU SHOULD ALWAYS LISTEN TO, JOE.
THERE'S GOING TO COME A TIME WHEN YOU'LL HAVE TO CHOOSE THE PATH FROM WHICH YOU CAN NEVER TURN BACK.
IS THAT WHAT YOU WERE DOING WHEN YOU HELPED US ESCAPE?
YES, BUT UNFORTUNATELY I TOOK TOO LONG TO GET TO THAT POINT.
I HAD NO FAMILY, NO FRIENDS. NO LIFE. I ONLY HAD MY WORK. I DIDN'T REALIZE THE CONSEQUENCES. IT NEVER SHOULD HAVE HAPPENED LIKE THIS.
NOW MAYBE WE CAN HELP OTHER PEOPLE.
YOU'RE STARTING TO SOUND LIKE A HERO, JOE.
I'M NO HERO, DR. GILMORE.
DON'T BE TOO SURE ABOUT THAT.

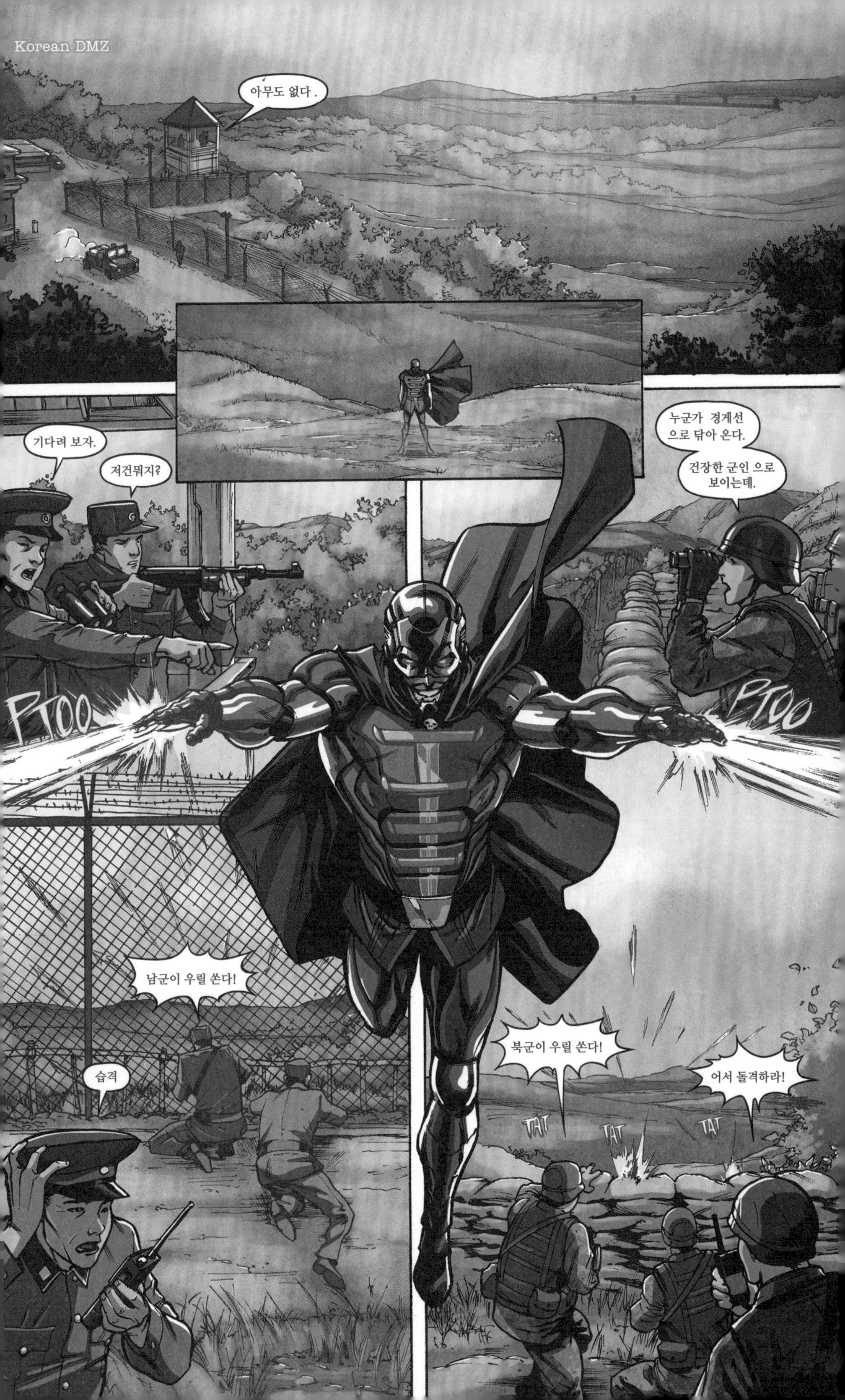
Korean DMZ
아무도 없다 .
기다려 보자.
저건뭐지?
누군가 경계선 으로 닦아 온다.
건장한 군인 으로 보이는데.
PTOO
PTOO
남군이 우릴 쏜다!
습격
북군이 우릴 쏜다!
TAT
TAT
TAT
어서 돌격하라!

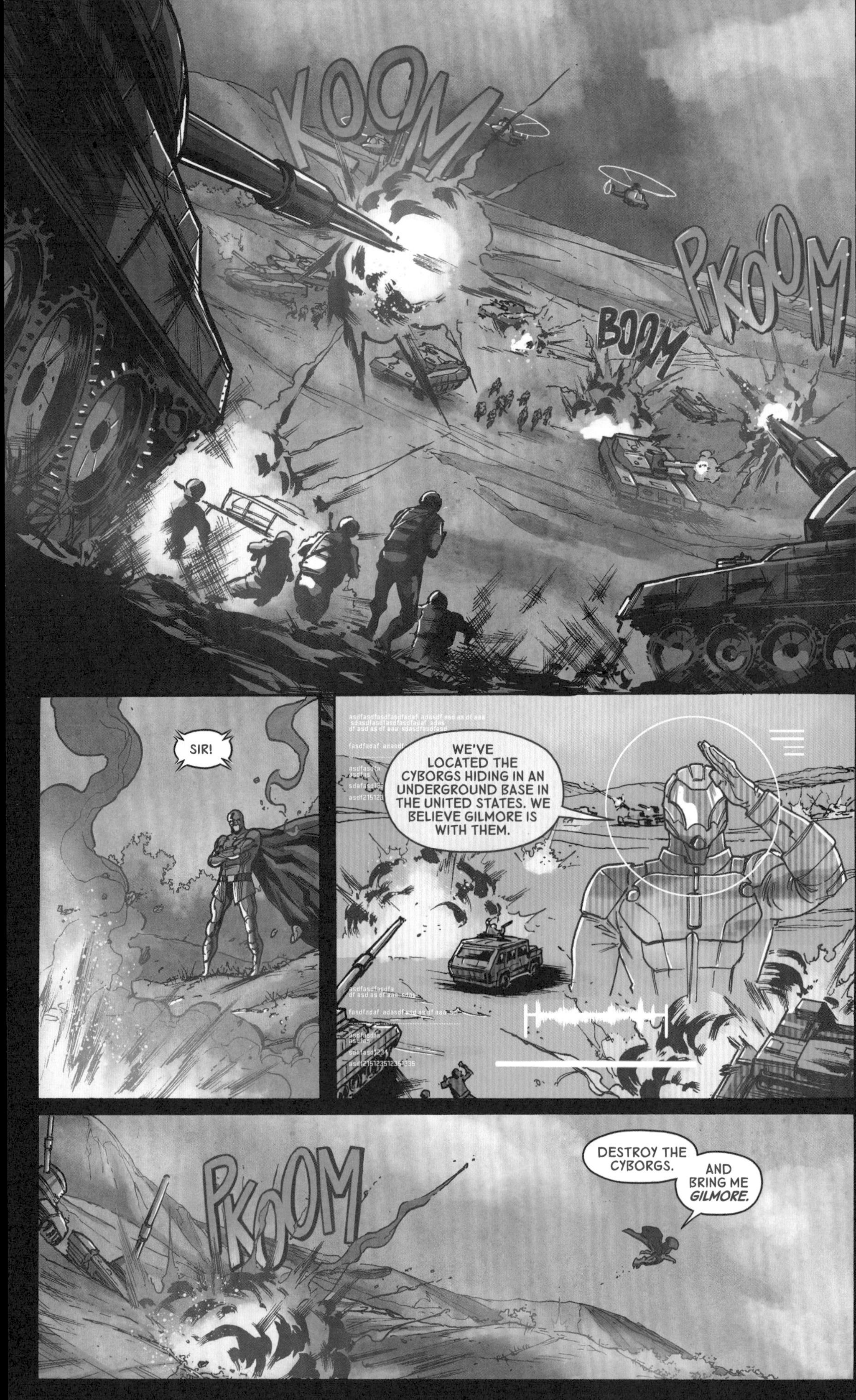
KOOM
PKOOM
BOOM
SIR!
WE'VE LOCATED THE CYBORGS HIDING IN AN UNDERGROUND BASE IN THE UNITED STATES. WE BELIEVE GILMORE IS WITH THEM.
PKOOM
DESTROY THE CYBORGS.
AND BRING ME *GILMORE.*

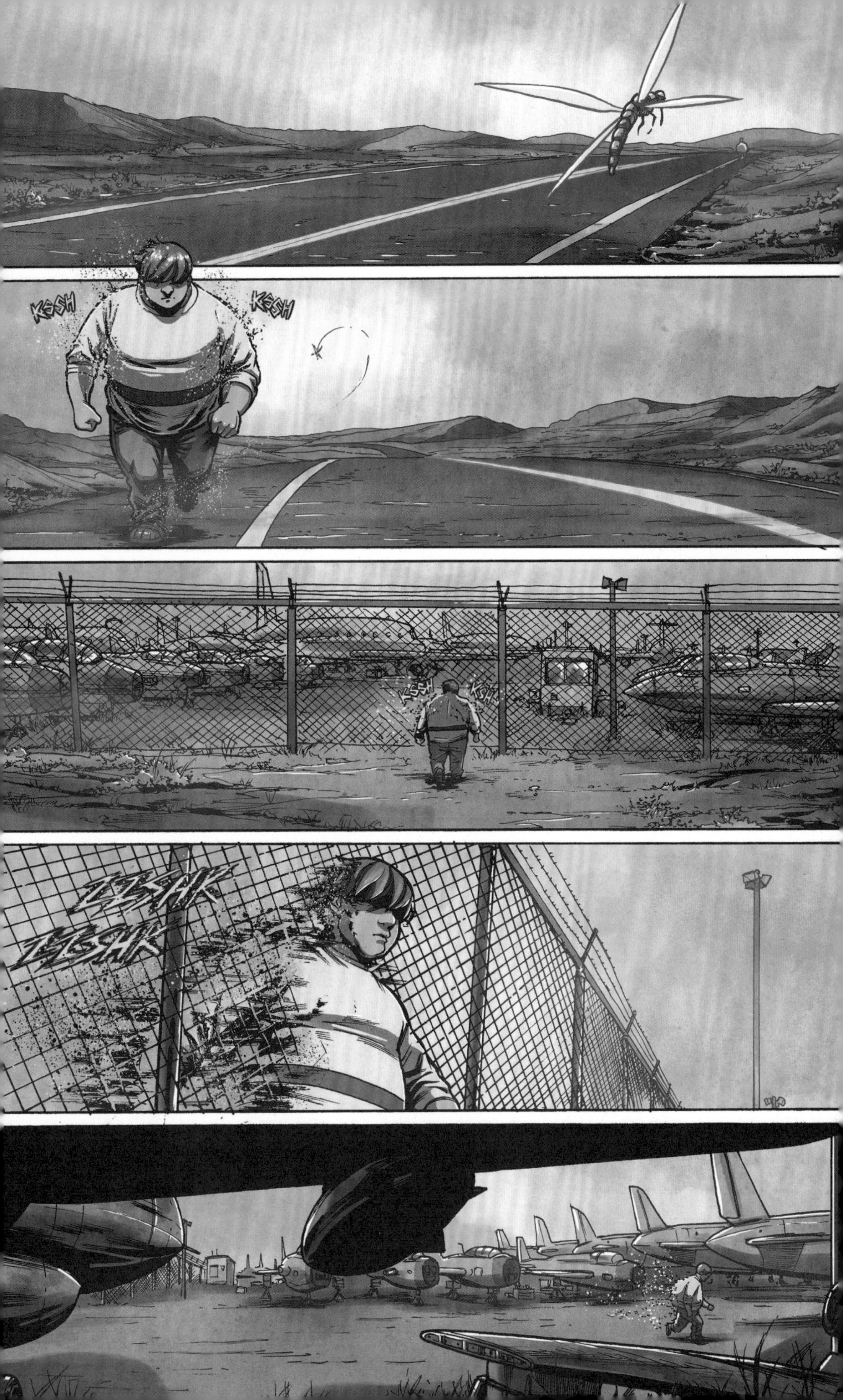
KSSH
KSSH
KSSH
KSSH
KSSHK
KSSHK

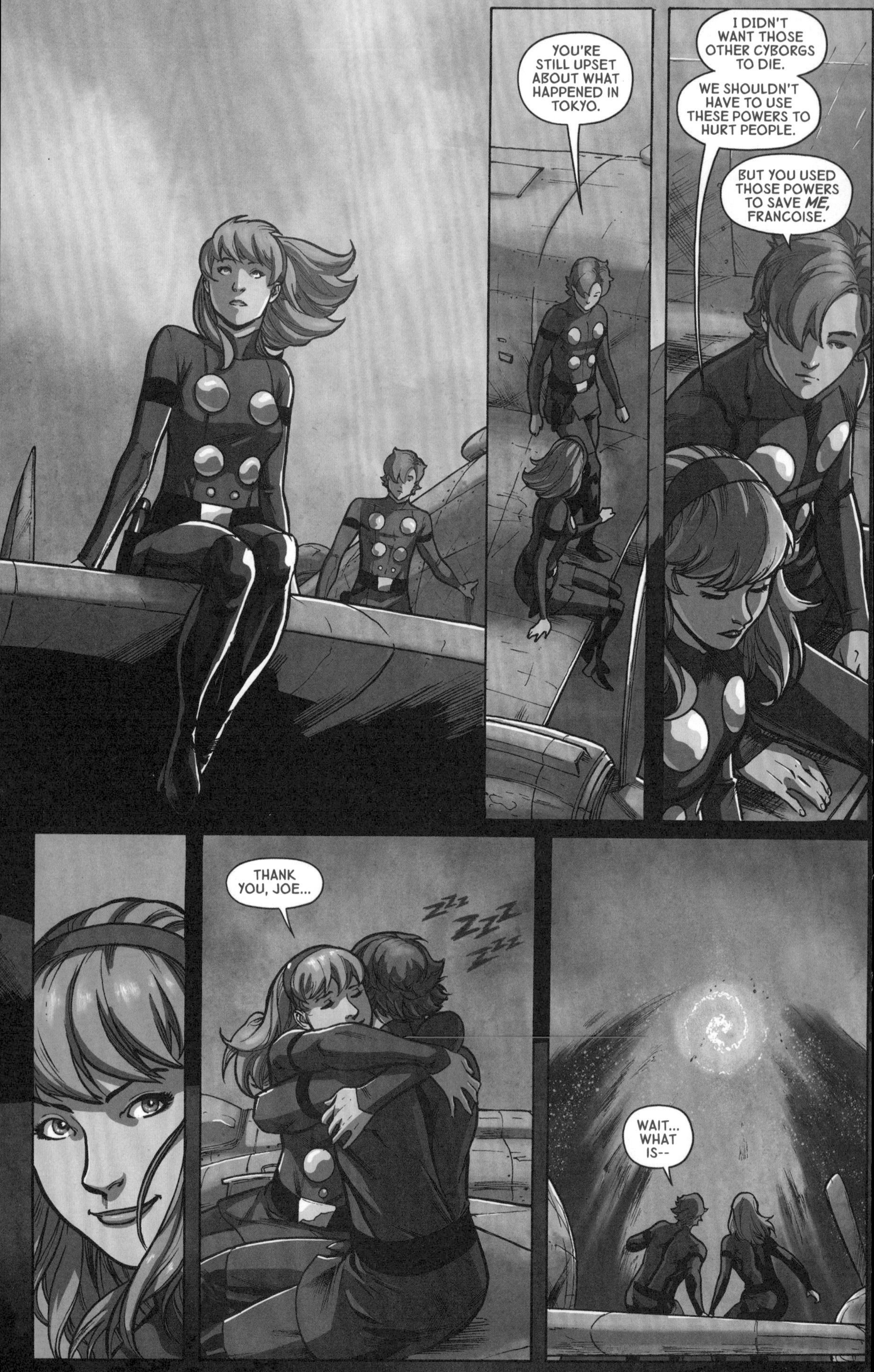
YOU'RE STILL UPSET ABOUT WHAT HAPPENED IN TOKYO.
I DIDN'T WANT THOSE OTHER CYBORGS TO DIE.
WE SHOULDN'T HAVE TO USE THESE POWERS TO HURT PEOPLE.
BUT YOU USED THOSE POWERS TO SAVE *ME,* FRANCOISE.
THANK YOU, JOE...
ZZZ
ZZZ
ZZZ
WAIT... WHAT IS--

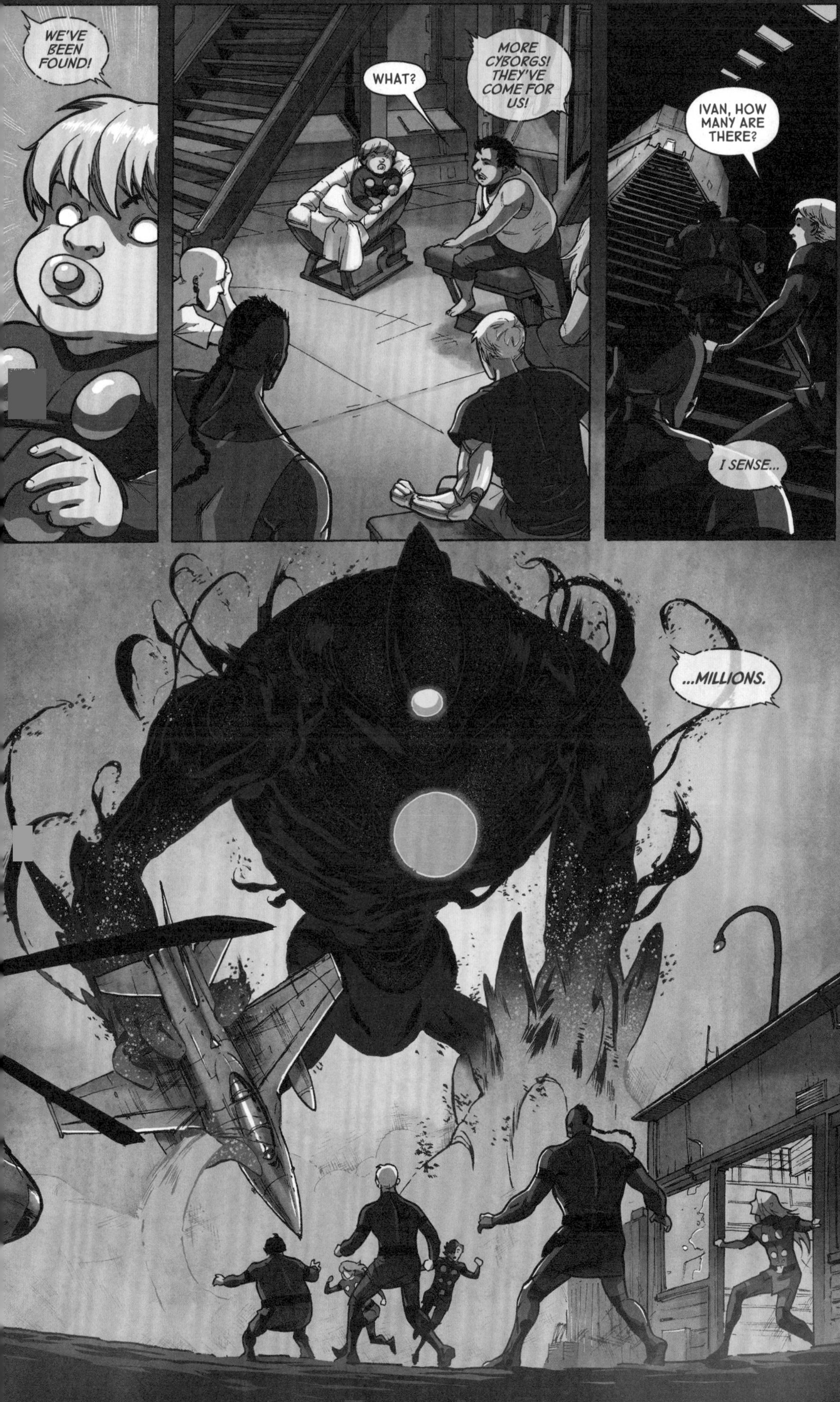
WE'VE BEEN FOUND!
WHAT?
MORE CYBORGS! THEY'VE COME FOR US!
IVAN, HOW MANY ARE THERE?
I SENSE...
...MILLIONS.

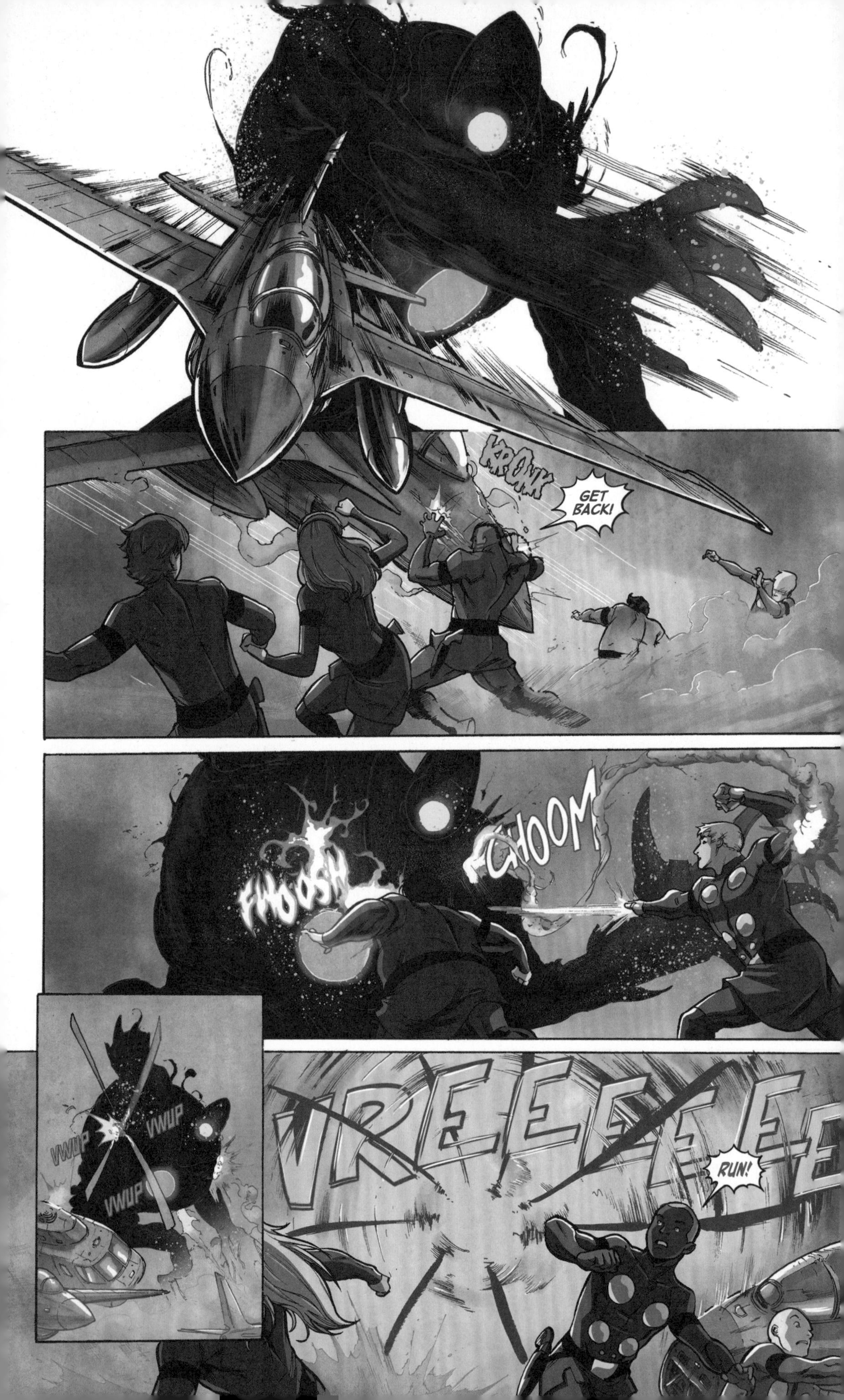
KRONK
GET BACK!
FWOOSH
CHOOM
VWUP
VWUP
VWUP
VREEEEEE
RUN!

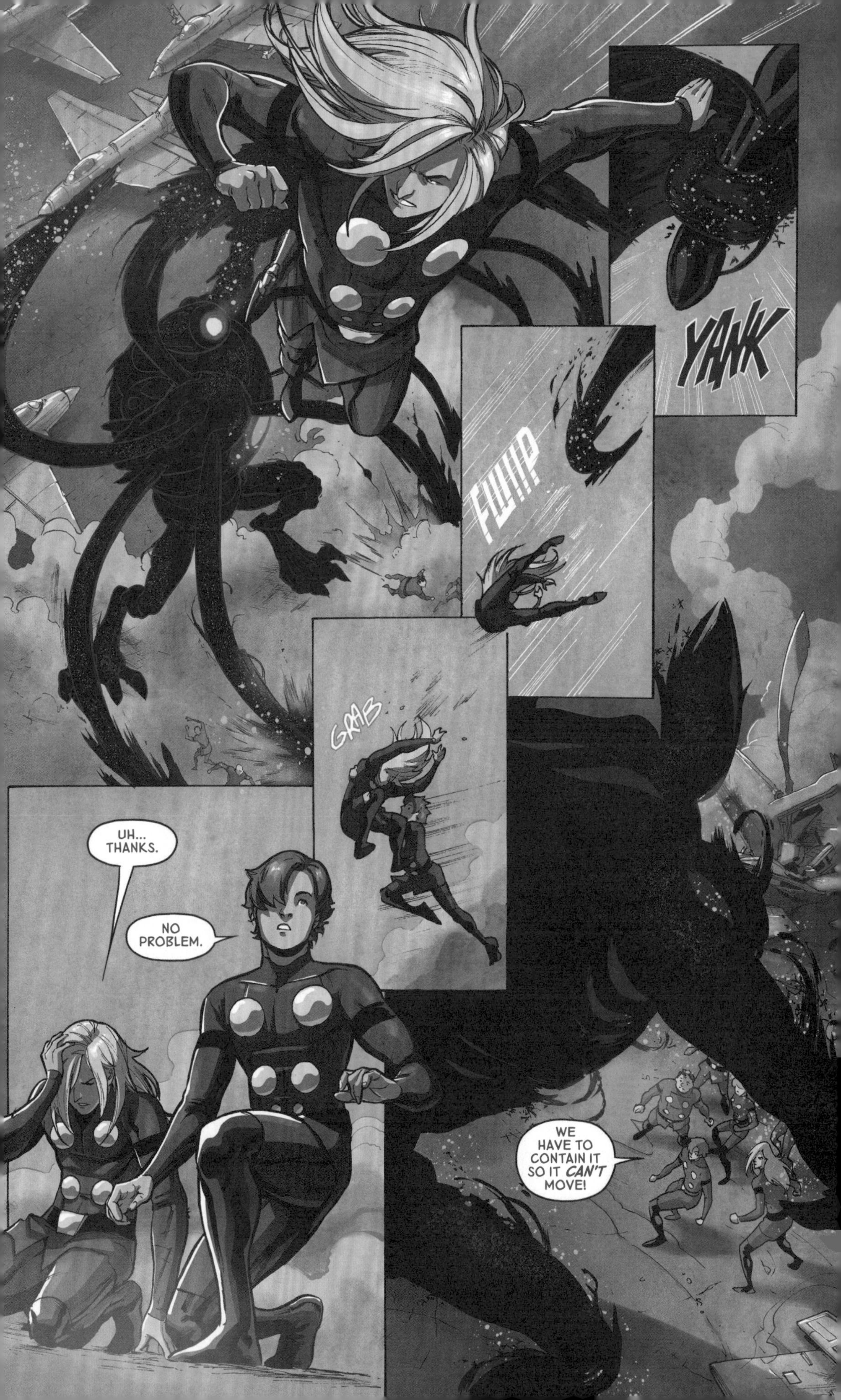
YANK
FWIP
GRAB
UH... THANKS.
NO PROBLEM.
WE HAVE TO CONTAIN IT SO IT *CAN'T* MOVE!

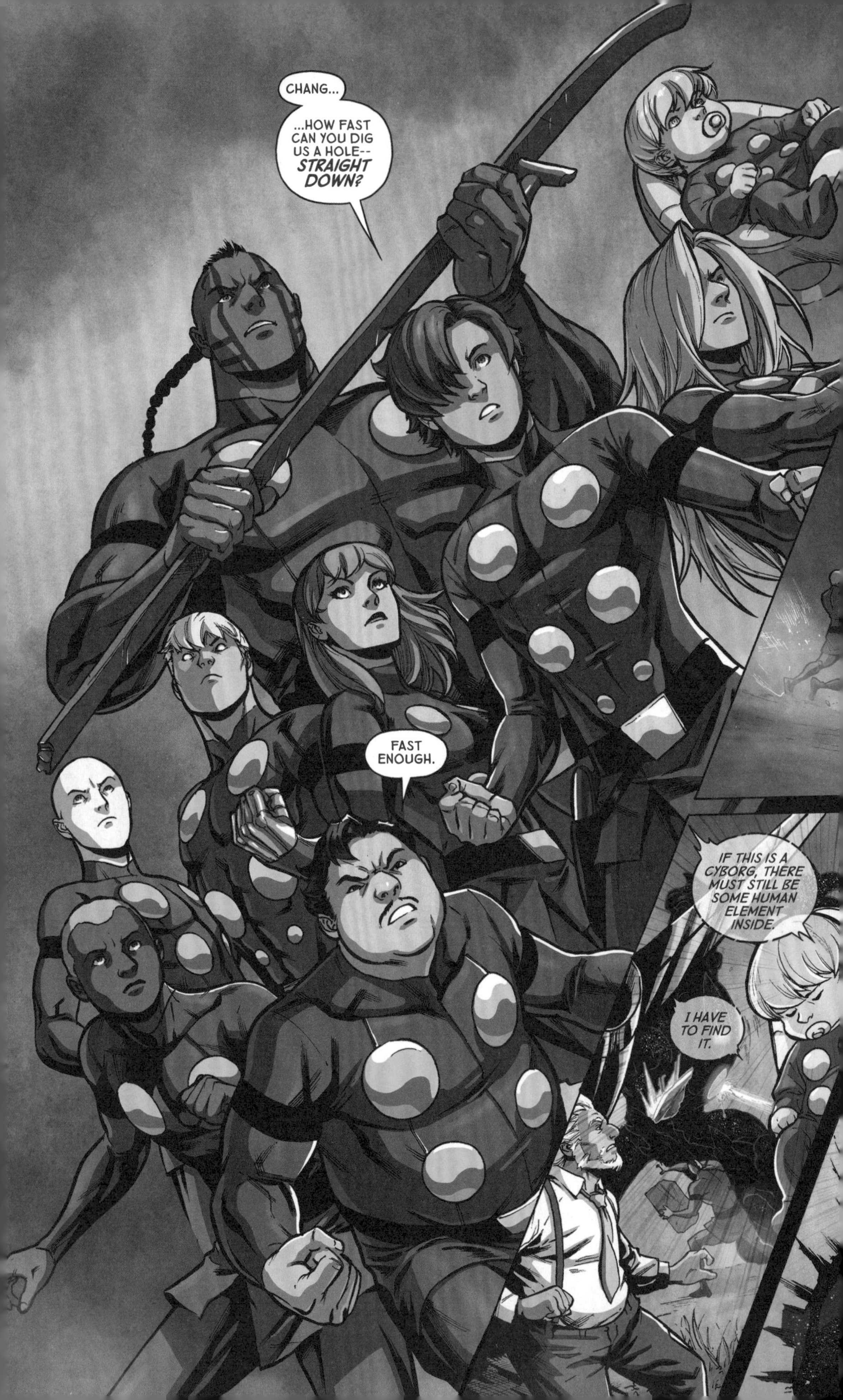
CHANG...
...HOW FAST CAN YOU DIG US A HOLE-- ***STRAIGHT DOWN?***
FAST ENOUGH.
IF THIS IS A CYBORG, THERE MUST STILL BE SOME HUMAN ELEMENT INSIDE.
I HAVE TO FIND IT.

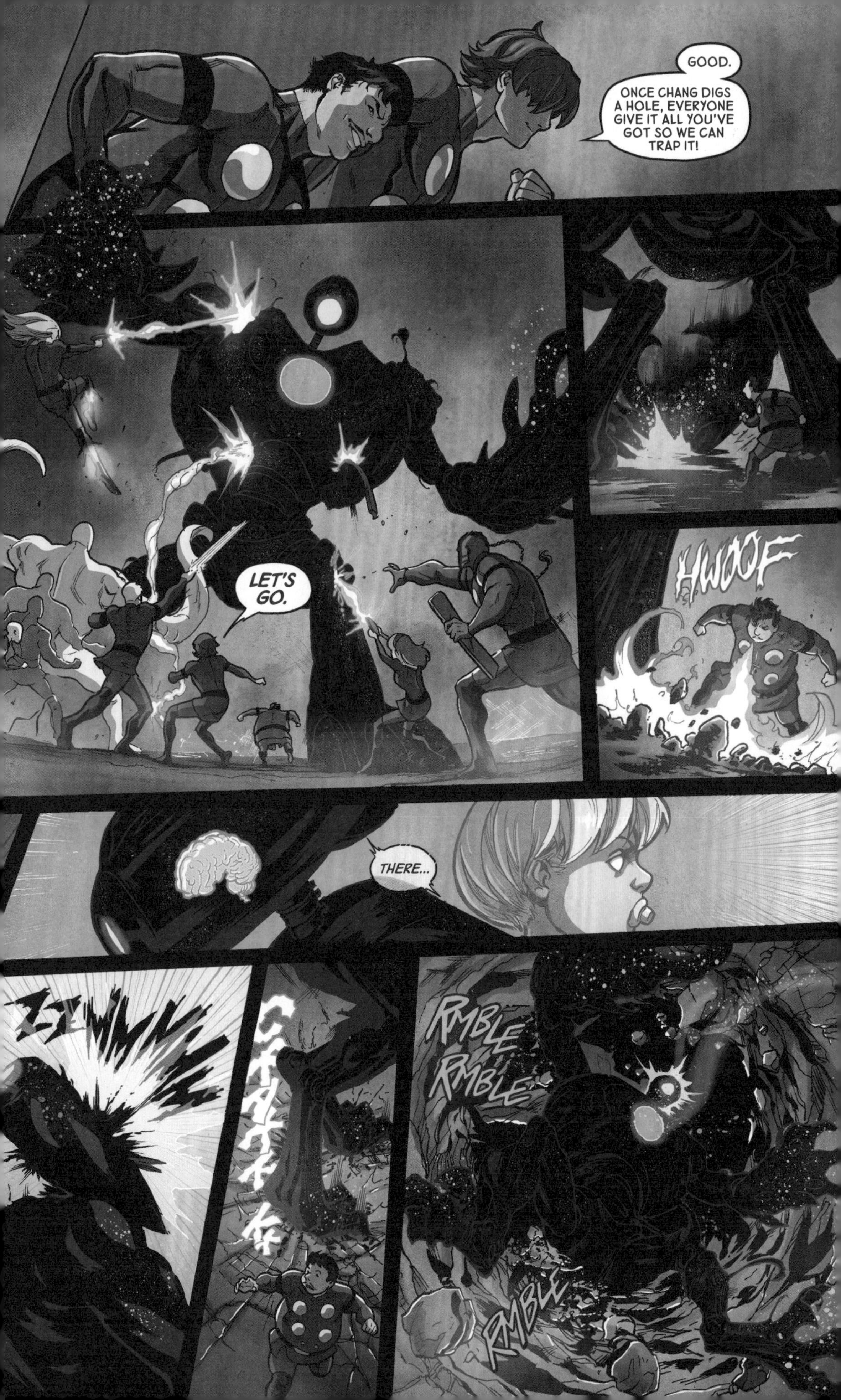
GOOD.
ONCE CHANG DIGS A HOLE, EVERYONE GIVE IT ALL YOU'VE GOT SO WE CAN TRAP IT!
LET'S GO.
HWOOF
THERE...
RMBLE
RMBLE
RMBLE

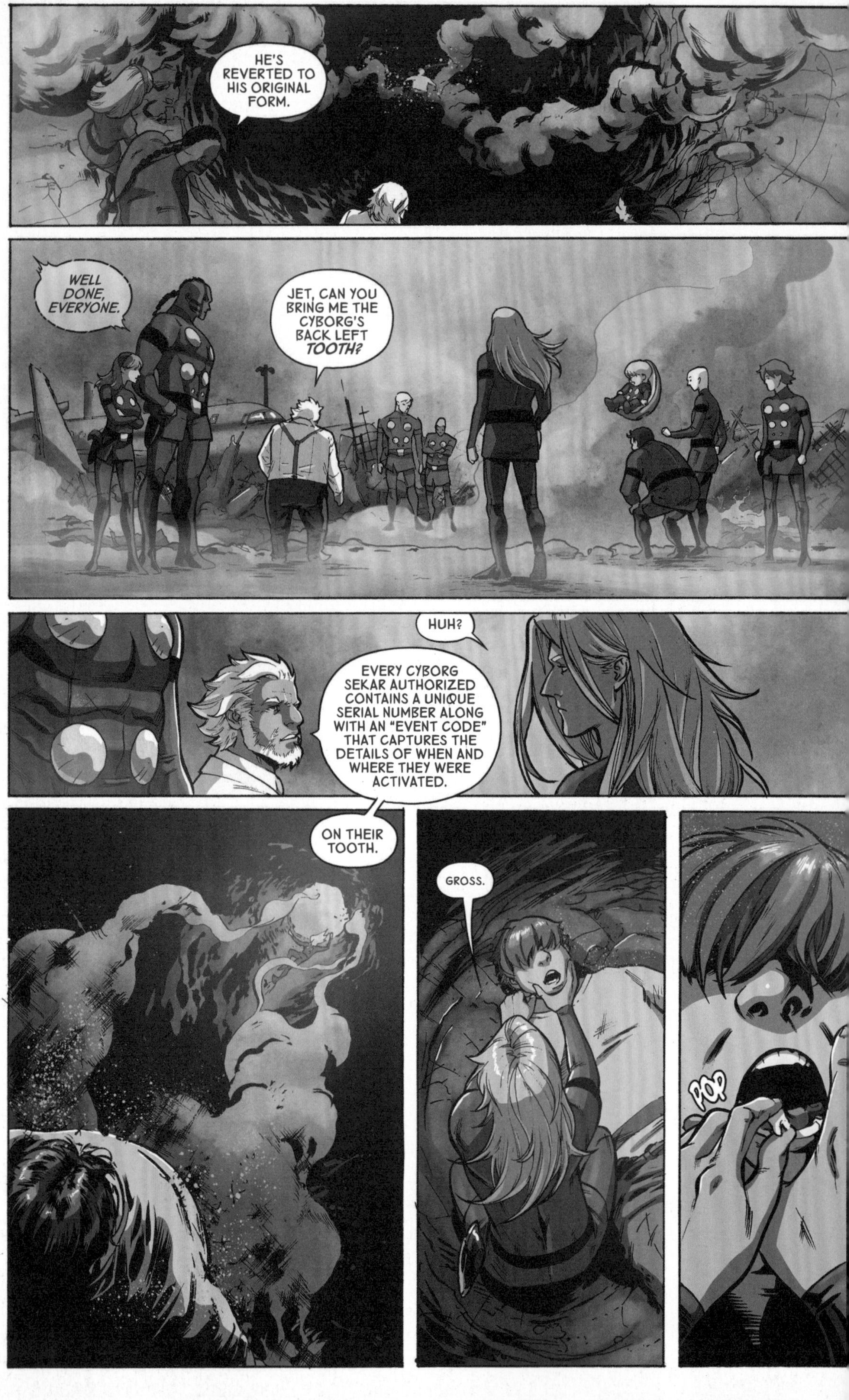
HE'S REVERTED TO HIS ORIGINAL FORM.
WELL DONE, EVERYONE.
JET, CAN YOU BRING ME THE CYBORG'S BACK LEFT *TOOTH?*
HUH?
EVERY CYBORG SEKAR AUTHORIZED CONTAINS A UNIQUE SERIAL NUMBER ALONG WITH AN "EVENT CODE" THAT CAPTURES THE DETAILS OF WHEN AND WHERE THEY WERE ACTIVATED.
ON THEIR TOOTH.
GROSS.
POP

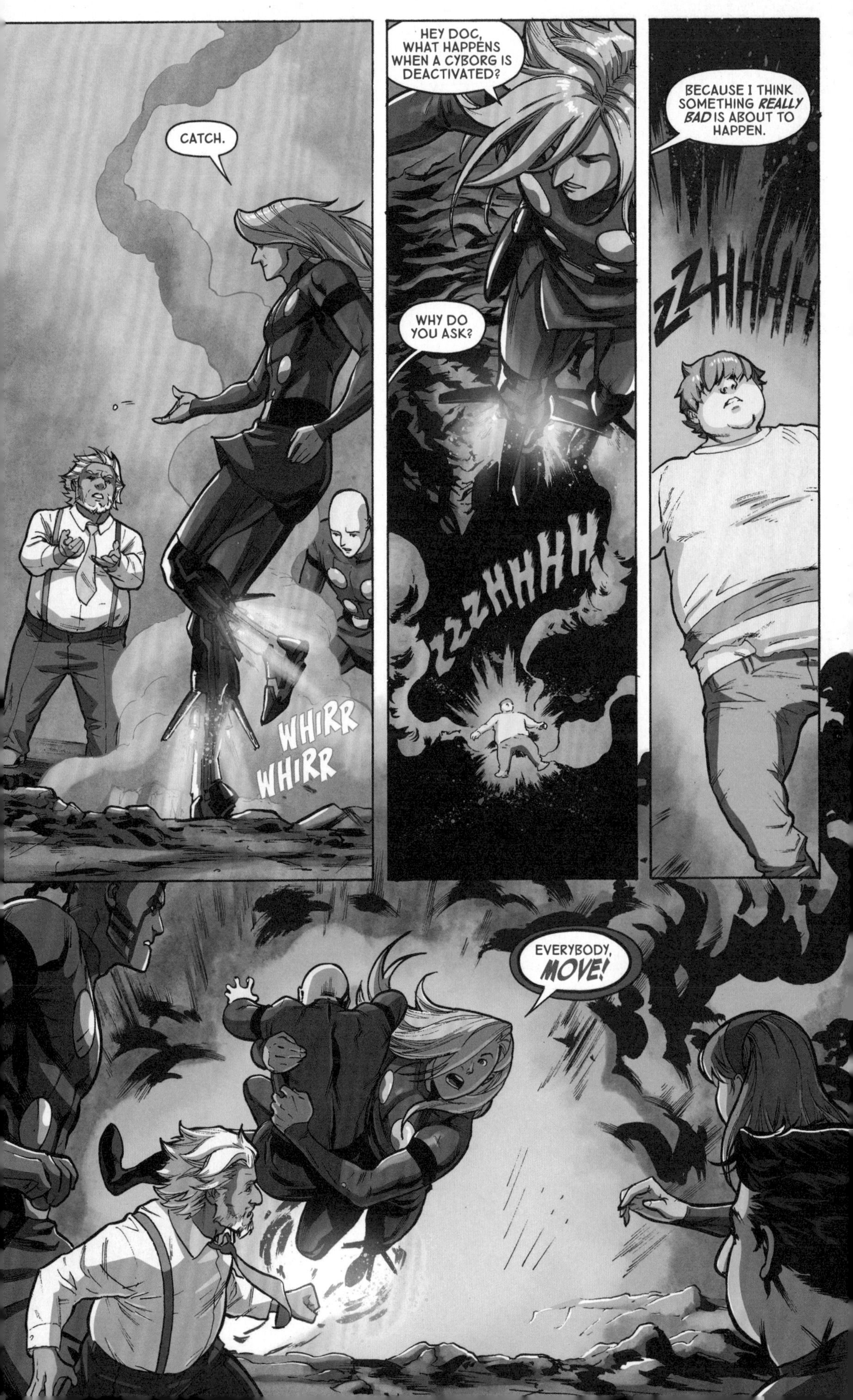
CATCH.
WHIRR
WHIRR
HEY DOC, WHAT HAPPENS WHEN A CYBORG IS DEACTIVATED?
WHY DO YOU ASK?
ZZZHHHH
BECAUSE I THINK SOMETHING *REALLY BAD* IS ABOUT TO HAPPEN.
ZZHHHH
EVERYBODY, *MOVE!*

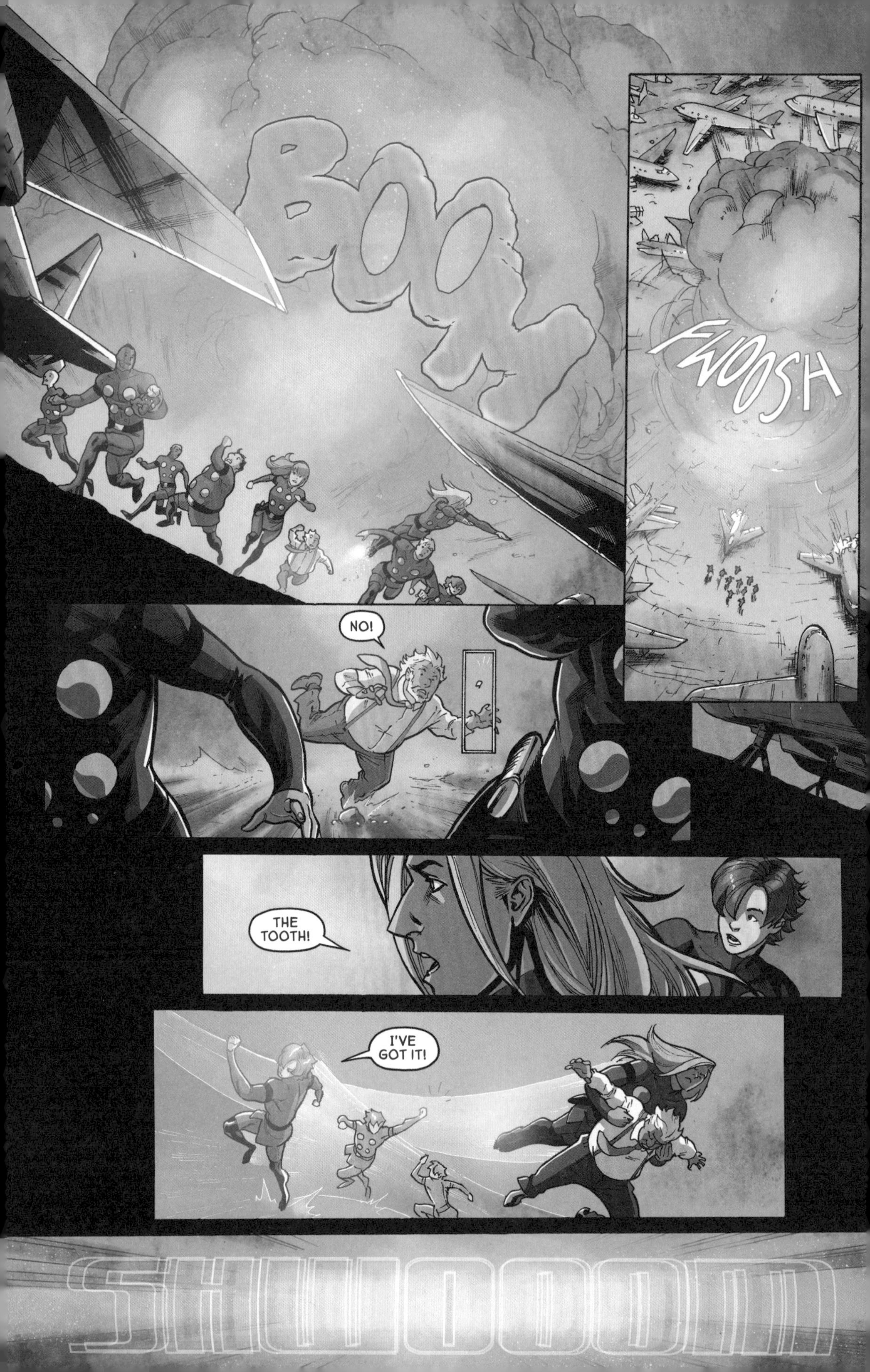
BOOM
FWOOSH
NO!
THE TOOTH!
I'VE GOT IT!
SHHOOOM

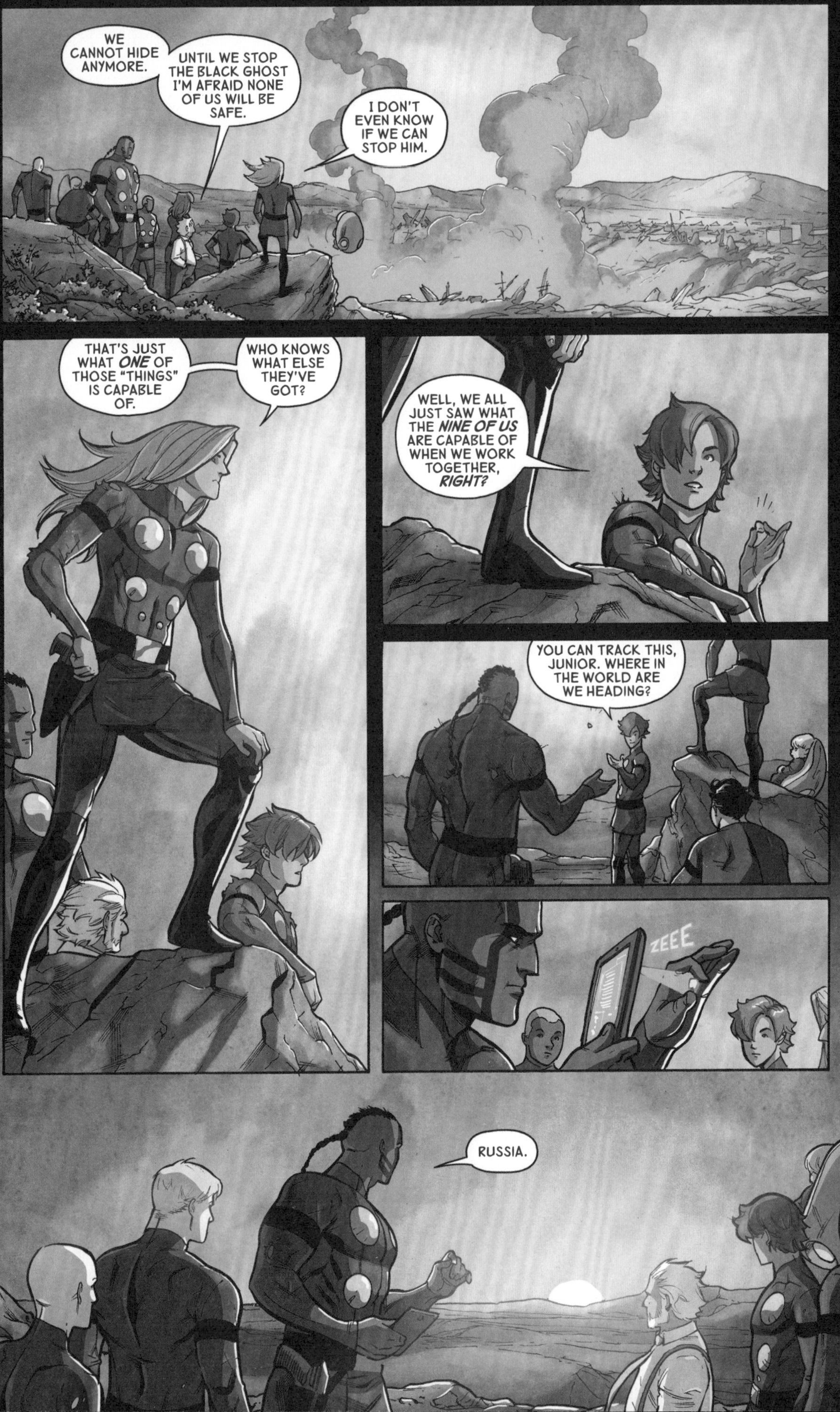
WE CANNOT HIDE ANYMORE.
UNTIL WE STOP THE BLACK GHOST I'M AFRAID NONE OF US WILL BE SAFE.
I DON'T EVEN KNOW IF WE CAN STOP HIM.
THAT'S JUST WHAT *ONE* OF THOSE "THINGS" IS CAPABLE OF.
WHO KNOWS WHAT ELSE THEY'VE GOT?
WELL, WE ALL JUST SAW WHAT THE *NINE OF US* ARE CAPABLE OF WHEN WE WORK TOGETHER, *RIGHT?*
YOU CAN TRACK THIS, JUNIOR. WHERE IN THE WORLD ARE WE HEADING?
ZEEE
RUSSIA.

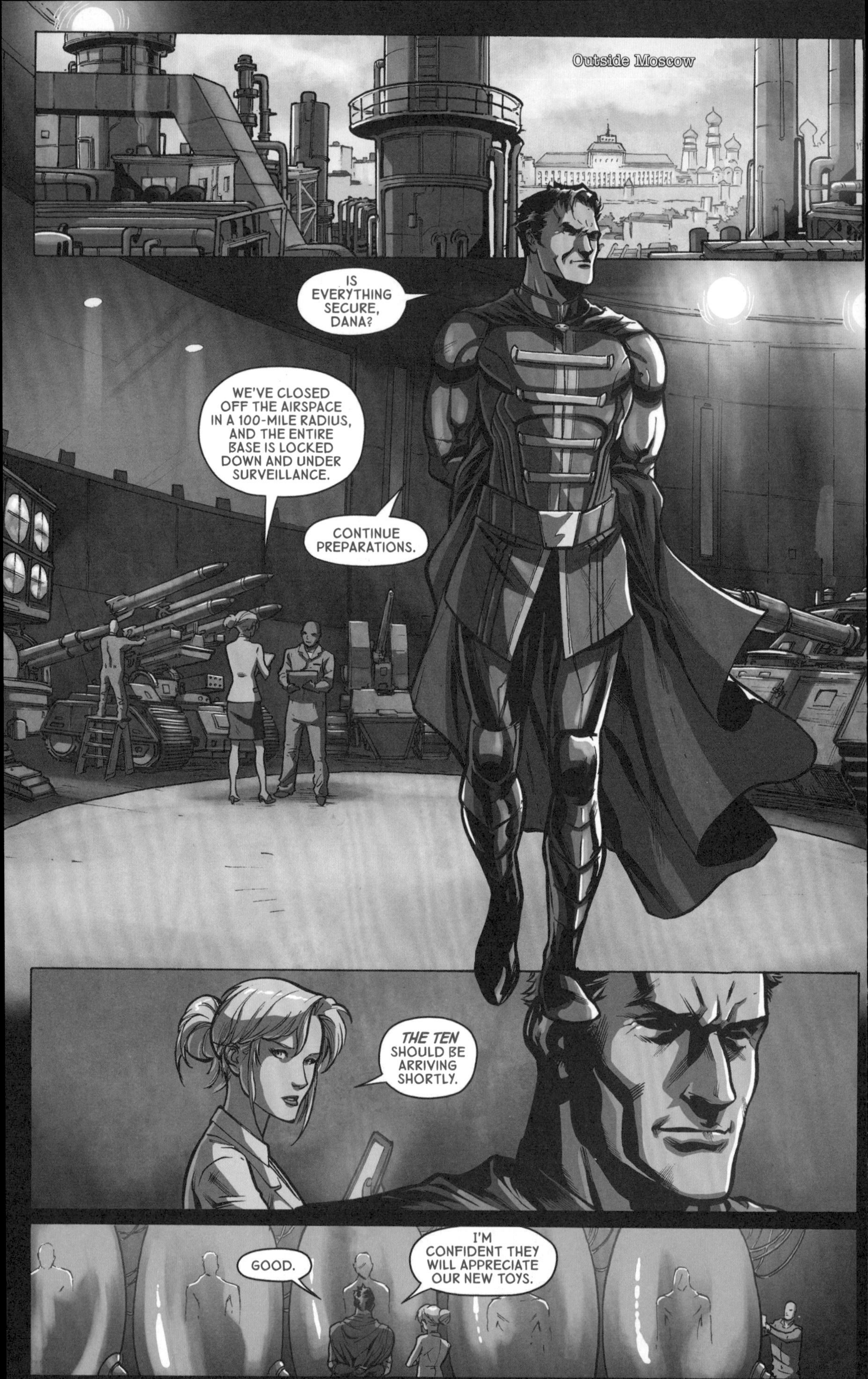
Outside Moscow
IS EVERYTHING SECURE, DANA?
WE'VE CLOSED OFF THE AIRSPACE IN A 100-MILE RADIUS, AND THE ENTIRE BASE IS LOCKED DOWN AND UNDER SURVEILLANCE.
CONTINUE PREPARATIONS.
THE TEN SHOULD BE ARRIVING SHORTLY.
GOOD.
I'M CONFIDENT THEY WILL APPRECIATE OUR NEW TOYS.

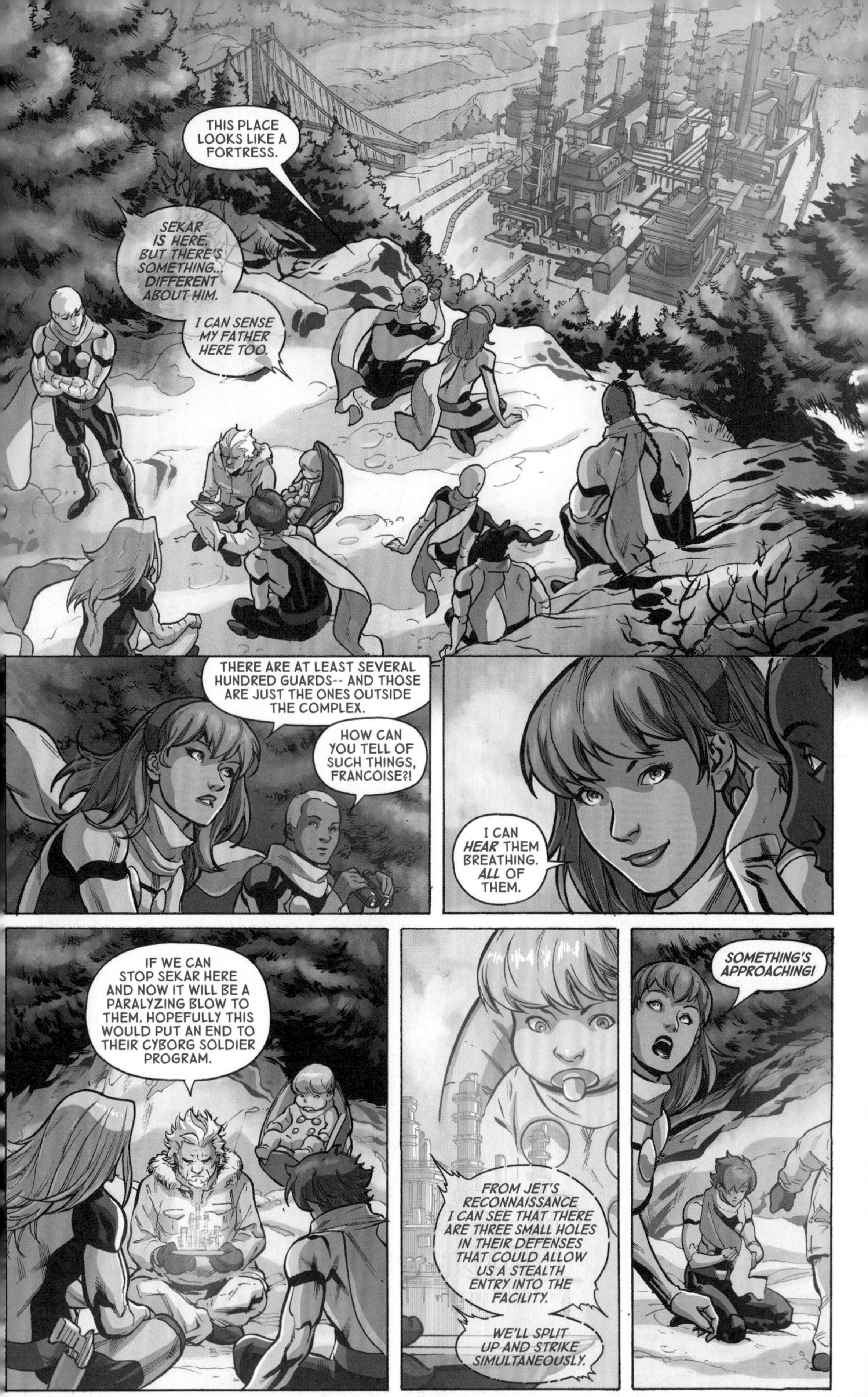
THIS PLACE LOOKS LIKE A FORTRESS.
SEKAR IS HERE. BUT THERE'S SOMETHING... DIFFERENT ABOUT HIM.
I CAN SENSE MY FATHER HERE TOO.
THERE ARE AT LEAST SEVERAL HUNDRED GUARDS-- AND THOSE ARE JUST THE ONES OUTSIDE THE COMPLEX.
HOW CAN YOU TELL OF SUCH THINGS, FRANCOISE?!
I CAN *HEAR* THEM BREATHING. *ALL* OF THEM.
IF WE CAN STOP SEKAR HERE AND NOW IT WILL BE A PARALYZING BLOW TO THEM. HOPEFULLY THIS WOULD PUT AN END TO THEIR CYBORG SOLDIER PROGRAM.
FROM JET'S RECONNAISSANCE I CAN SEE THAT THERE ARE THREE SMALL HOLES IN THEIR DEFENSES THAT COULD ALLOW US A STEALTH ENTRY INTO THE FACILITY.
WE'LL SPLIT UP AND STRIKE SIMULTANEOUSLY.
SOMETHING'S APPROACHING!

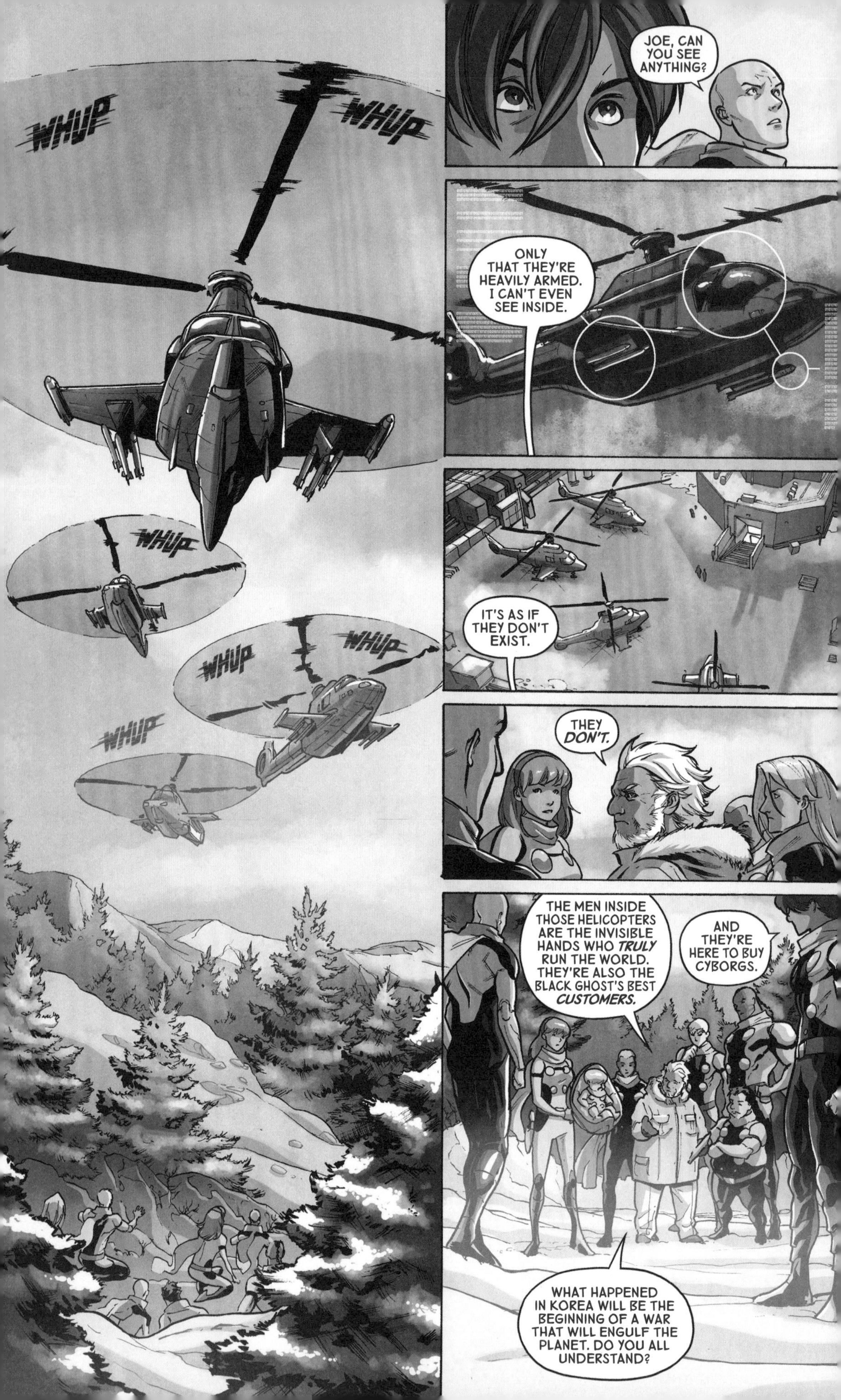
WHUP
WHUP
WHUP
WHUP
WHUP
WHUP
JOE, CAN YOU SEE ANYTHING?
ONLY THAT THEY'RE HEAVILY ARMED. I CAN'T EVEN SEE INSIDE.
IT'S AS IF THEY DON'T EXIST.
THEY *DON'T.*
THE MEN INSIDE THOSE HELICOPTERS ARE THE INVISIBLE HANDS WHO *TRULY* RUN THE WORLD. THEY'RE ALSO THE BLACK GHOST'S BEST *CUSTOMERS.*
AND THEY'RE HERE TO BUY CYBORGS.
WHAT HAPPENED IN KOREA WILL BE THE BEGINNING OF A WAR THAT WILL ENGULF THE PLANET. DO YOU ALL UNDERSTAND?

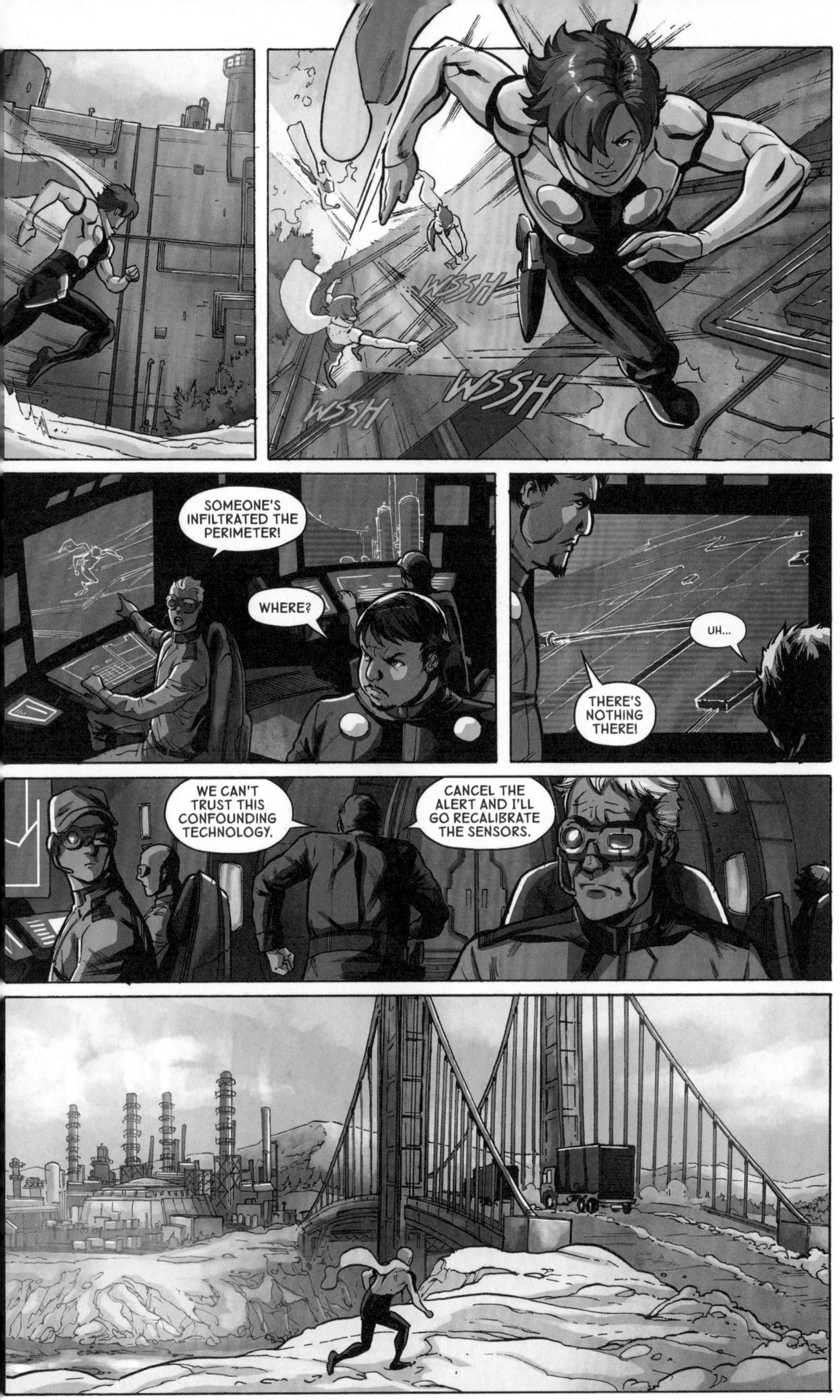
WSSH
WSSH
WSSH
SOMEONE'S INFILTRATED THE PERIMETER!
WHERE?
UH...
THERE'S NOTHING THERE!
WE CAN'T TRUST THIS CONFOUNDING TECHNOLOGY.
CANCEL THE ALERT AND I'LL GO RECALIBRATE THE SENSORS.

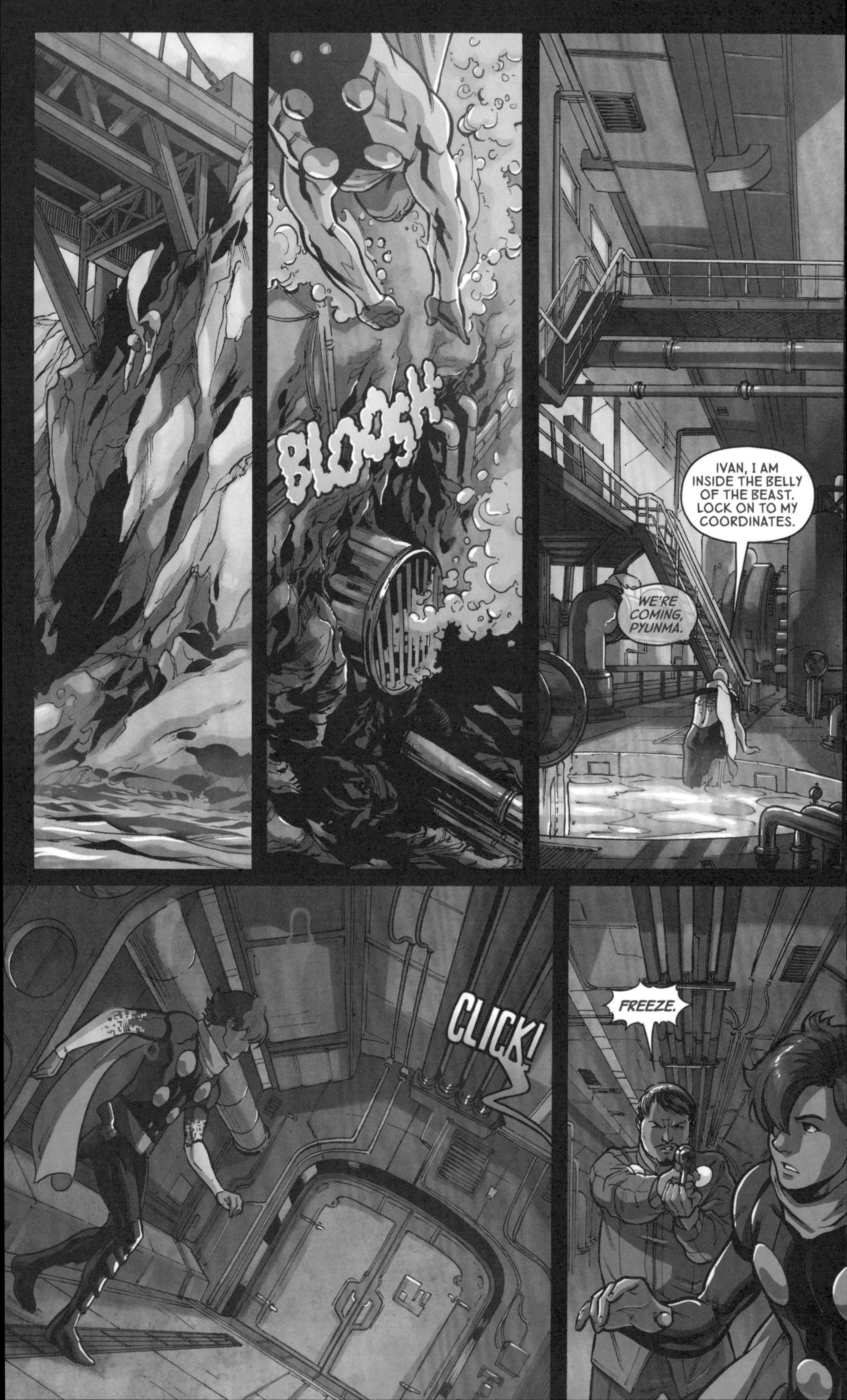
BLOOSH
IVAN, I AM INSIDE THE BELLY OF THE BEAST. LOCK ON TO MY COORDINATES.
WE'RE COMING, PYUNMA.
CLICK!
FREEZE.

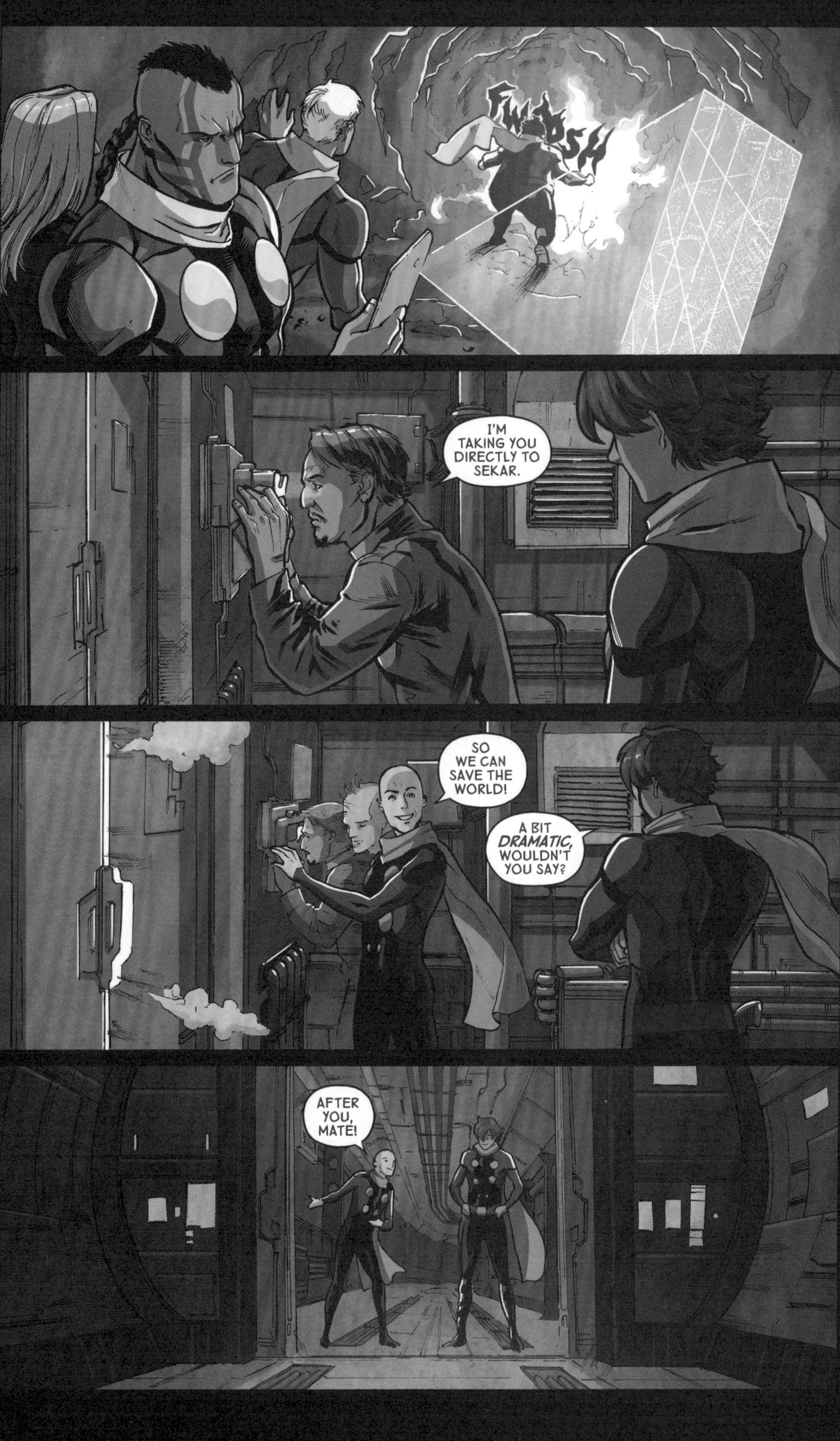
I'M TAKING YOU DIRECTLY TO SEKAR.
SO WE CAN SAVE THE WORLD!
A BIT *DRAMATIC*, WOULDN'T YOU SAY?
AFTER YOU, MATE!

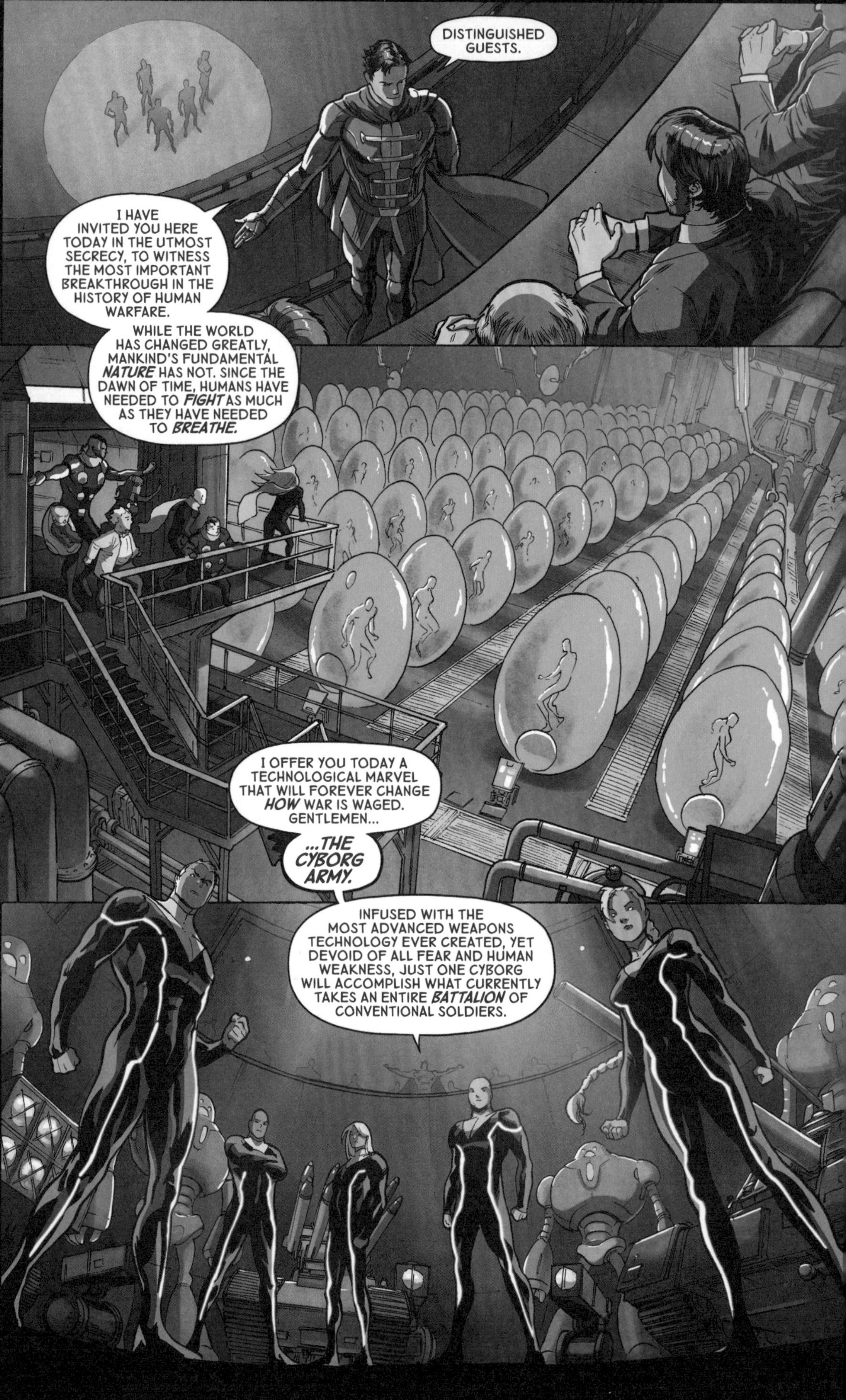
DISTINGUISHED GUESTS.
I HAVE INVITED YOU HERE TODAY IN THE UTMOST SECRECY, TO WITNESS THE MOST IMPORTANT BREAKTHROUGH IN THE HISTORY OF HUMAN WARFARE.
WHILE THE WORLD HAS CHANGED GREATLY, MANKIND'S FUNDAMENTAL NATURE HAS NOT. SINCE THE DAWN OF TIME, HUMANS HAVE NEEDED TO FIGHT AS MUCH AS THEY HAVE NEEDED TO BREATHE.
I OFFER YOU TODAY A TECHNOLOGICAL MARVEL THAT WILL FOREVER CHANGE HOW WAR IS WAGED. GENTLEMEN...
...THE CYBORG ARMY.
INFUSED WITH THE MOST ADVANCED WEAPONS TECHNOLOGY EVER CREATED, YET DEVOID OF ALL FEAR AND HUMAN WEAKNESS, JUST ONE CYBORG WILL ACCOMPLISH WHAT CURRENTLY TAKES AN ENTIRE BATTALION OF CONVENTIONAL SOLDIERS.

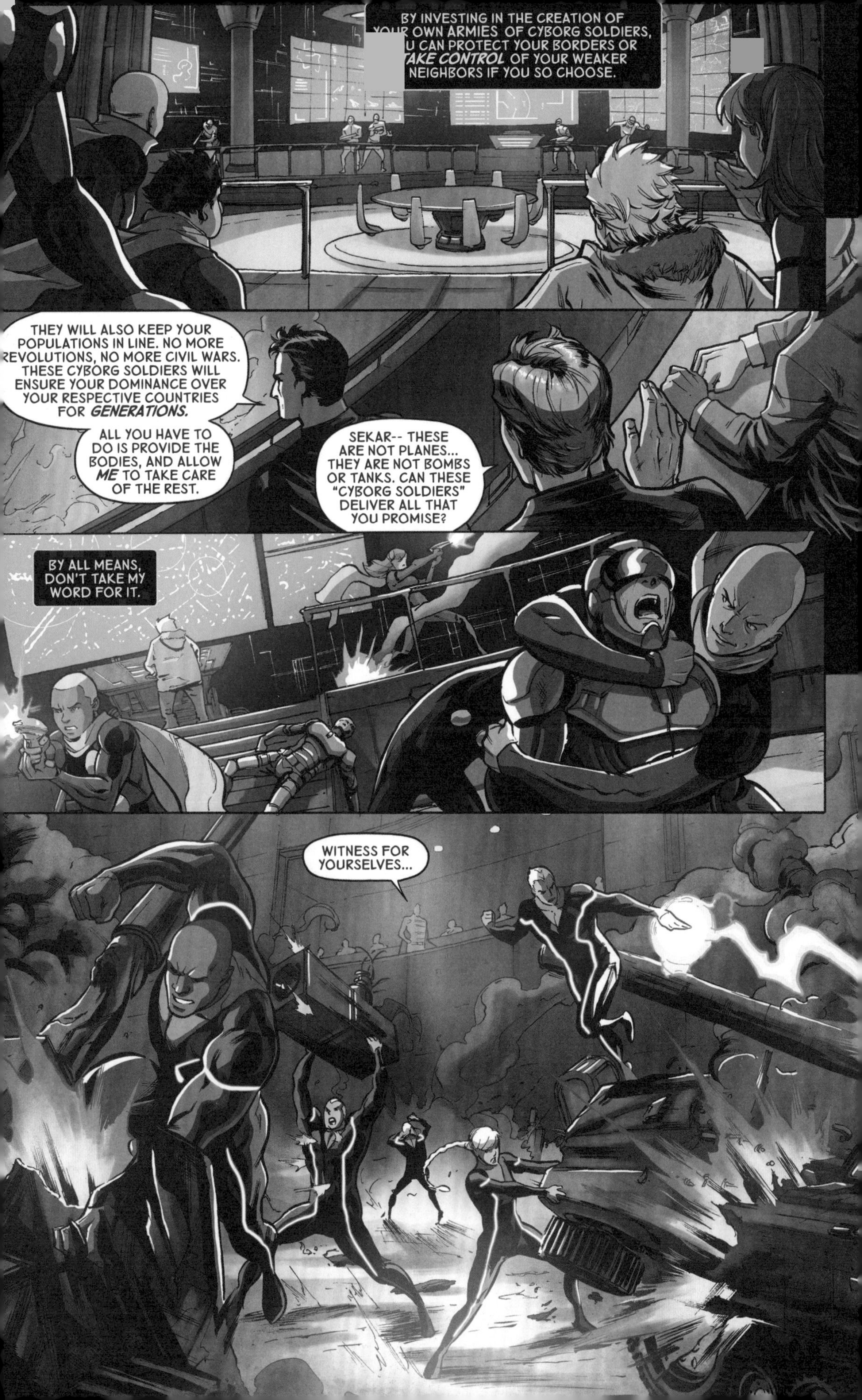
BY INVESTING IN THE CREATION OF YOUR OWN ARMIES OF CYBORG SOLDIERS, U CAN PROTECT YOUR BORDERS OR AKE CONTROL OF YOUR WEAKER NEIGHBORS IF YOU SO CHOOSE.
THEY WILL ALSO KEEP YOUR POPULATIONS IN LINE. NO MORE REVOLUTIONS, NO MORE CIVIL WARS. THESE CYBORG SOLDIERS WILL ENSURE YOUR DOMINANCE OVER YOUR RESPECTIVE COUNTRIES FOR *GENERATIONS.*
ALL YOU HAVE TO DO IS PROVIDE THE BODIES, AND ALLOW *ME* TO TAKE CARE OF THE REST.
SEKAR-- THESE ARE NOT PLANES... THEY ARE NOT BOMBS OR TANKS. CAN THESE "CYBORG SOLDIERS" DELIVER ALL THAT YOU PROMISE?
BY ALL MEANS, DON'T TAKE MY WORD FOR IT.
WITNESS FOR YOURSELVES...

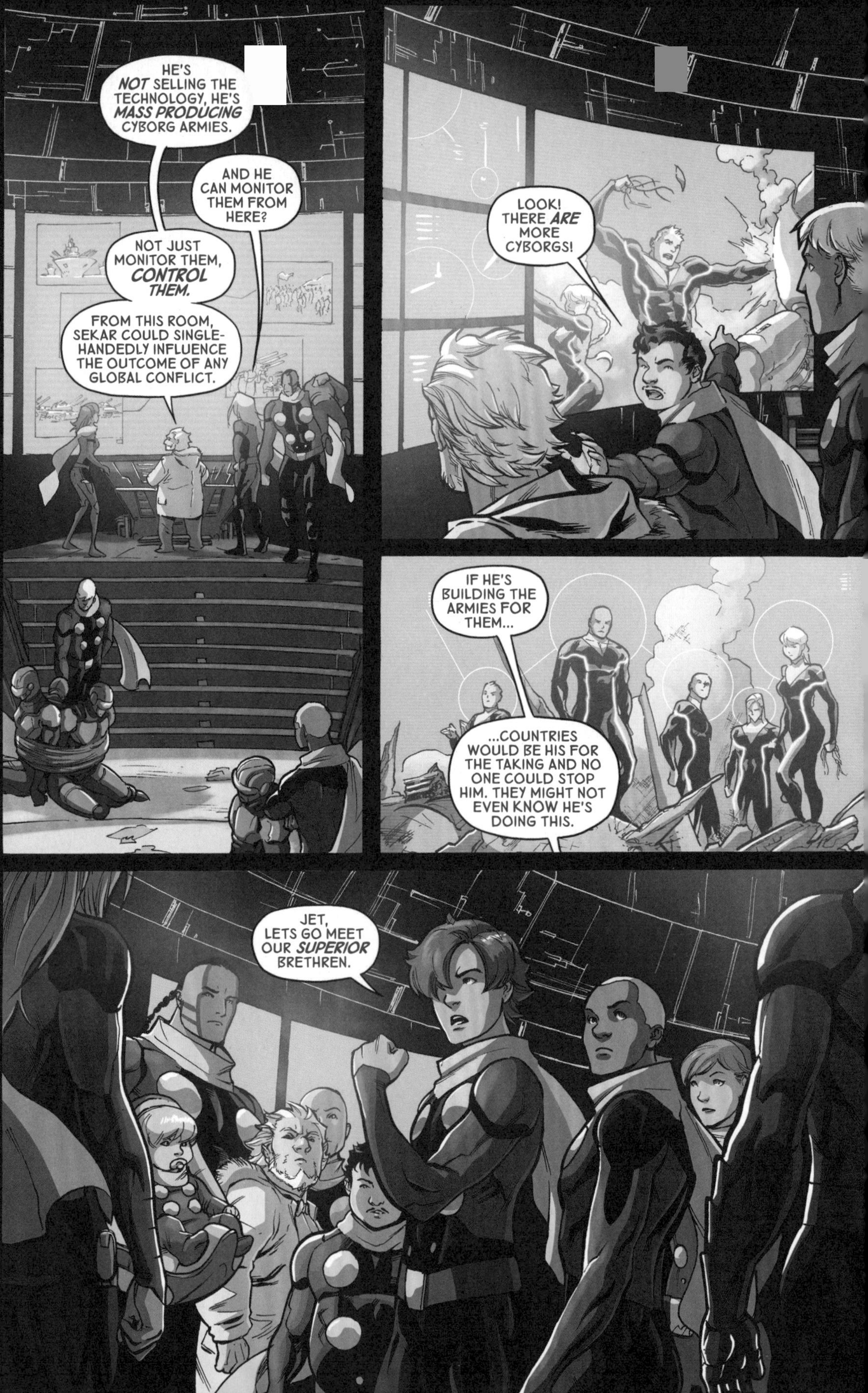
HE'S *NOT* SELLING THE TECHNOLOGY, HE'S *MASS PRODUCING* CYBORG ARMIES.
AND HE CAN MONITOR THEM FROM HERE?
NOT JUST MONITOR THEM, *CONTROL THEM.*
FROM THIS ROOM, SEKAR COULD SINGLE-HANDEDLY INFLUENCE THE OUTCOME OF ANY GLOBAL CONFLICT.
LOOK! THERE *ARE* MORE CYBORGS!
IF HE'S BUILDING THE ARMIES FOR THEM...
...COUNTRIES WOULD BE HIS FOR THE TAKING AND NO ONE COULD STOP HIM. THEY MIGHT NOT EVEN KNOW HE'S DOING THIS.
JET, LETS GO MEET OUR *SUPERIOR* BRETHREN.

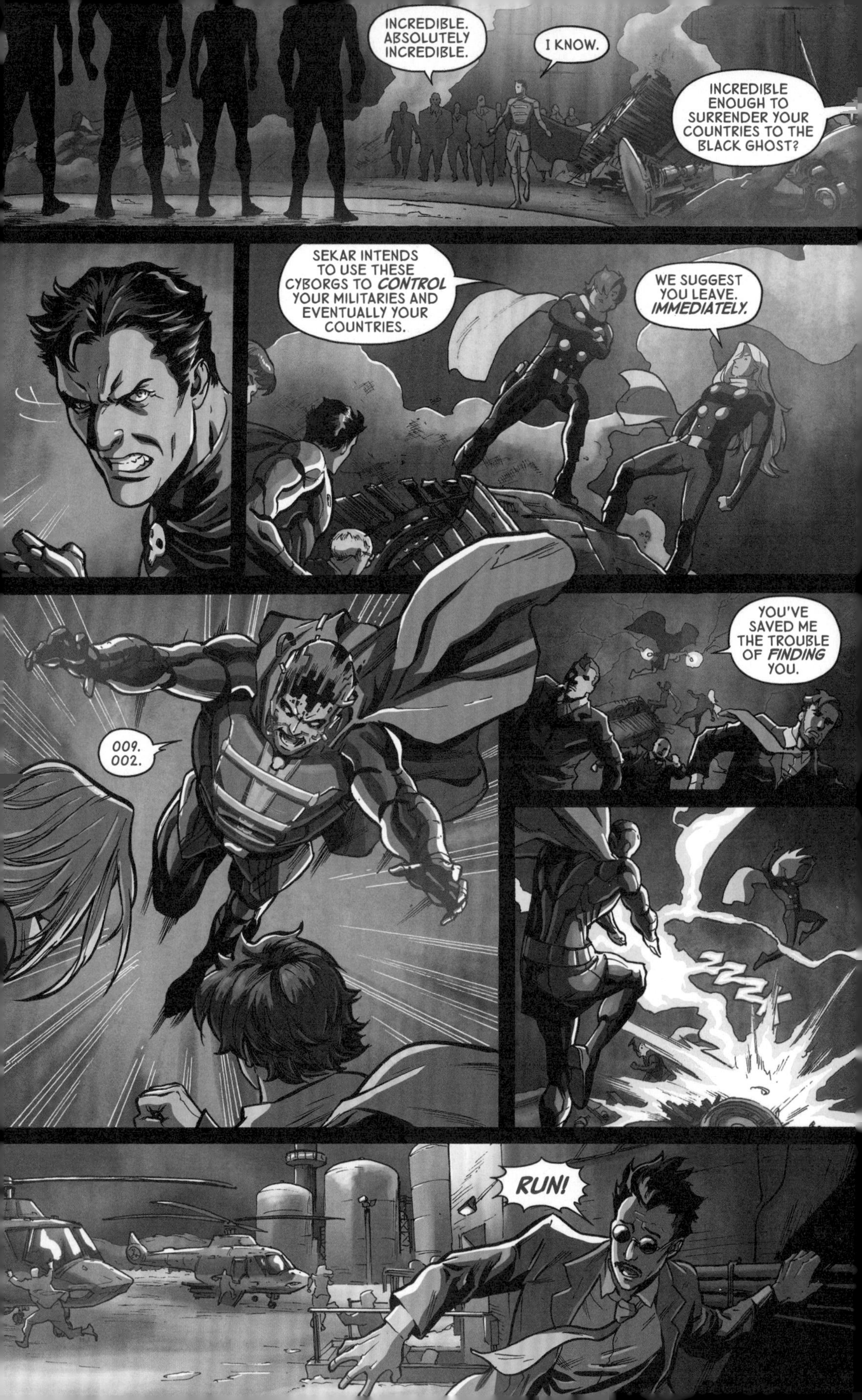
INCREDIBLE. ABSOLUTELY INCREDIBLE.
I KNOW.
INCREDIBLE ENOUGH TO SURRENDER YOUR COUNTRIES TO THE BLACK GHOST?
SEKAR INTENDS TO USE THESE CYBORGS TO *CONTROL* YOUR MILITARIES AND EVENTUALLY YOUR COUNTRIES.
WE SUGGEST YOU LEAVE. *IMMEDIATELY.*
009. 002.
YOU'VE SAVED ME THE TROUBLE OF *FINDING* YOU.
ZZZZK
RUN!

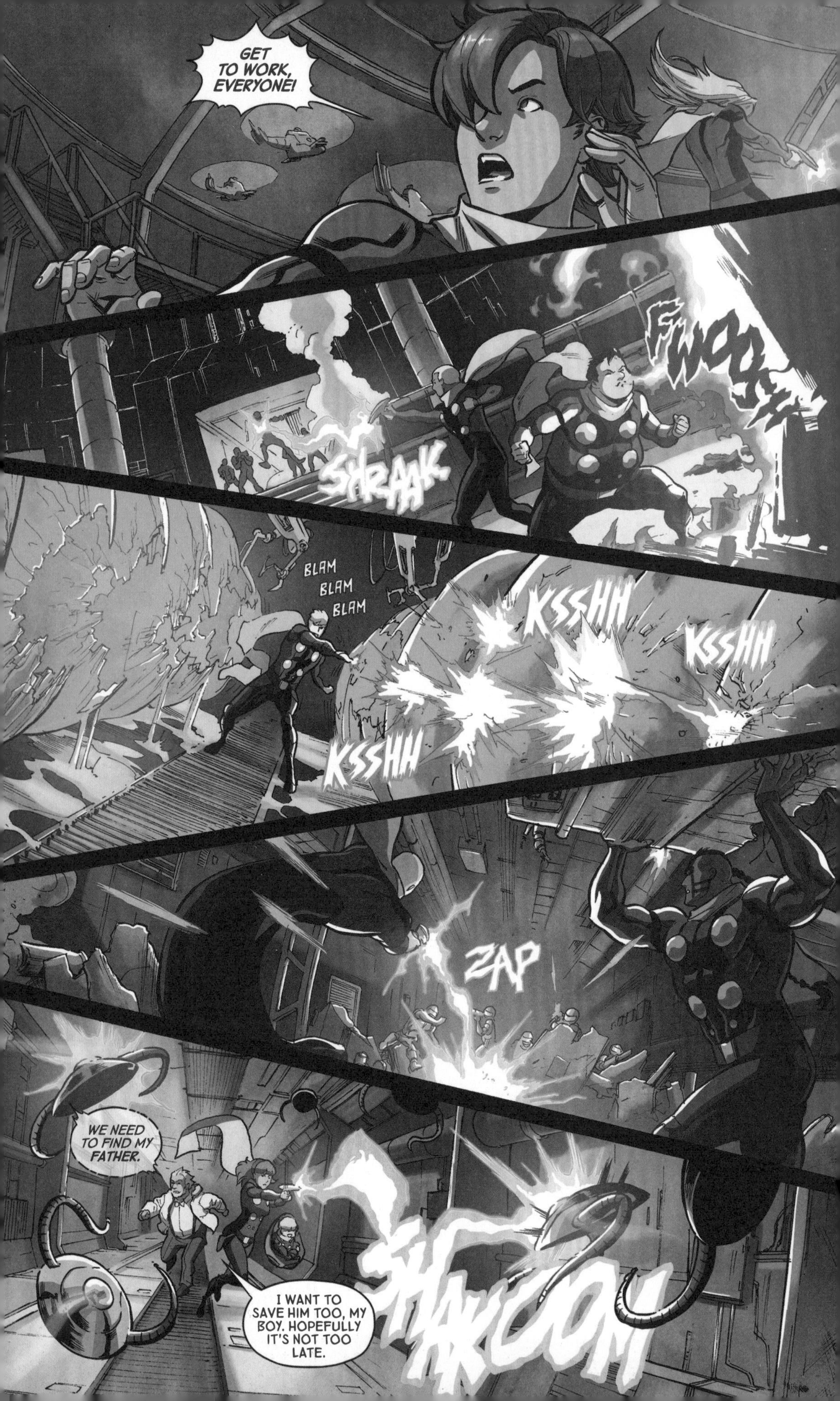
GET TO WORK, EVERYONE!
FWOOSH
SHRAAK
BLAM BLAM BLAM
KSSHH
KSSHH
KSSHH
ZAP
WE NEED TO FIND MY FATHER.
I WANT TO SAVE HIM TOO, MY BOY. HOPEFULLY IT'S NOT TOO LATE.
SHAKOOM

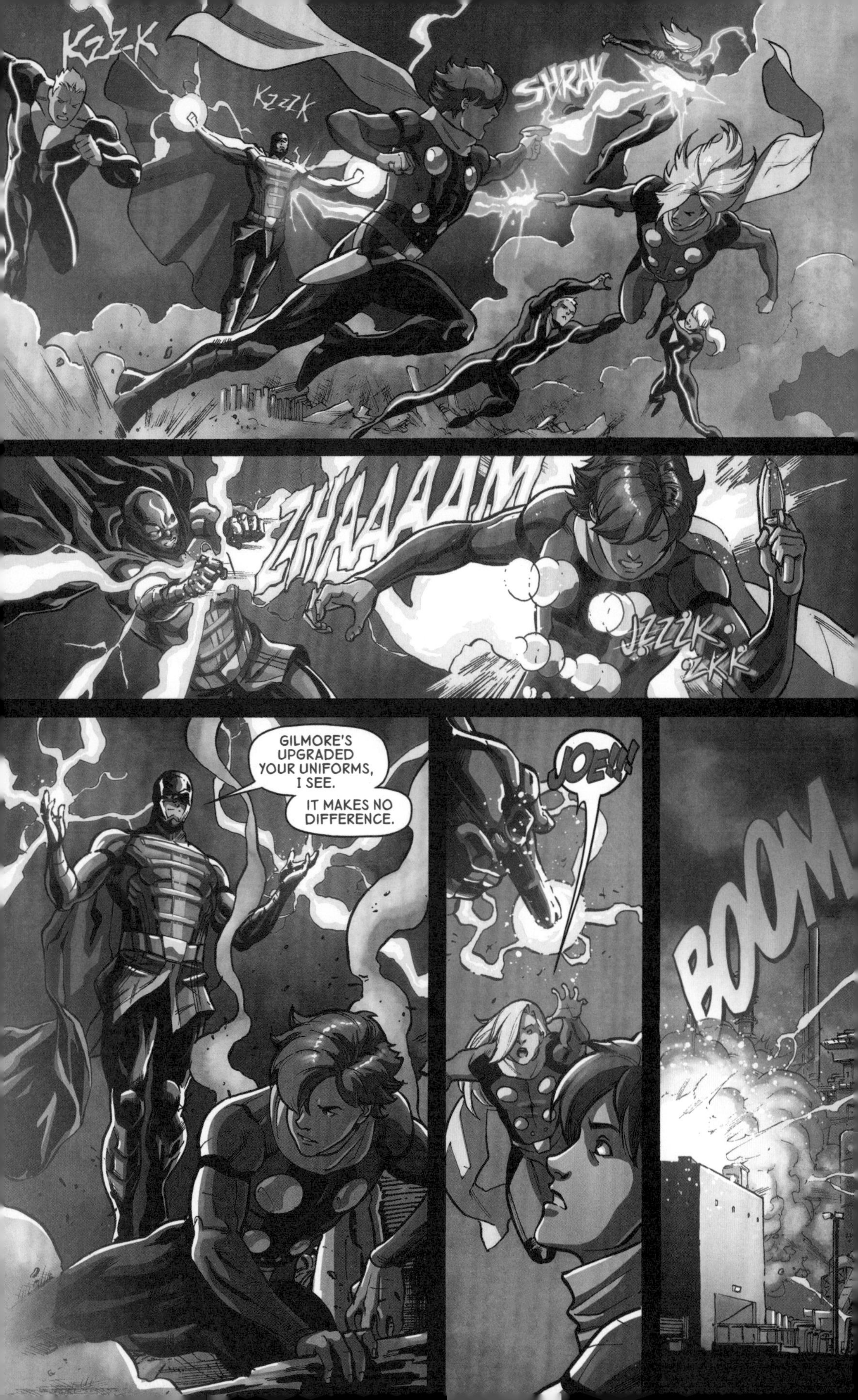
KZZ-K
KZZZK
SHRAK
ZHAAAAM
JZZZK
ZKK
GILMORE'S UPGRADED YOUR UNIFORMS, I SEE.
IT MAKES NO DIFFERENCE.
JOE!!!
BOOM

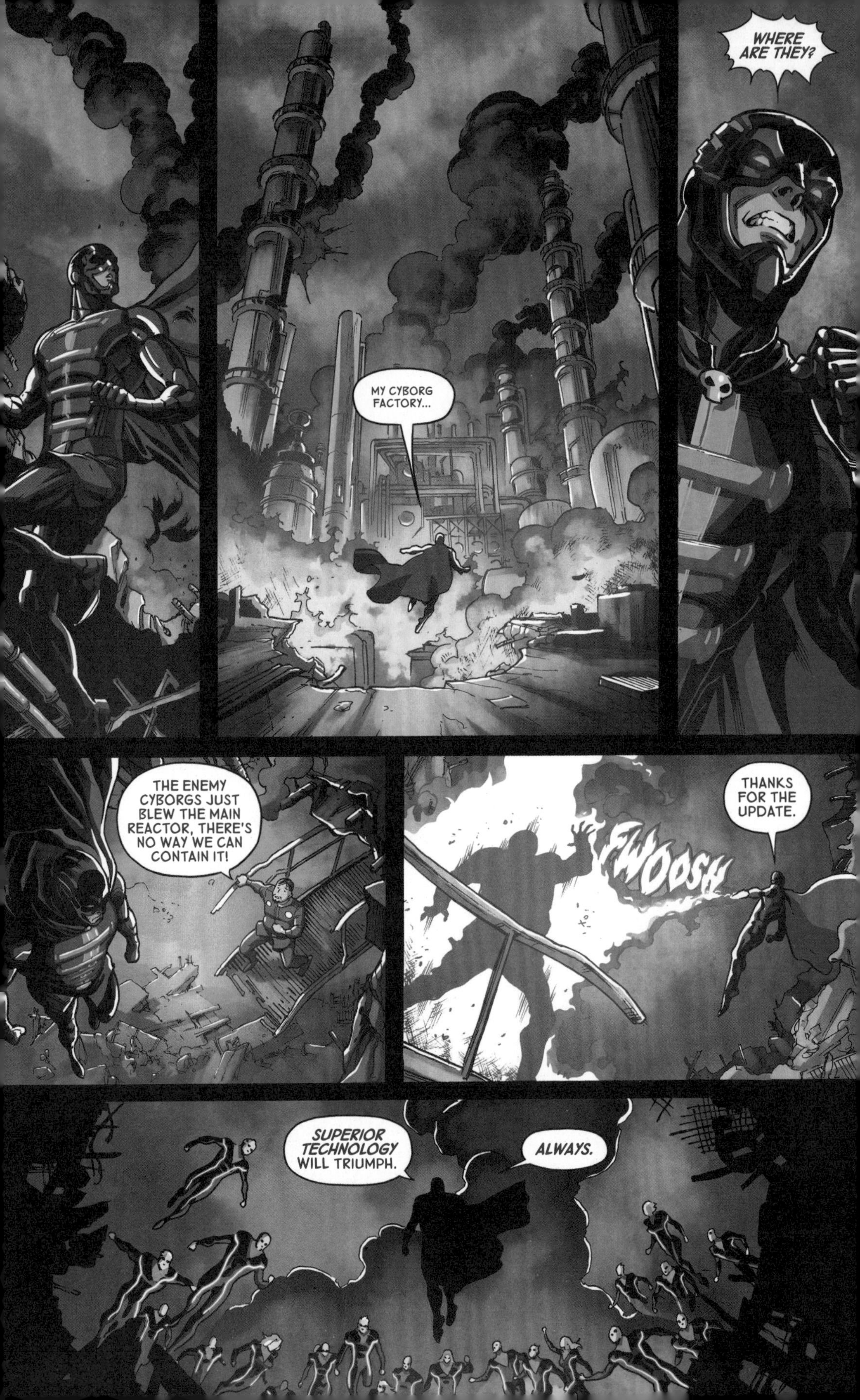
MY CYBORG FACTORY...
WHERE ARE THEY?
THE ENEMY CYBORGS JUST BLEW THE MAIN REACTOR, THERE'S NO WAY WE CAN CONTAIN IT!
FWOOSH
THANKS FOR THE UPDATE.
SUPERIOR TECHNOLOGY WILL TRIUMPH.
ALWAYS.

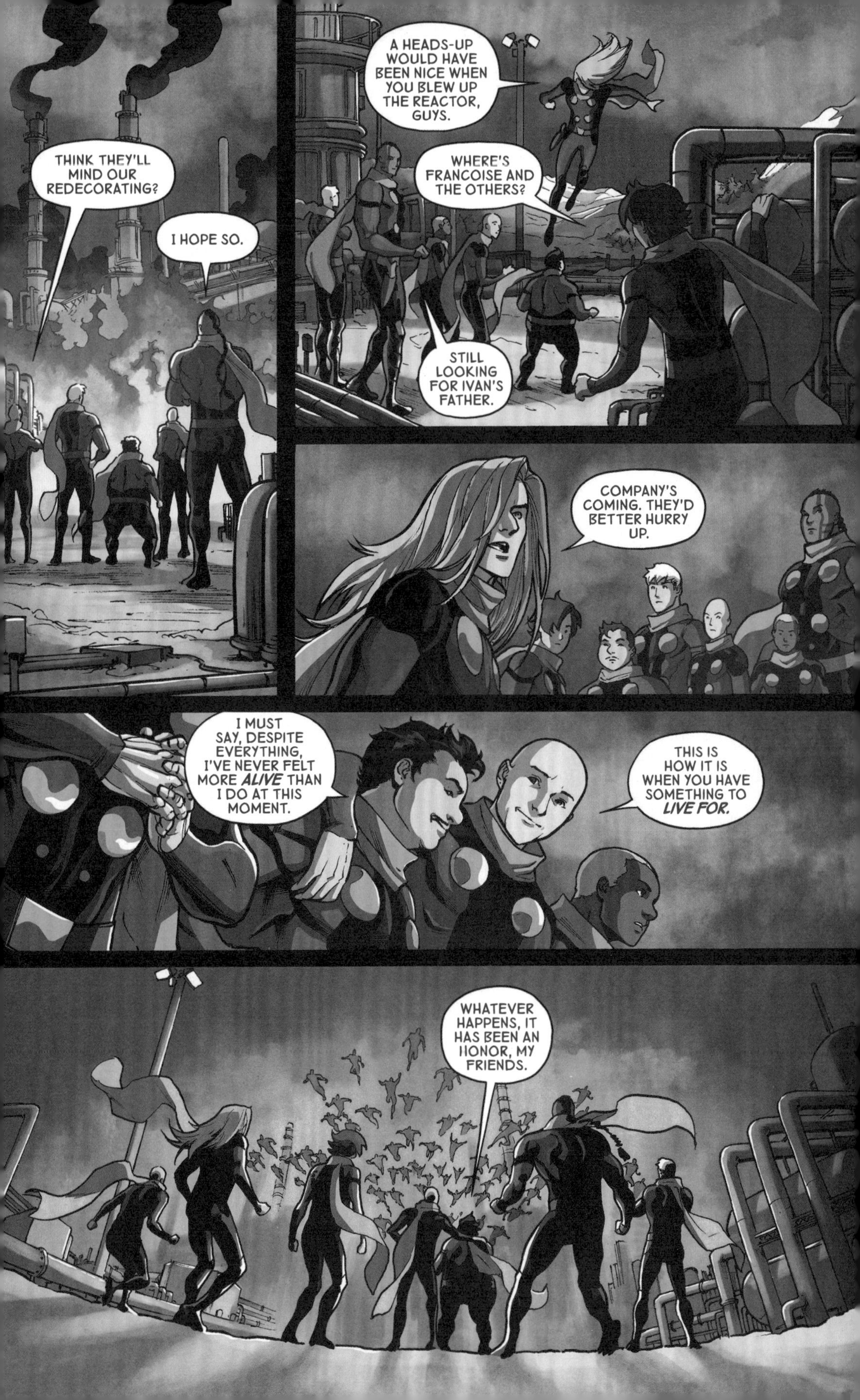

THINK THEY'LL MIND OUR REDECORATING?
I HOPE SO.
A HEADS-UP WOULD HAVE BEEN NICE WHEN YOU BLEW UP THE REACTOR, GUYS.
WHERE'S FRANCOISE AND THE OTHERS?
STILL LOOKING FOR IVAN'S FATHER.
COMPANY'S COMING. THEY'D BETTER HURRY UP.
I MUST SAY, DESPITE EVERYTHING, I'VE NEVER FELT MORE *ALIVE* THAN I DO AT THIS MOMENT.
THIS IS HOW IT IS WHEN YOU HAVE SOMETHING TO ***LIVE FOR.***
WHATEVER HAPPENS, IT HAS BEEN AN HONOR, MY FRIENDS.

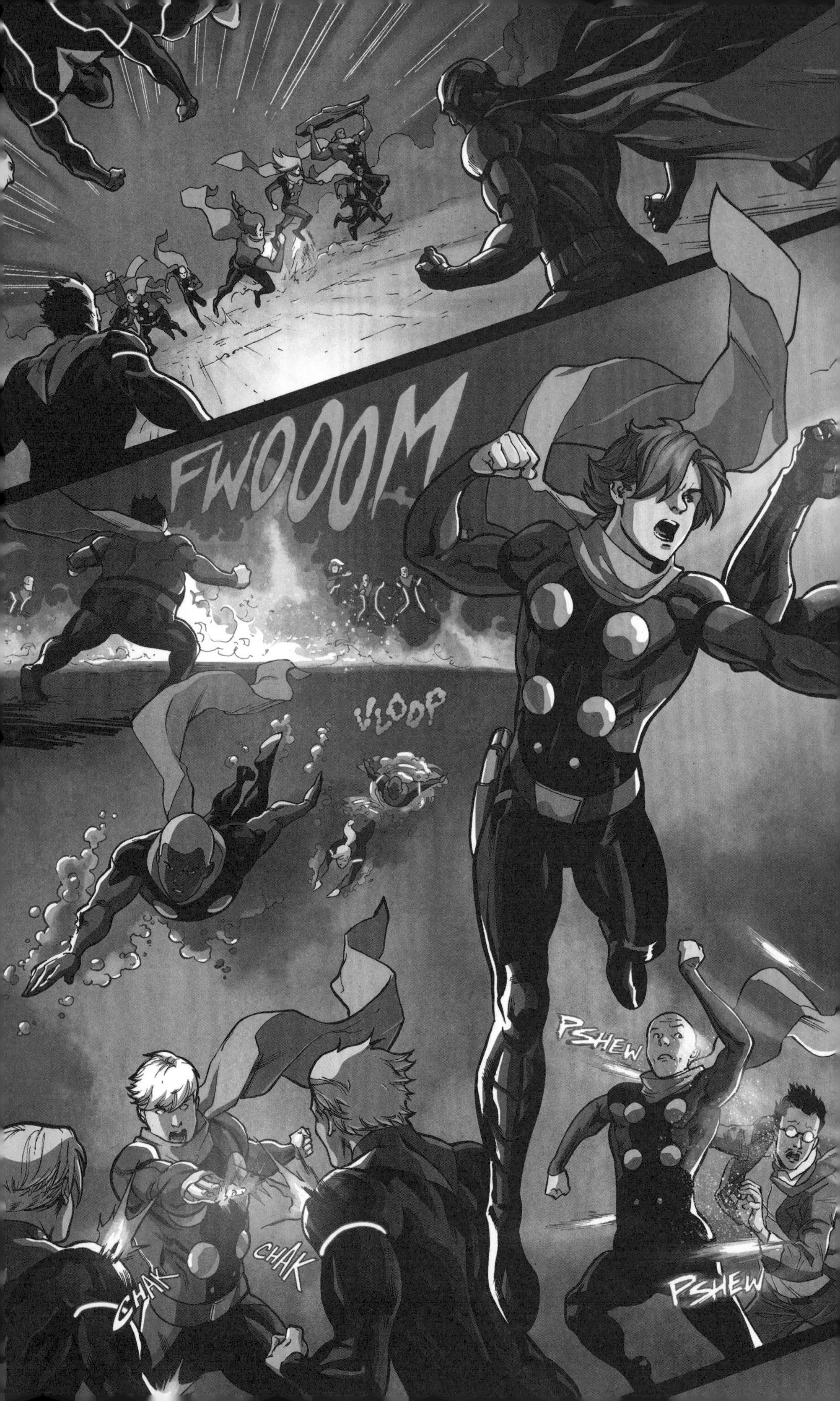
FWOOOM
VLOOP
CHAK
CHAK
PSHEW
PSHEW

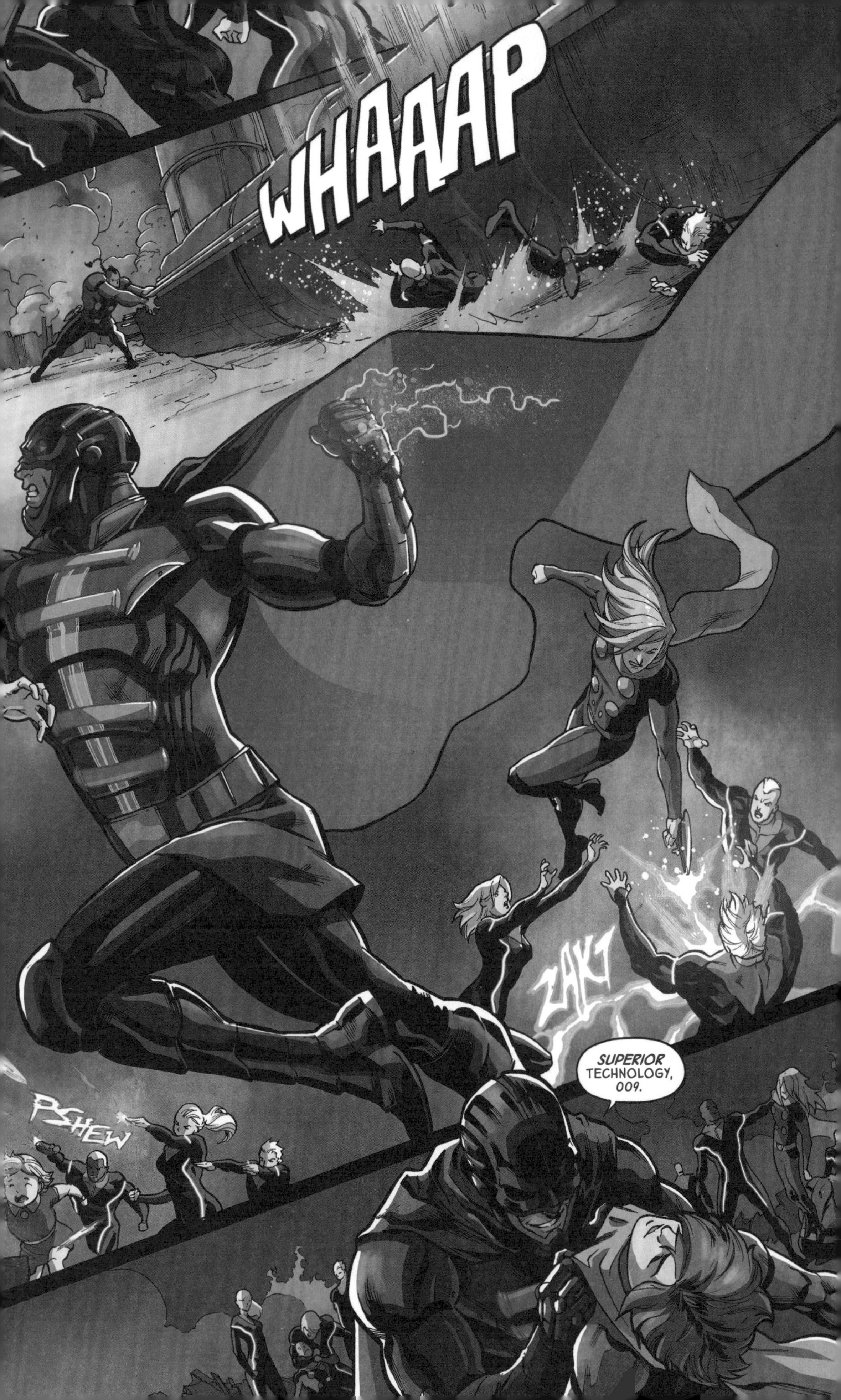
WHAAAP
ZAK!
PSHEW
SUPERIOR TECHNOLOGY, 009.

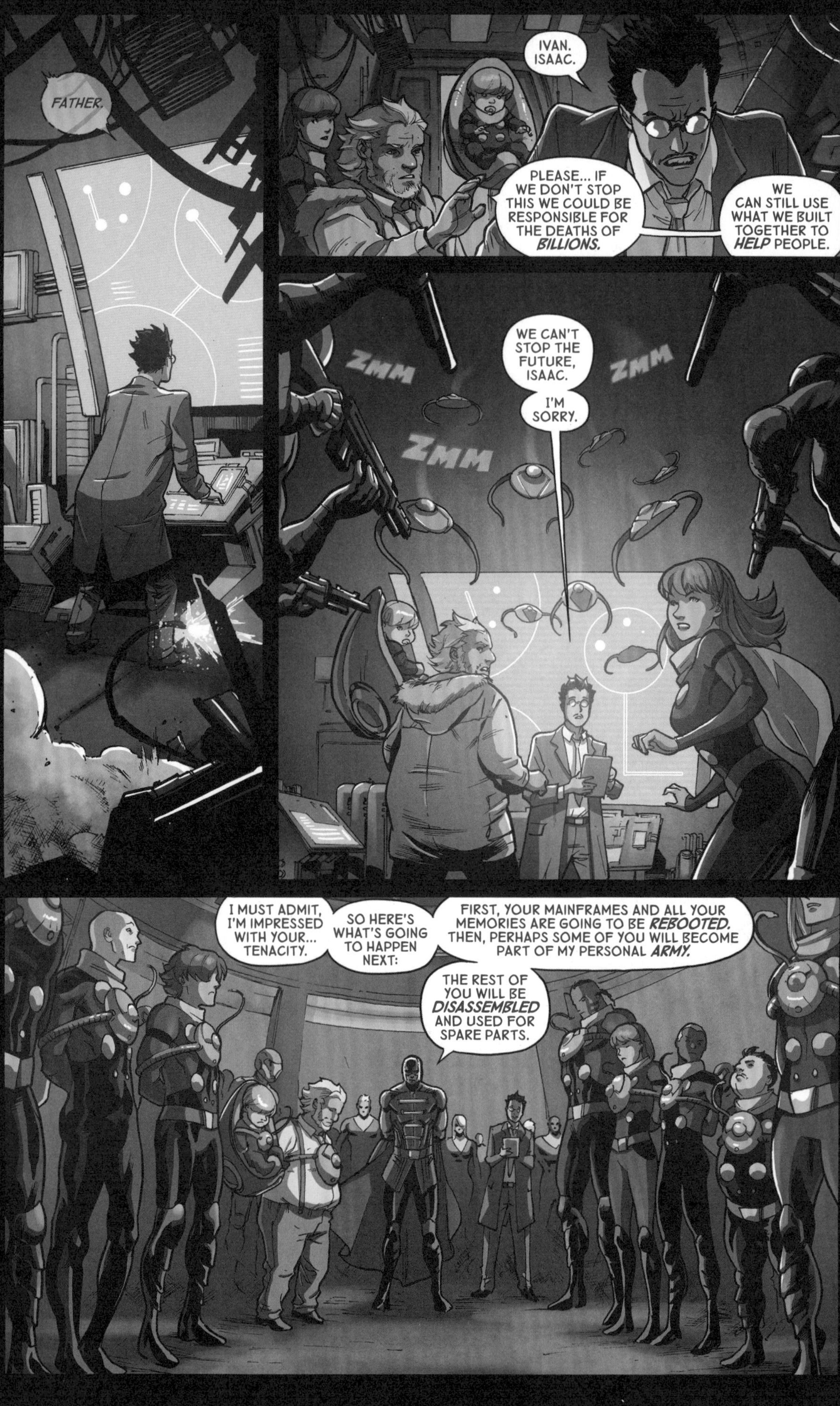
FATHER.
IVAN. ISAAC.
PLEASE... IF WE DON'T STOP THIS WE COULD BE RESPONSIBLE FOR THE DEATHS OF BILLIONS.
WE CAN STILL USE WHAT WE BUILT TOGETHER TO HELP PEOPLE.
WE CAN'T STOP THE FUTURE, ISAAC.
I'M SORRY.
ZMM
ZMM
ZMM
I MUST ADMIT, I'M IMPRESSED WITH YOUR... TENACITY.
SO HERE'S WHAT'S GOING TO HAPPEN NEXT:
FIRST, YOUR MAINFRAMES AND ALL YOUR MEMORIES ARE GOING TO BE REBOOTED. THEN, PERHAPS SOME OF YOU WILL BECOME PART OF MY PERSONAL ARMY.
THE REST OF YOU WILL BE DISASSEMBLED AND USED FOR SPARE PARTS.

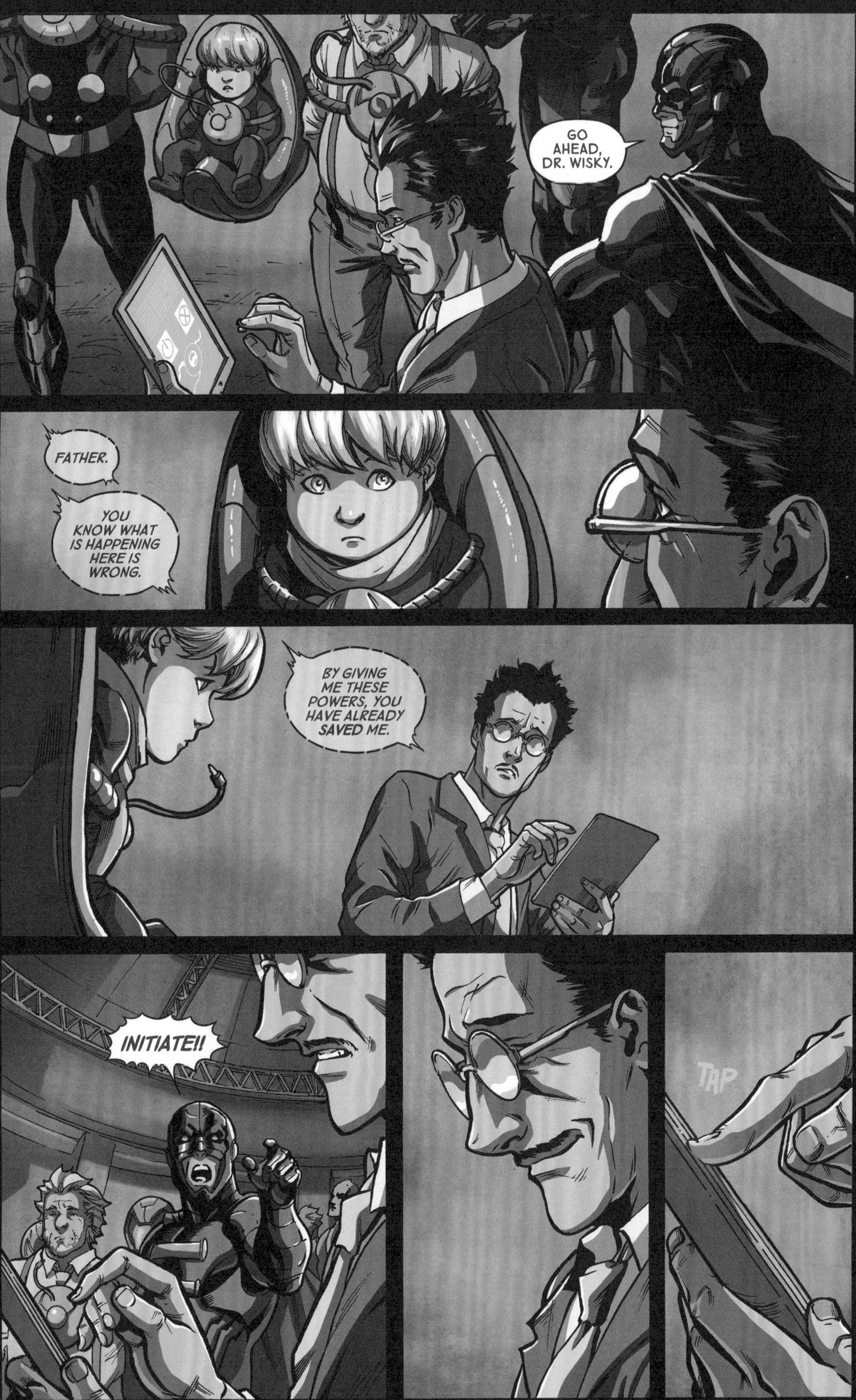
GO AHEAD, DR. WISKY.
FATHER.
YOU KNOW WHAT IS HAPPENING HERE IS WRONG.
BY GIVING ME THESE POWERS, YOU HAVE ALREADY SAVED ME.
INITIATE!!
TAP

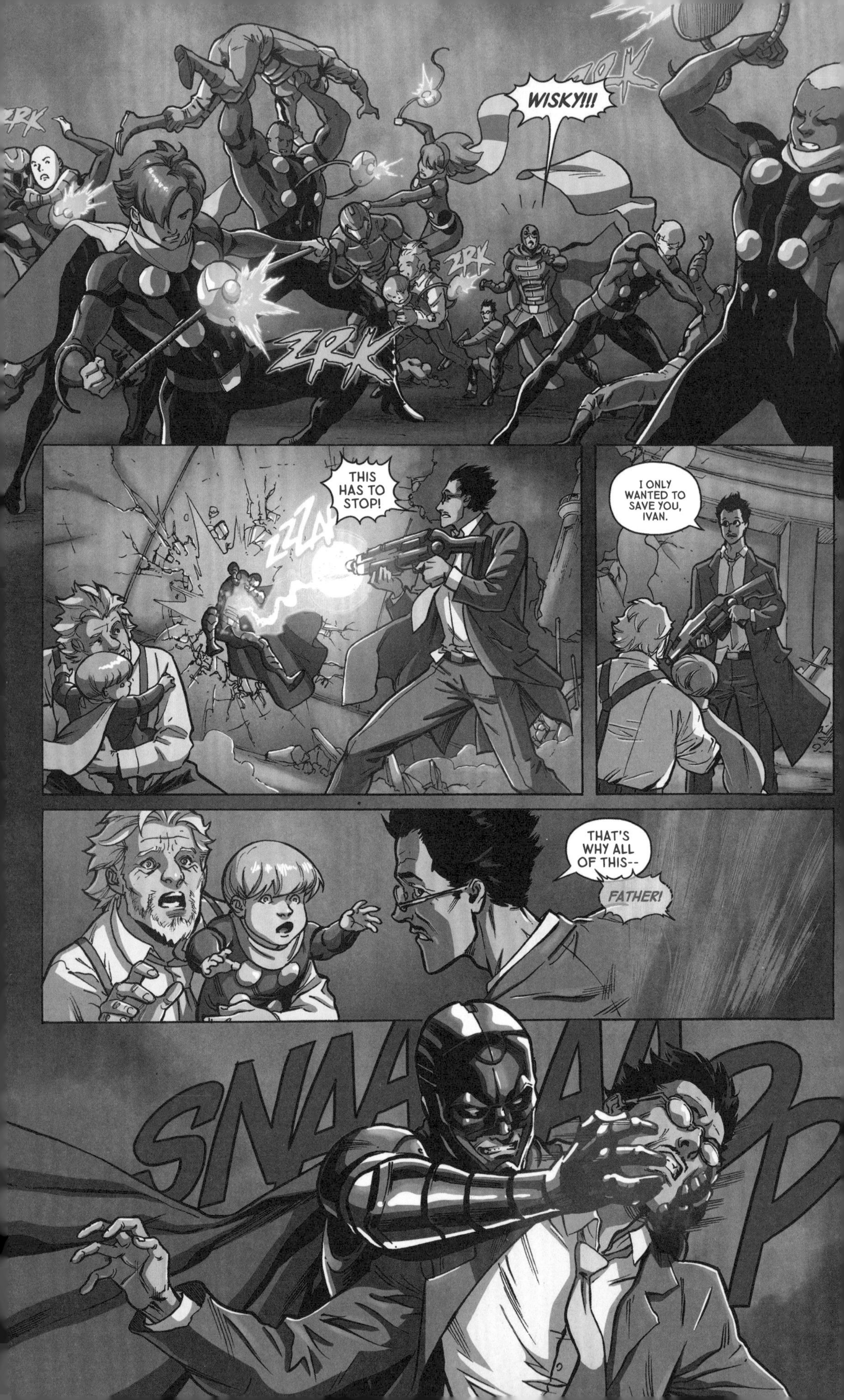
ZRK
WISKY!!!
ZRK
ZRK
ZRK
THIS HAS TO STOP!
ZZZAP
I ONLY WANTED TO SAVE YOU, IVAN.
THAT'S WHY ALL OF THIS--
FATHER!
SNAAAAP

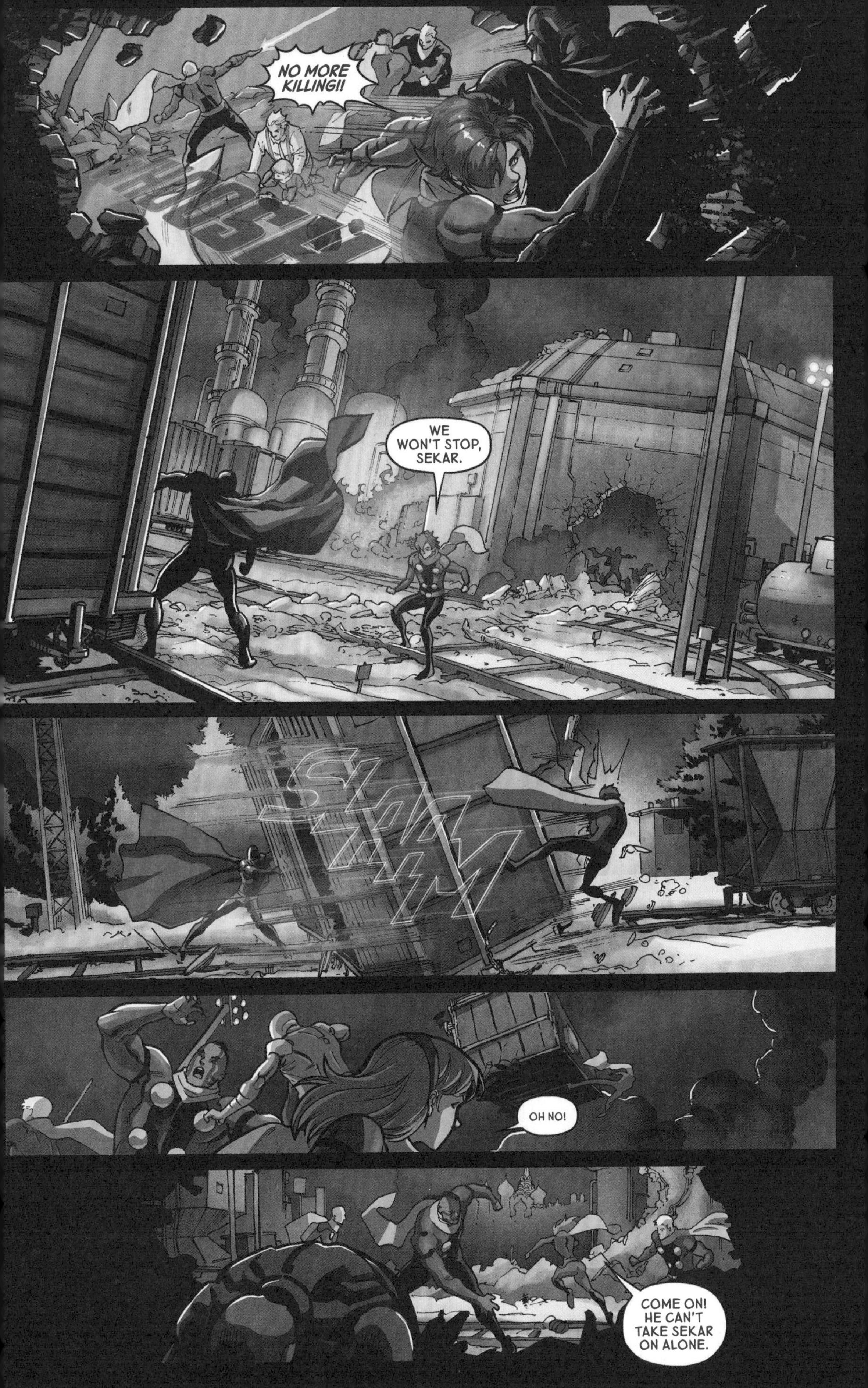
NO MORE KILLING!!
WE WON'T STOP, SEKAR.
OH NO!
COME ON! HE CAN'T TAKE SEKAR ON ALONE.

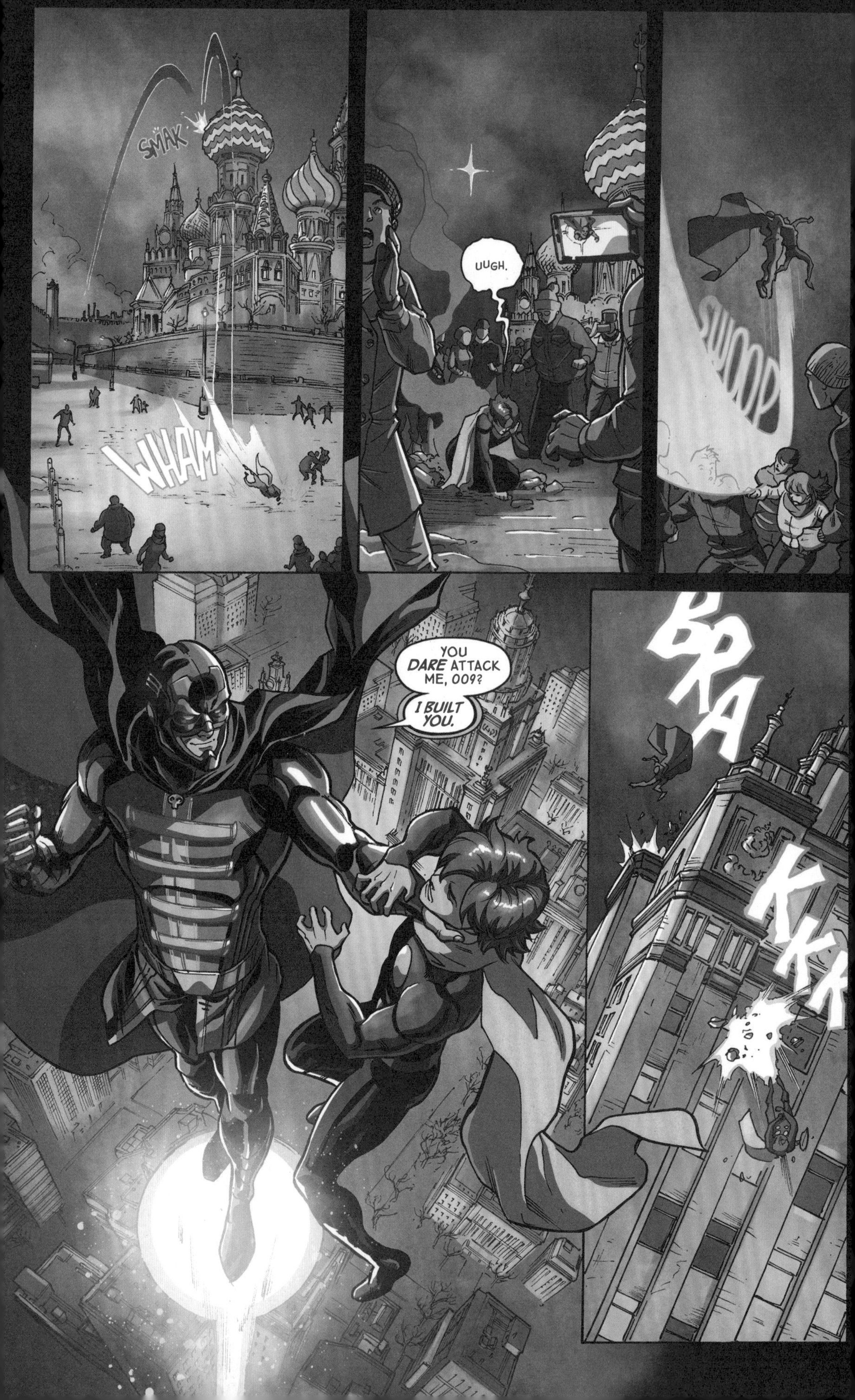
SMAK
WHAM
UUGH.
SWOOP
YOU *DARE* ATTACK ME, 009?
I BUILT YOU.
BRAKKK

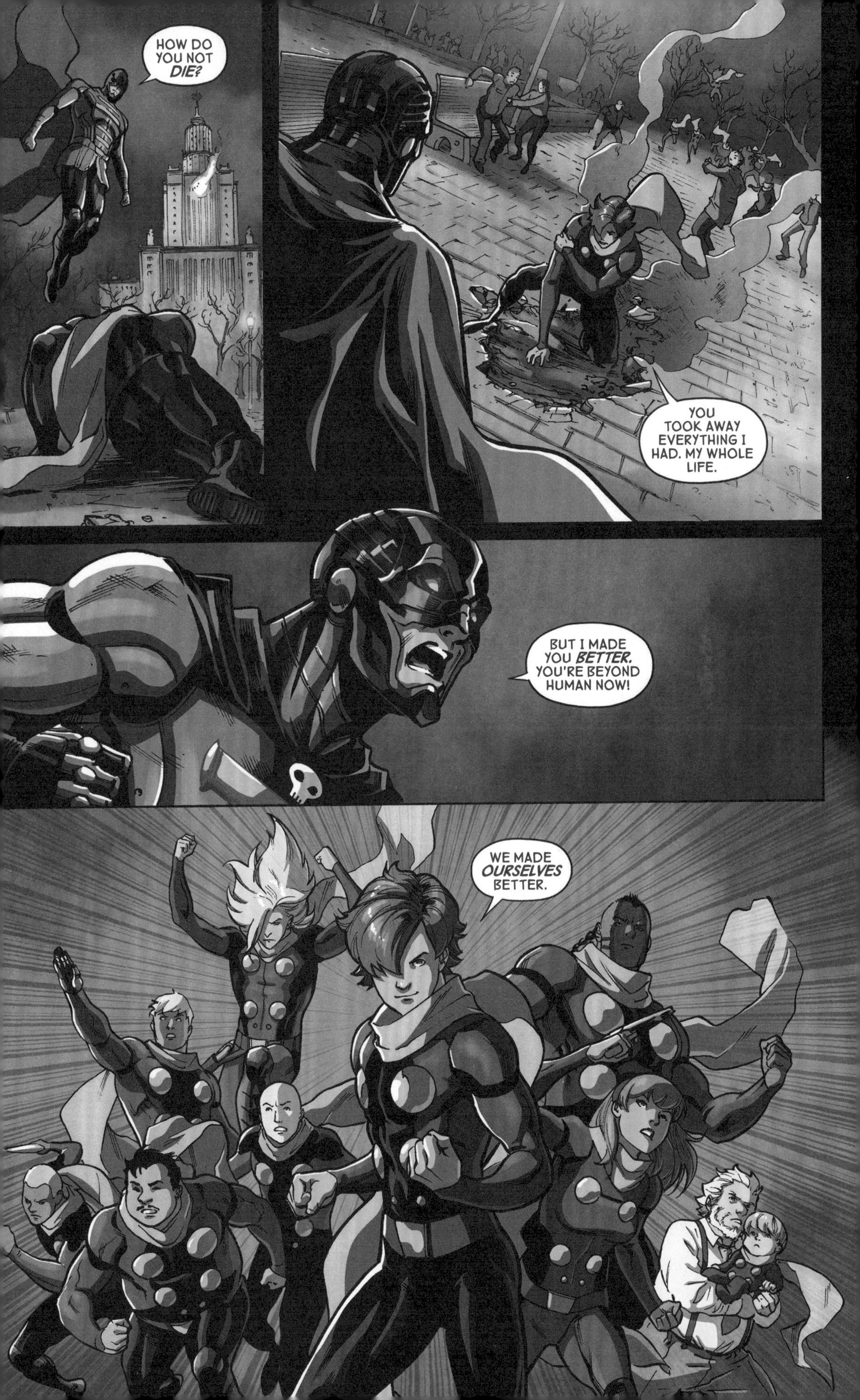
HOW DO YOU NOT *DIE?*
YOU TOOK AWAY EVERYTHING I HAD. MY WHOLE LIFE.
BUT I MADE YOU *BETTER.* YOU'RE BEYOND HUMAN NOW!
WE MADE *OURSELVES* BETTER.

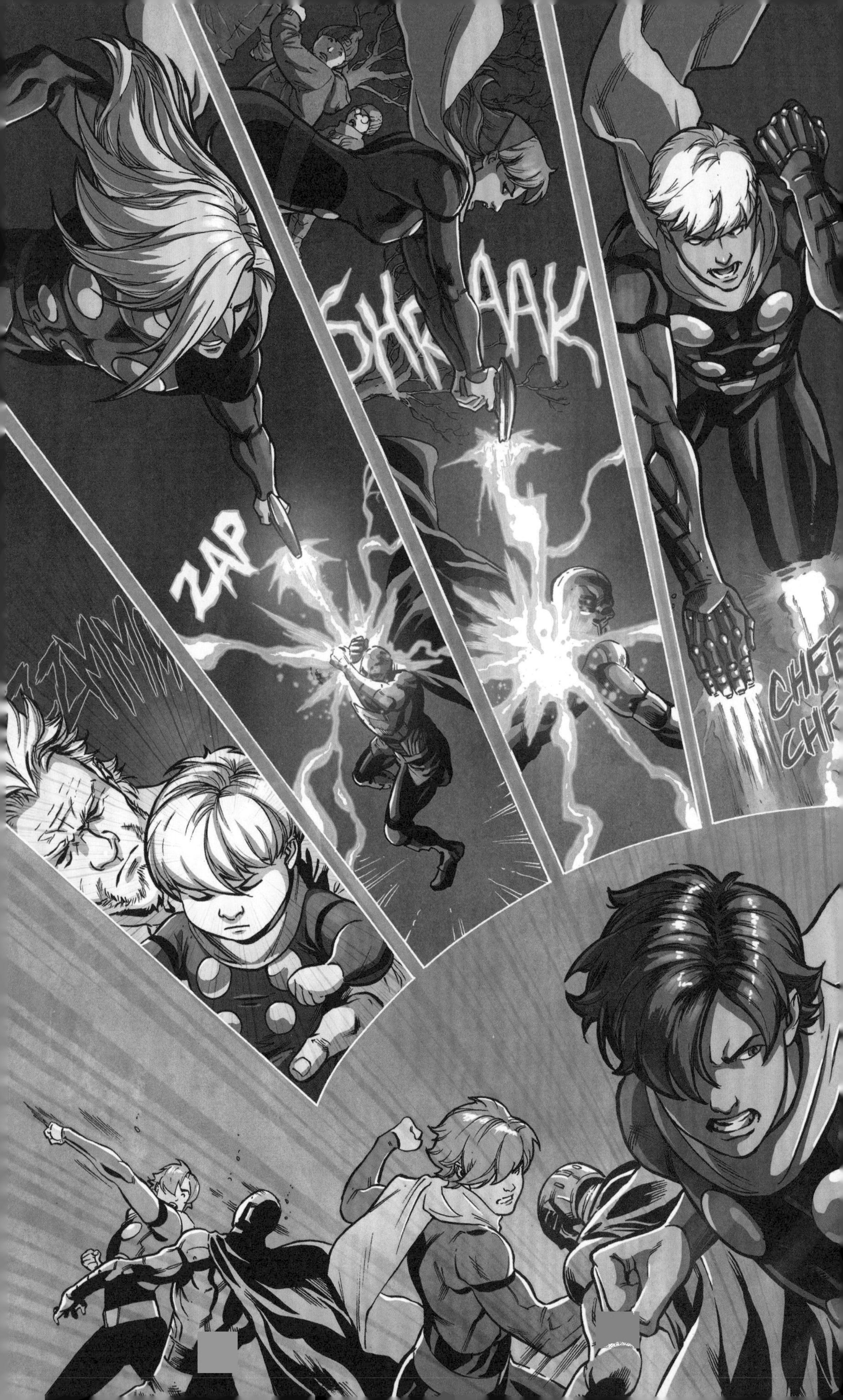
ZAP
CHFF
CHF

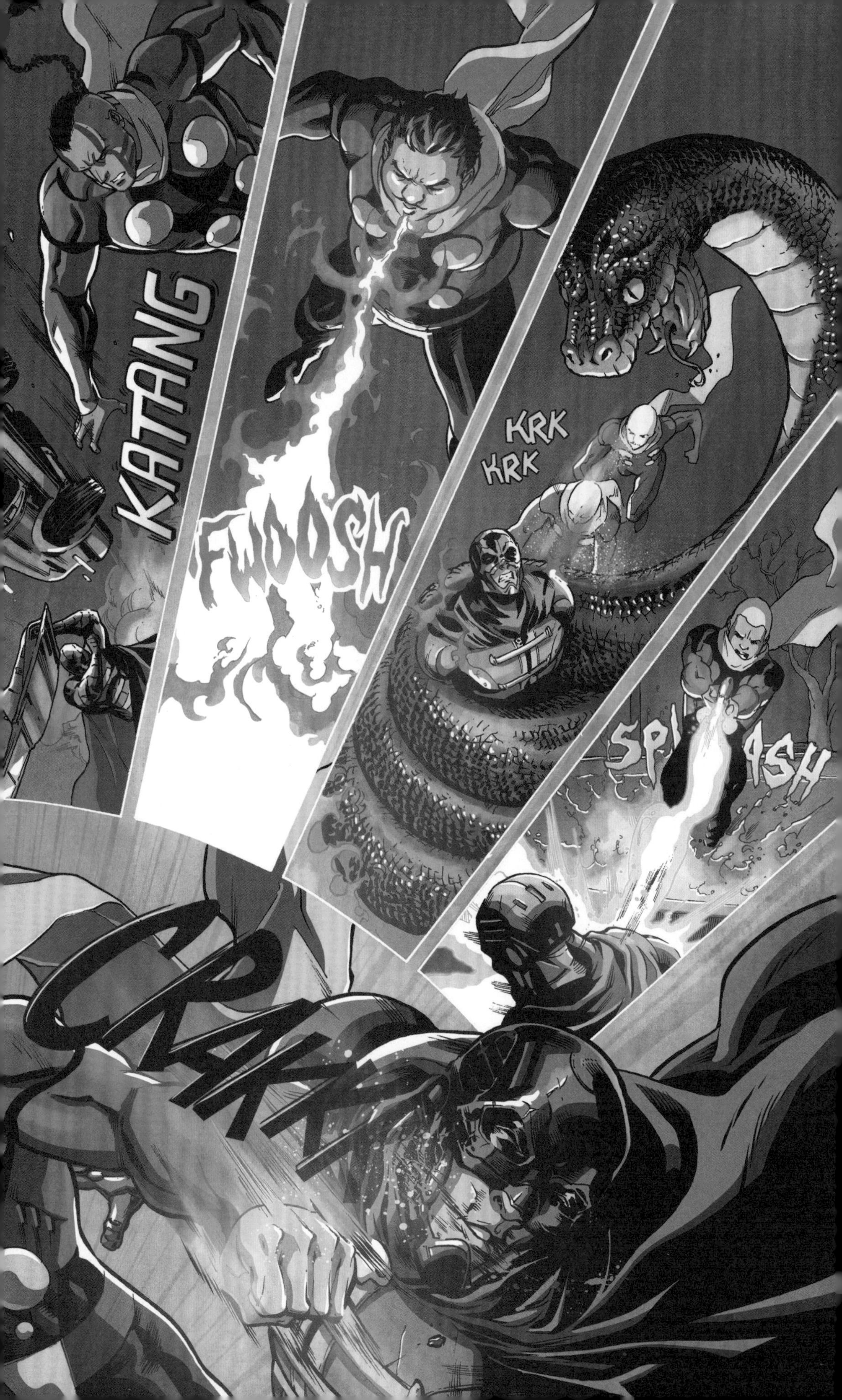
KATANG
FWOOSH
KRK
KRK
SPLASH
CRAKK

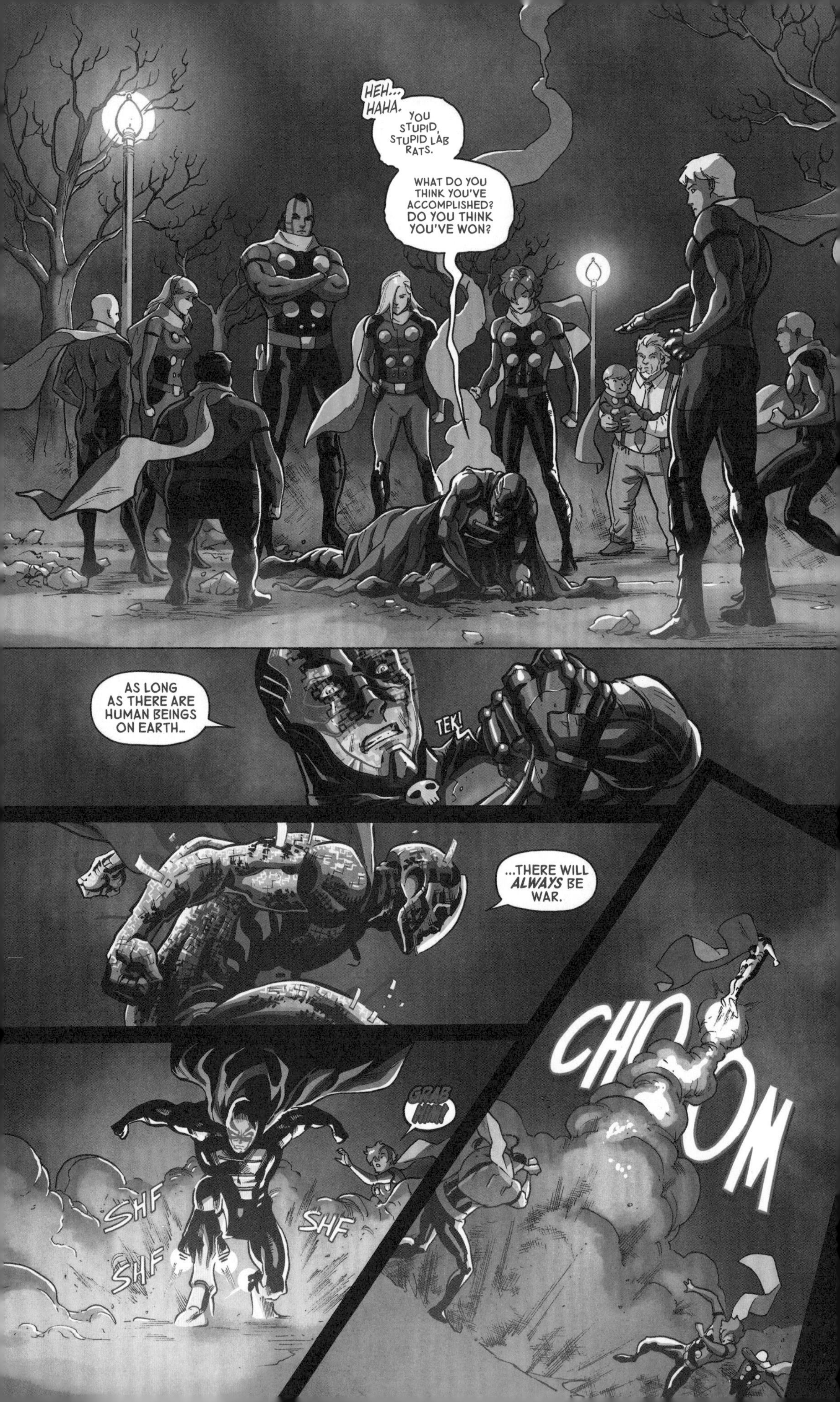
HEH... HAHA.
YOU STUPID, STUPID LAB RATS.
WHAT DO YOU THINK YOU'VE ACCOMPLISHED? DO YOU THINK YOU'VE WON?
AS LONG AS THERE ARE HUMAN BEINGS ON EARTH..
TEK!
...THERE WILL *ALWAYS* BE WAR.
GRAB
SHF
SHF
SHF
CHOOOM

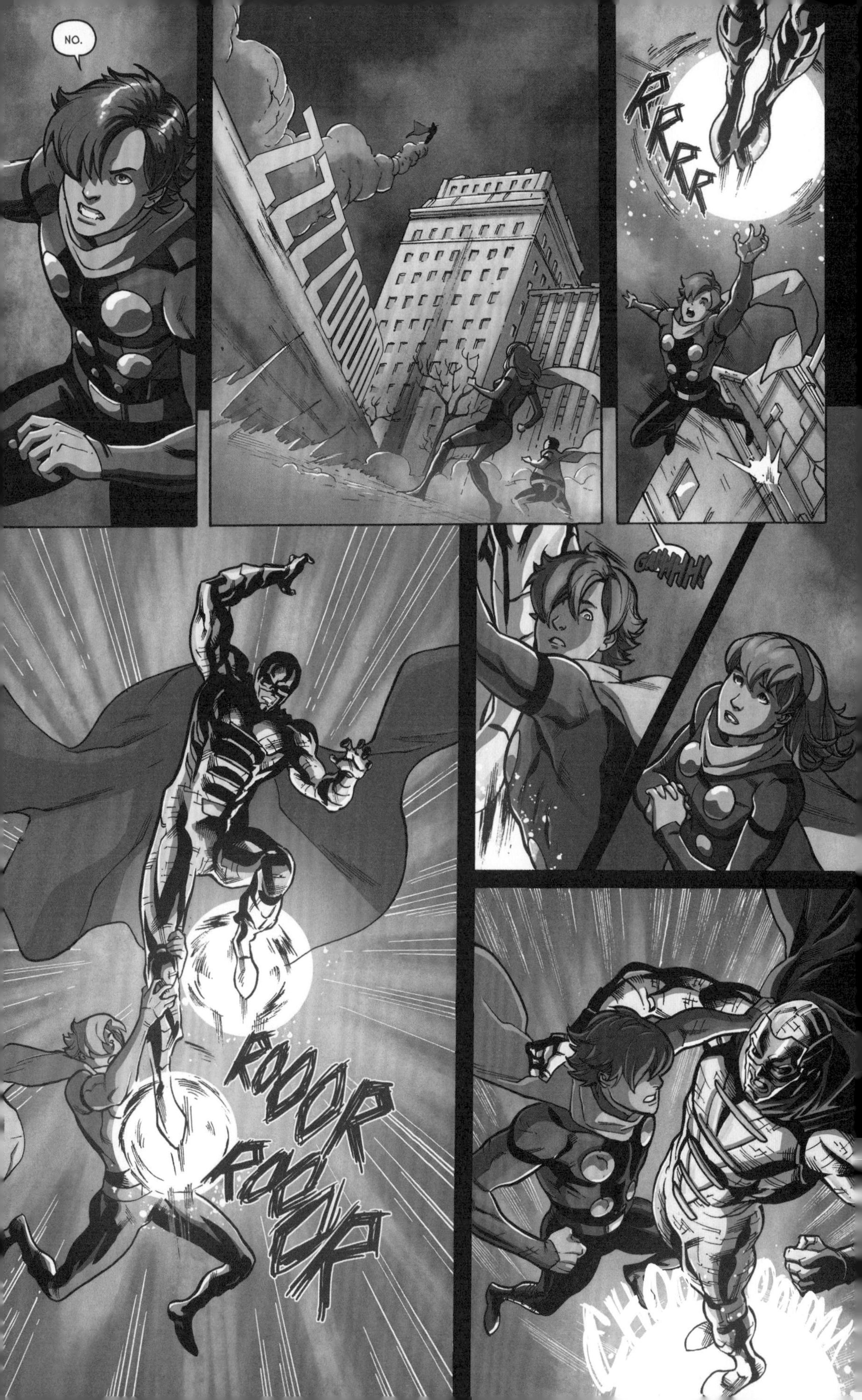
NO.
RRRR
GAHHHH!
ROOOR
ROOOK

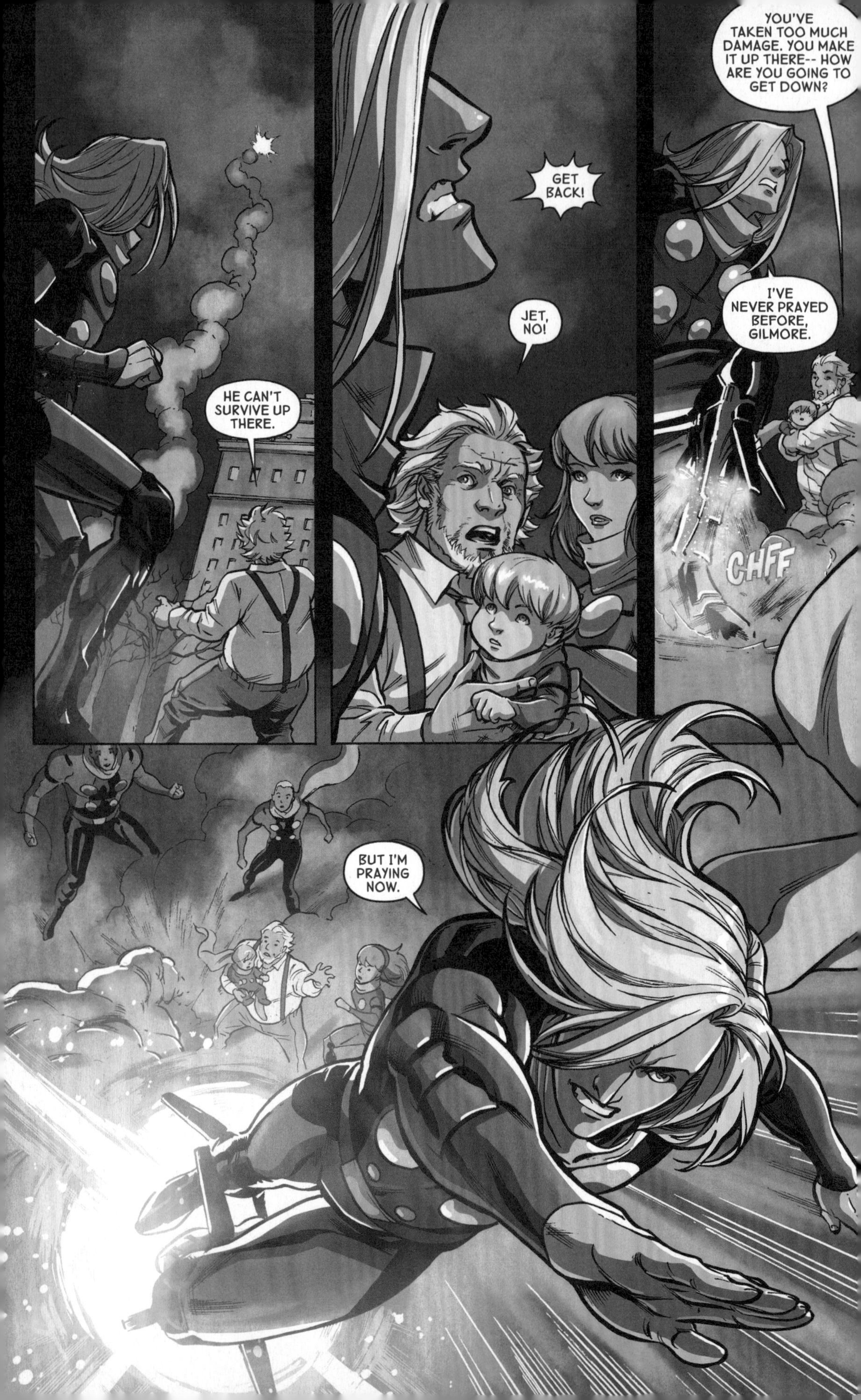
HE CAN'T SURVIVE UP THERE.
GET BACK!
JET, NO!
YOU'VE TAKEN TOO MUCH DAMAGE. YOU MAKE IT UP THERE-- HOW ARE YOU GOING TO GET DOWN?
I'VE NEVER PRAYED BEFORE, GILMORE.
CHFF
BUT I'M PRAYING NOW.

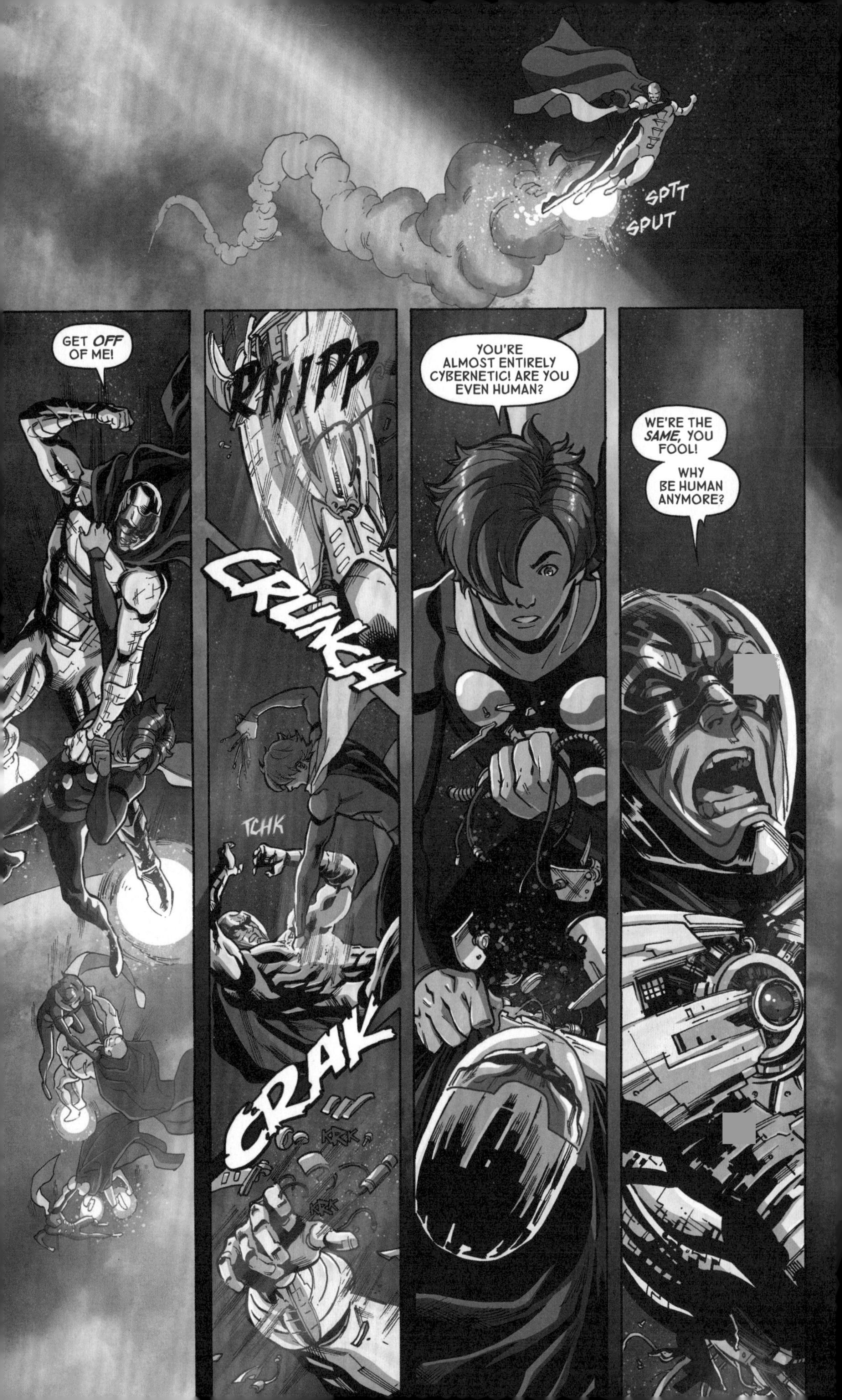
SPTT
SPUT
GET *OFF* OF ME!
RIIIPP
CRUNCH
TCHK
CRAK
KRK
KRK
YOU'RE ALMOST ENTIRELY CYBERNETIC! ARE YOU EVEN HUMAN?
WE'RE THE *SAME,* YOU FOOL!
WHY BE HUMAN ANYMORE?

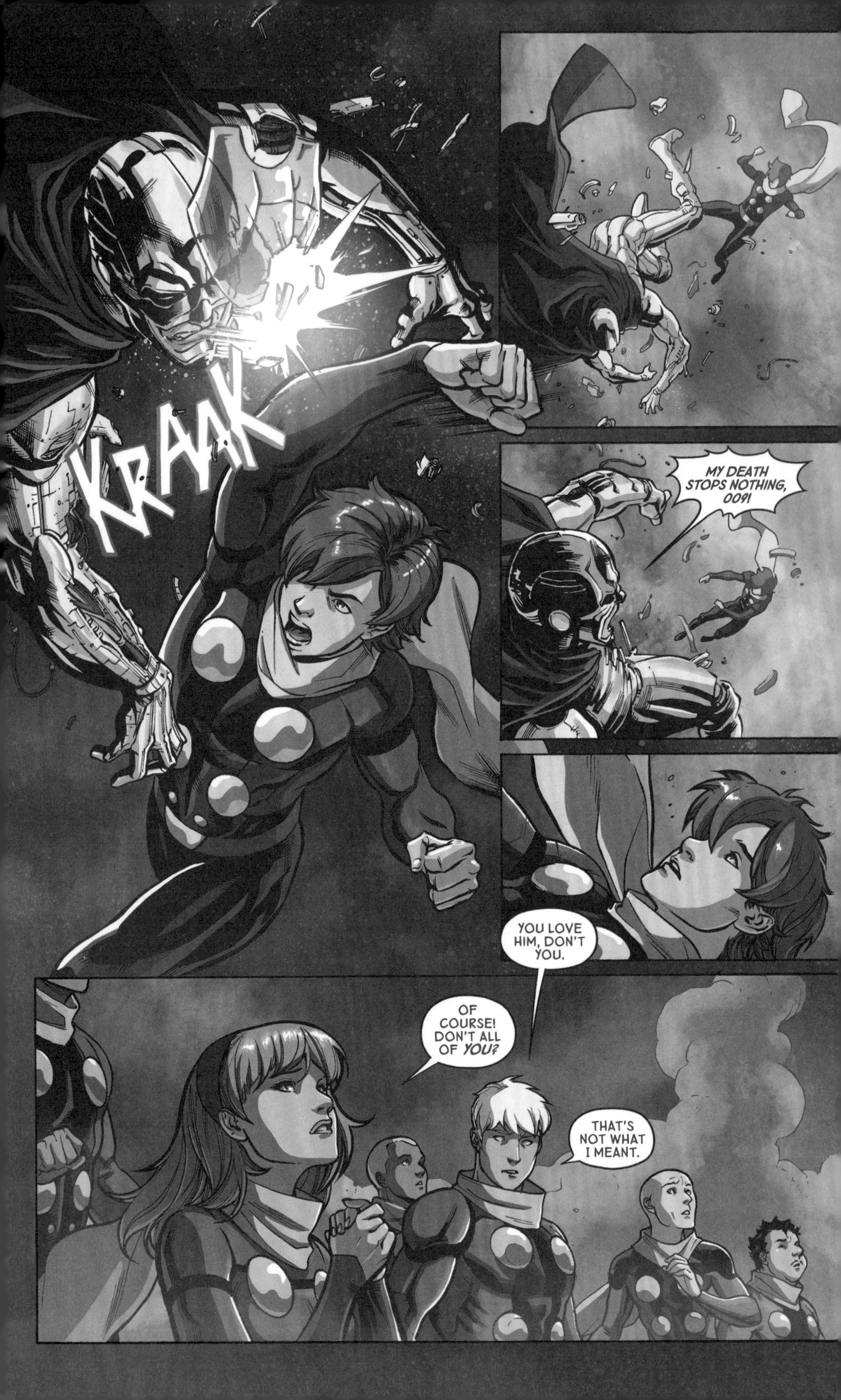
KRAAK
MY DEATH STOPS NOTHING, 009!
YOU LOVE HIM, DON'T YOU.
OF COURSE! DON'T ALL OF *YOU*?
THAT'S NOT WHAT I MEANT.

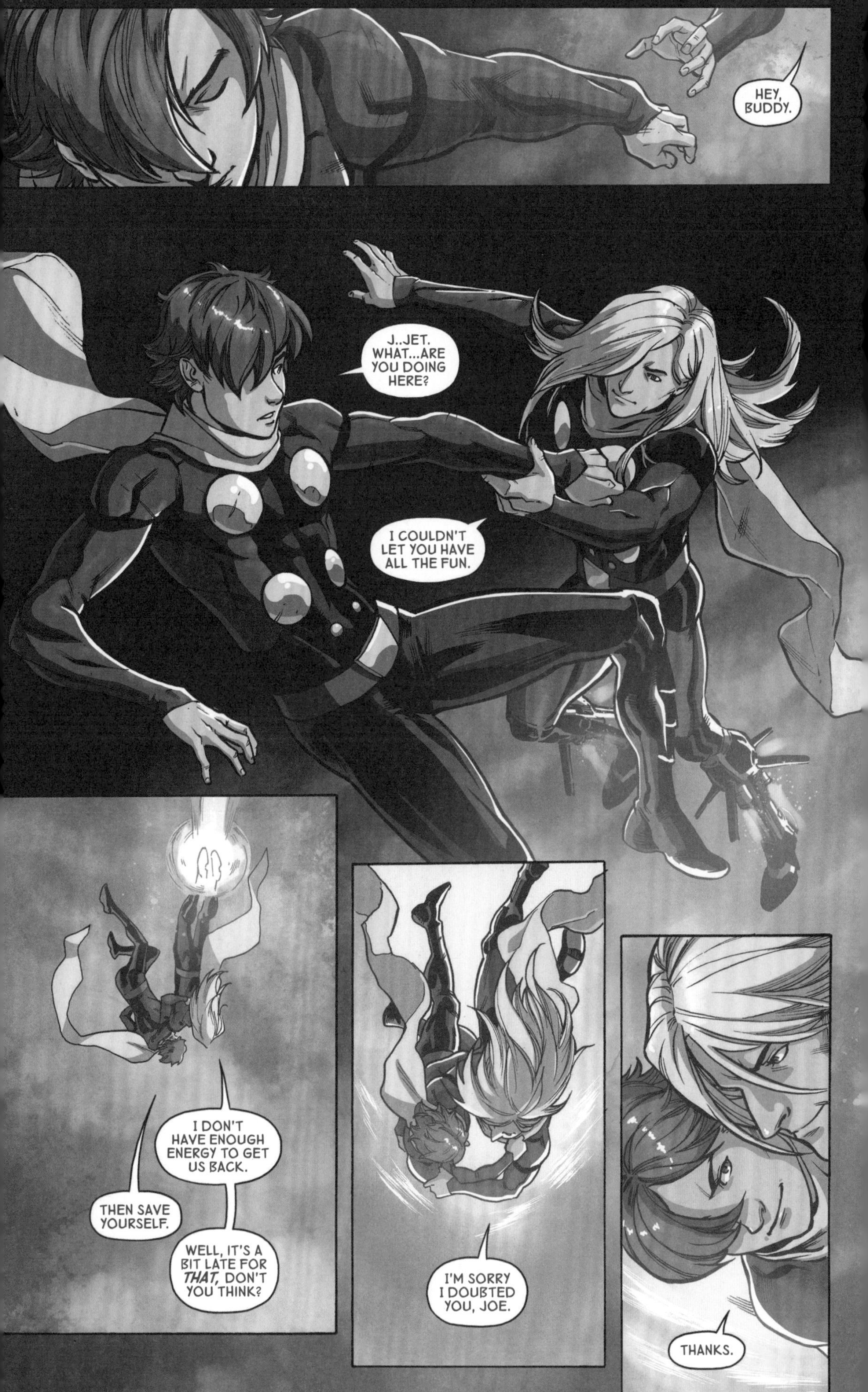
HEY, BUDDY.
J..JET. WHAT...ARE YOU DOING HERE?
I COULDN'T LET YOU HAVE ALL THE FUN.
I DON'T HAVE ENOUGH ENERGY TO GET US BACK.
THEN SAVE YOURSELF.
WELL, IT'S A BIT LATE FOR *THAT,* DON'T YOU THINK?
I'M SORRY I DOUBTED YOU, JOE.
THANKS.

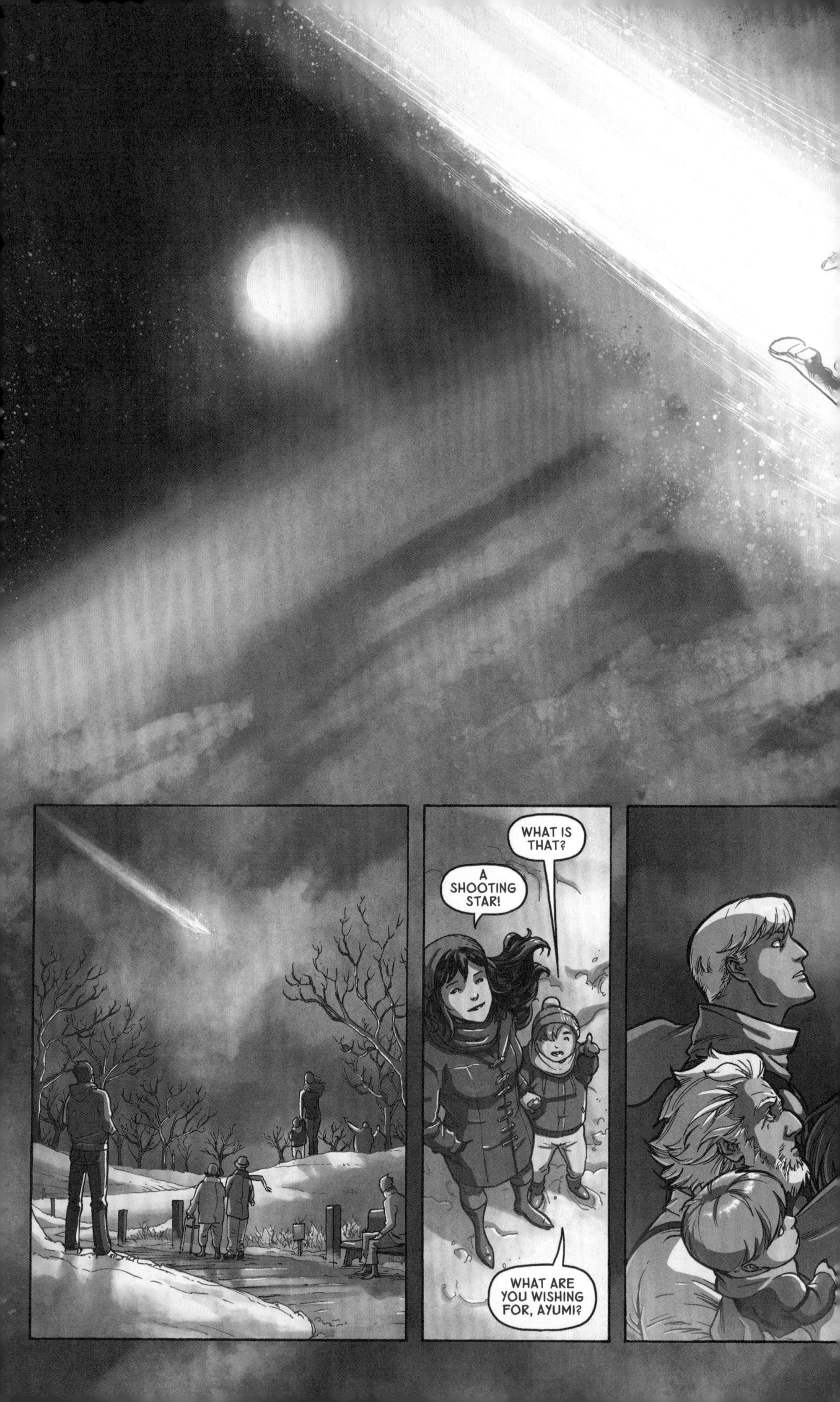
WHAT IS THAT?
A SHOOTING STAR!
WHAT ARE YOU WISHING FOR, AYUMI?

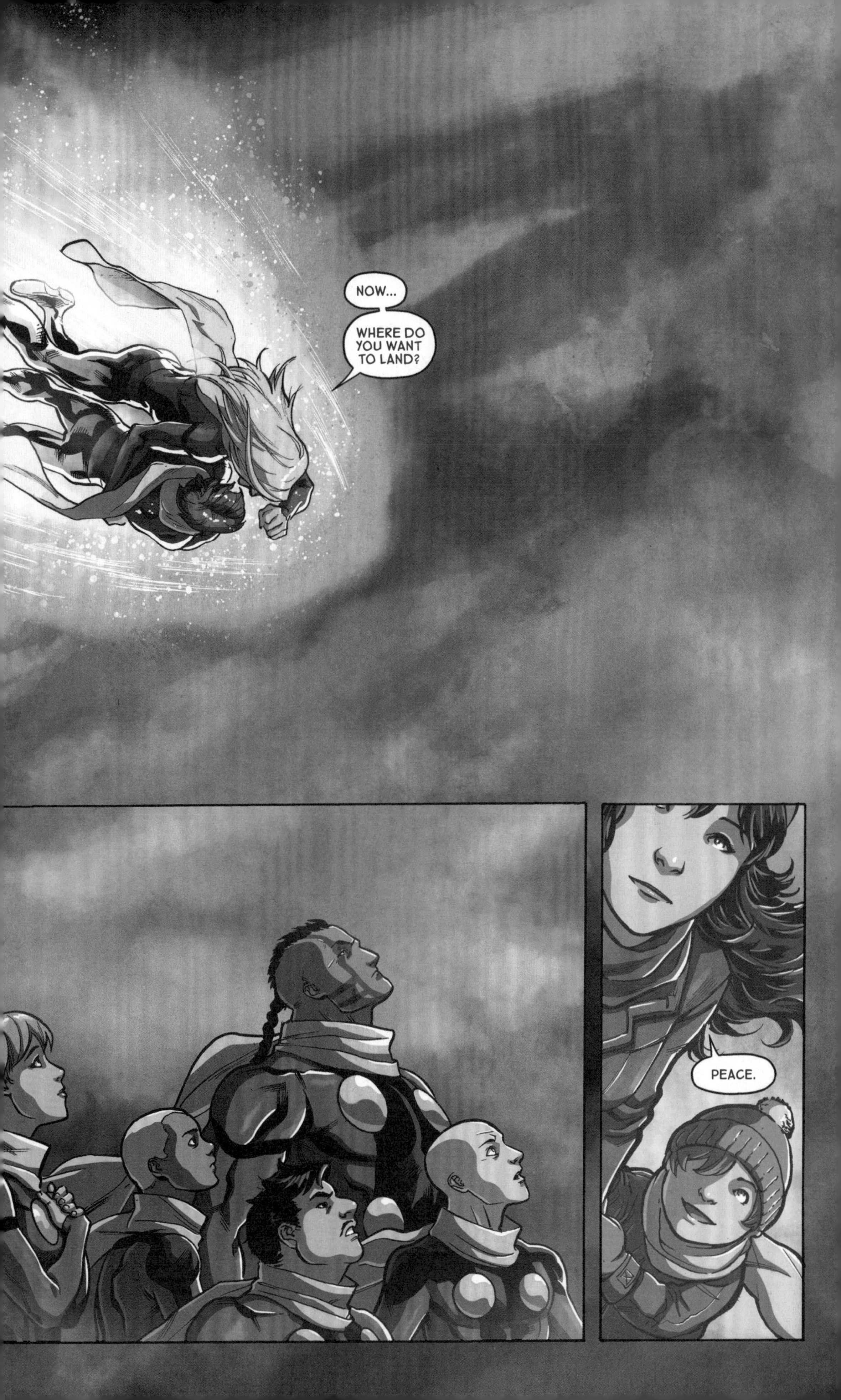
NOW...
WHERE DO YOU WANT TO LAND?
PEACE.

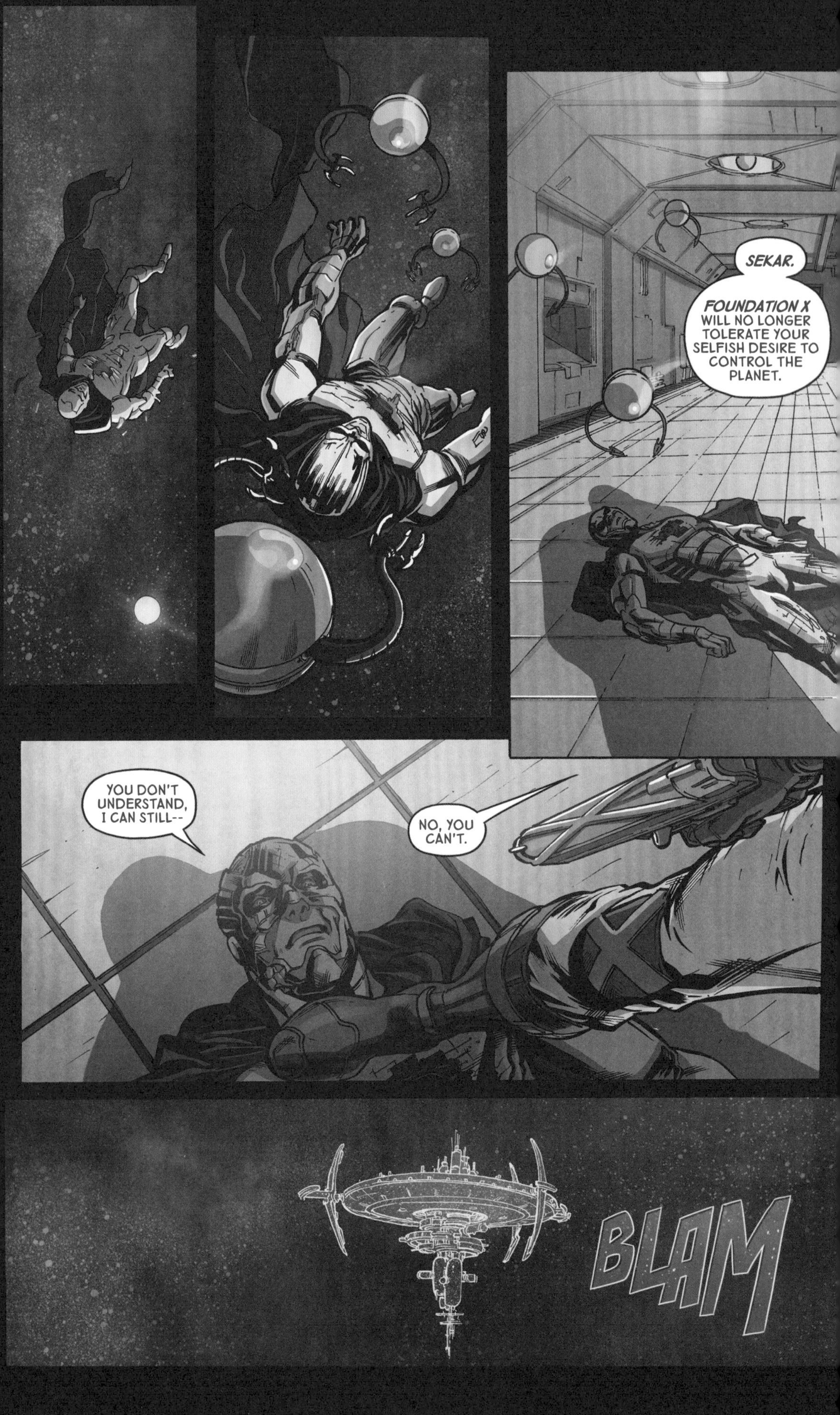
SEKAR.
FOUNDATION X WILL NO LONGER TOLERATE YOUR SELFISH DESIRE TO CONTROL THE PLANET.
YOU DON'T UNDERSTAND, I CAN STILL--
NO, YOU CAN'T.
BLAM

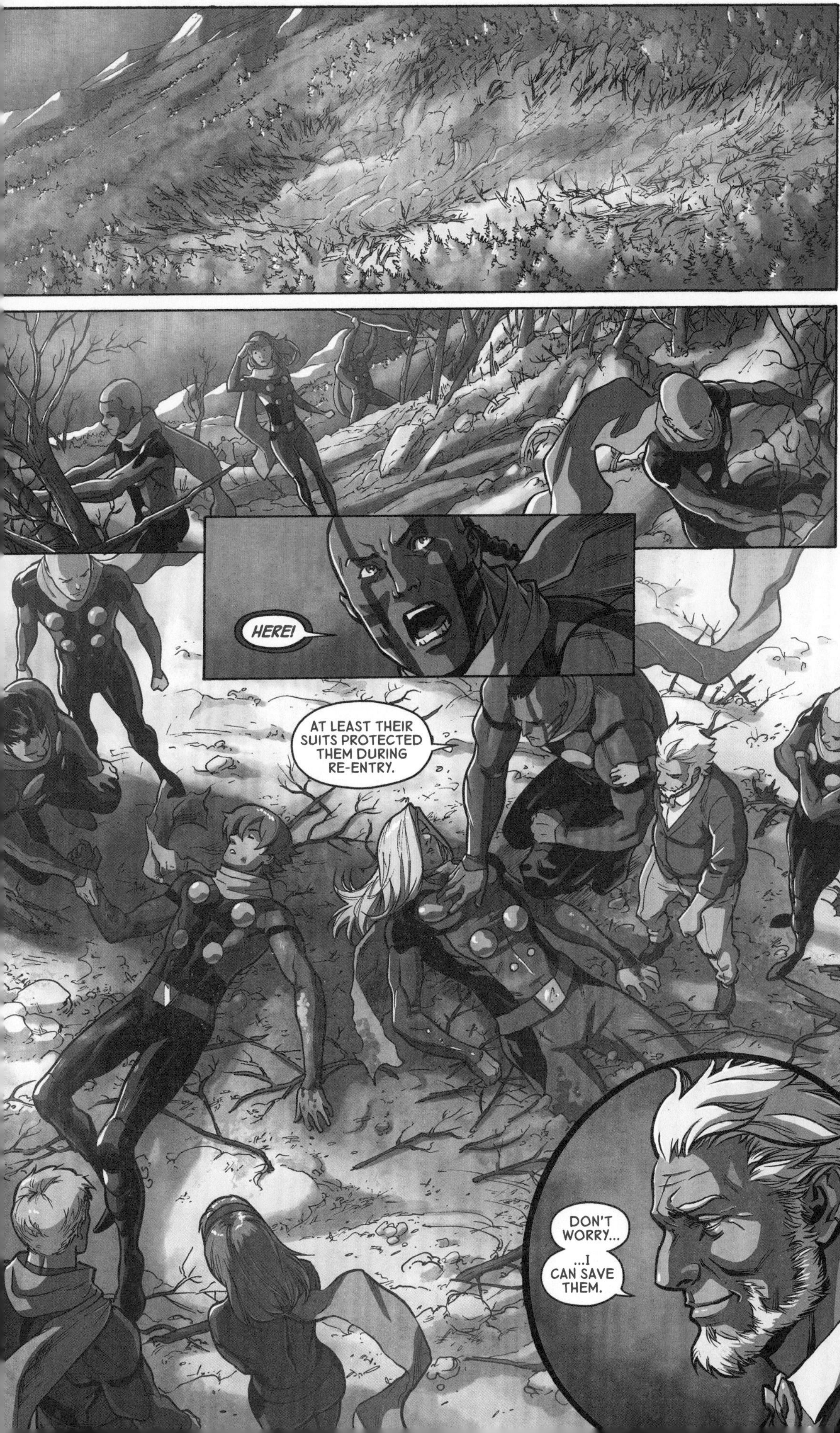
HERE!
AT LEAST THEIR SUITS PROTECTED THEM DURING RE-ENTRY.
DON'T WORRY...
...I CAN SAVE THEM.

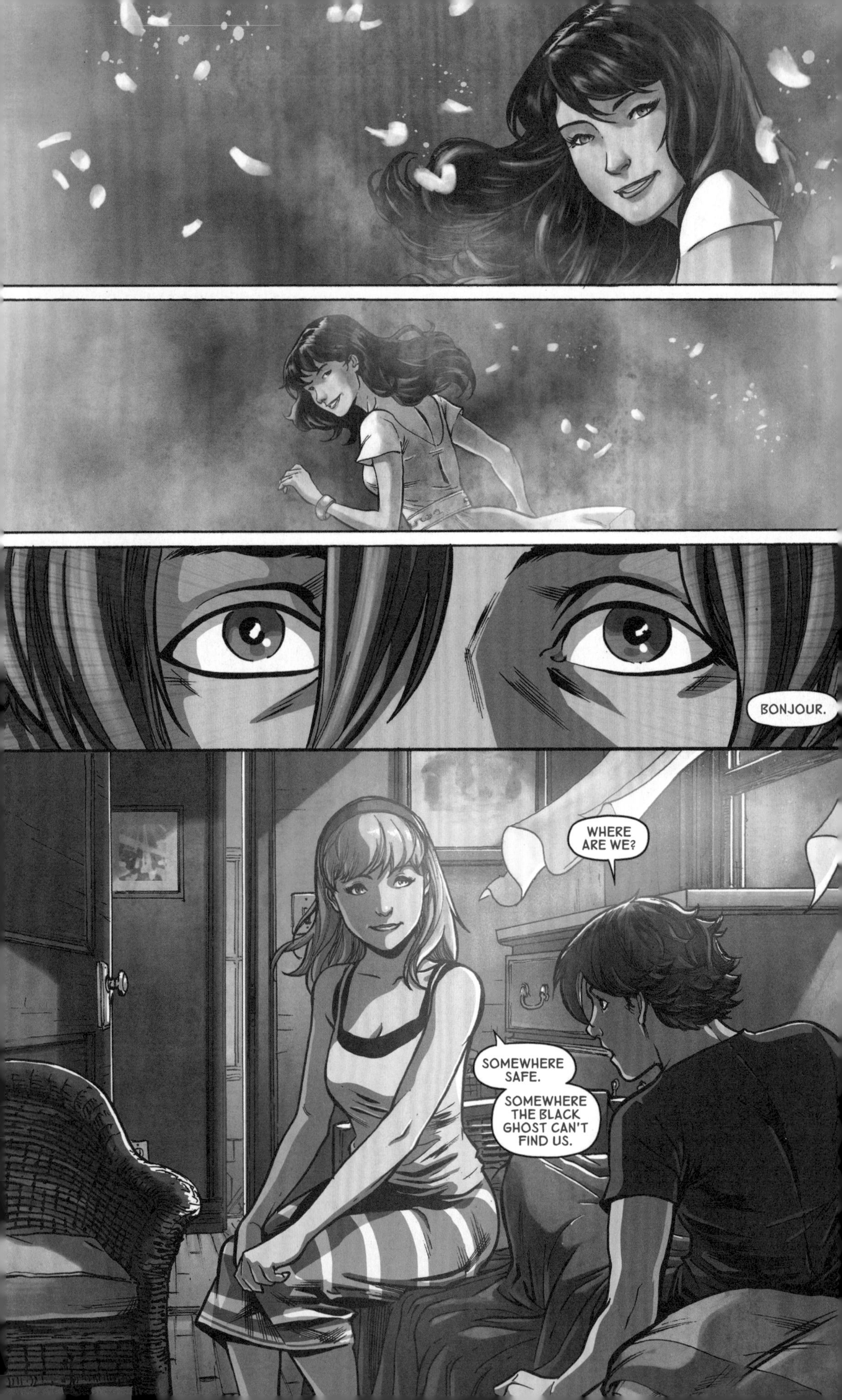
BONJOUR.
WHERE ARE WE?
SOMEWHERE SAFE.
SOMEWHERE THE BLACK GHOST CAN'T FIND US.

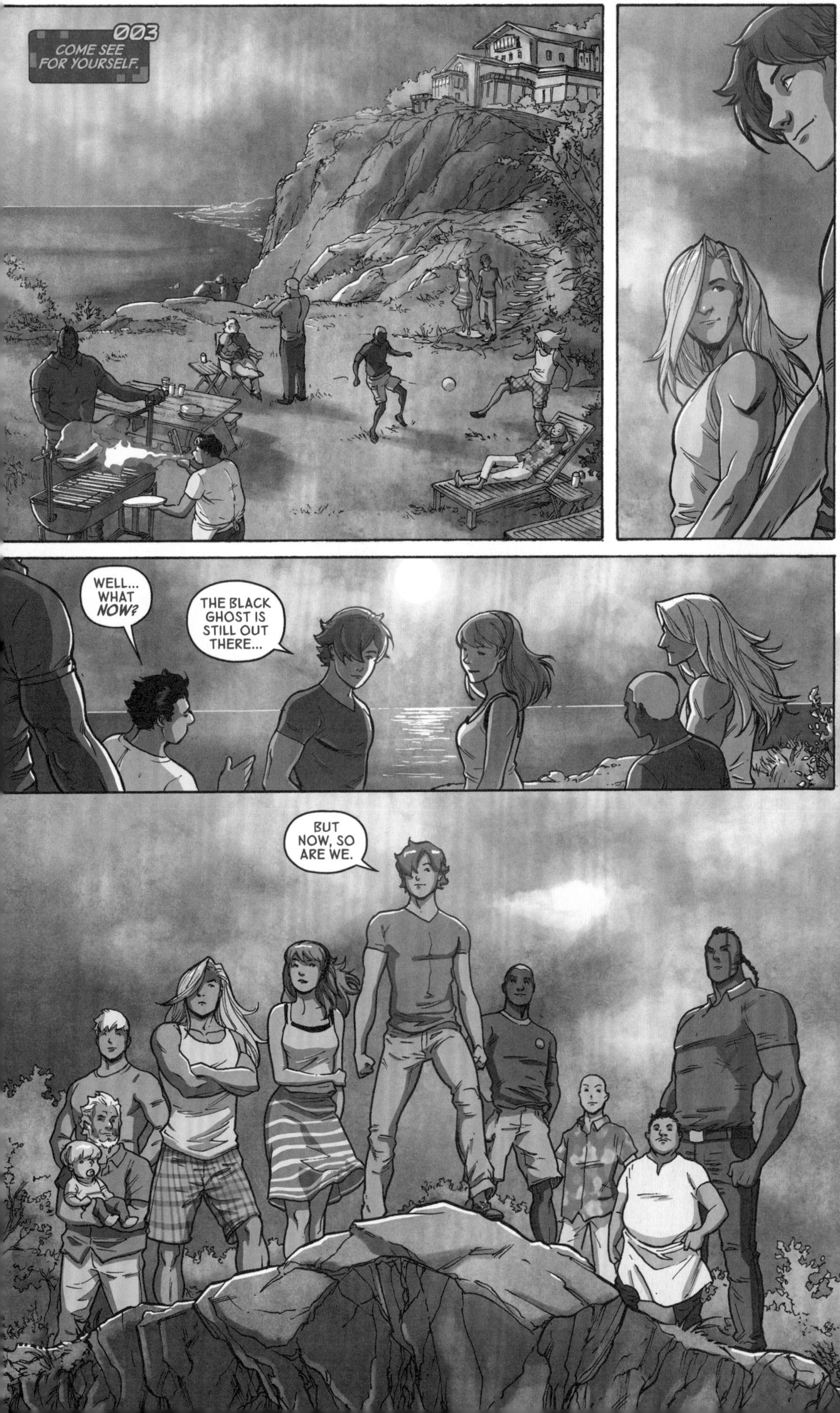
003
COME SEE FOR YOURSELF.
WELL... WHAT *NOW*?
THE BLACK GHOST IS STILL OUT THERE...
BUT NOW, SO ARE WE.

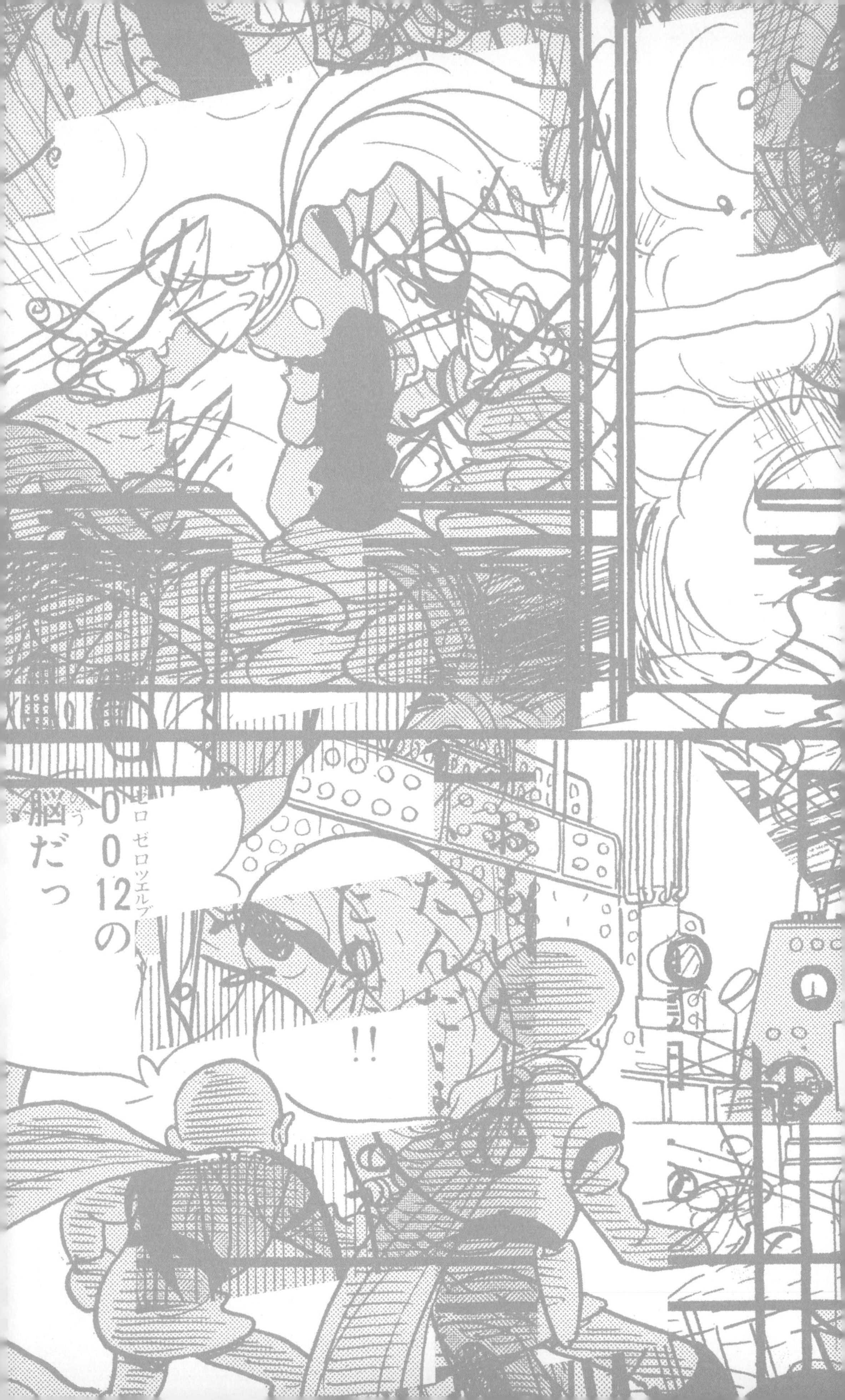

0012(ゼロゼロツエルブ)の脳(のう)だっ
!!

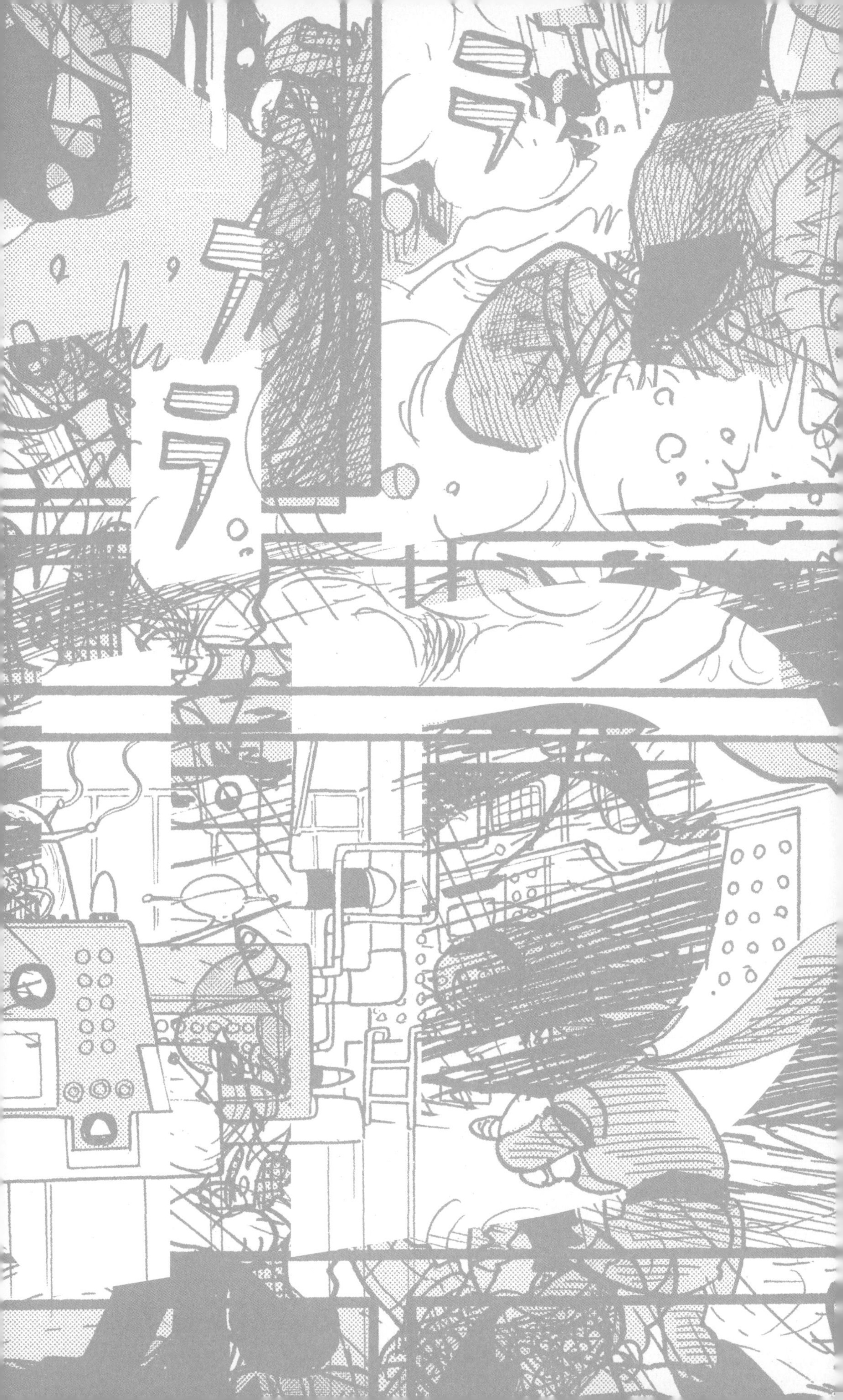

AND WE ARE ALL CYBORGS

BY DAVID BROTHERS

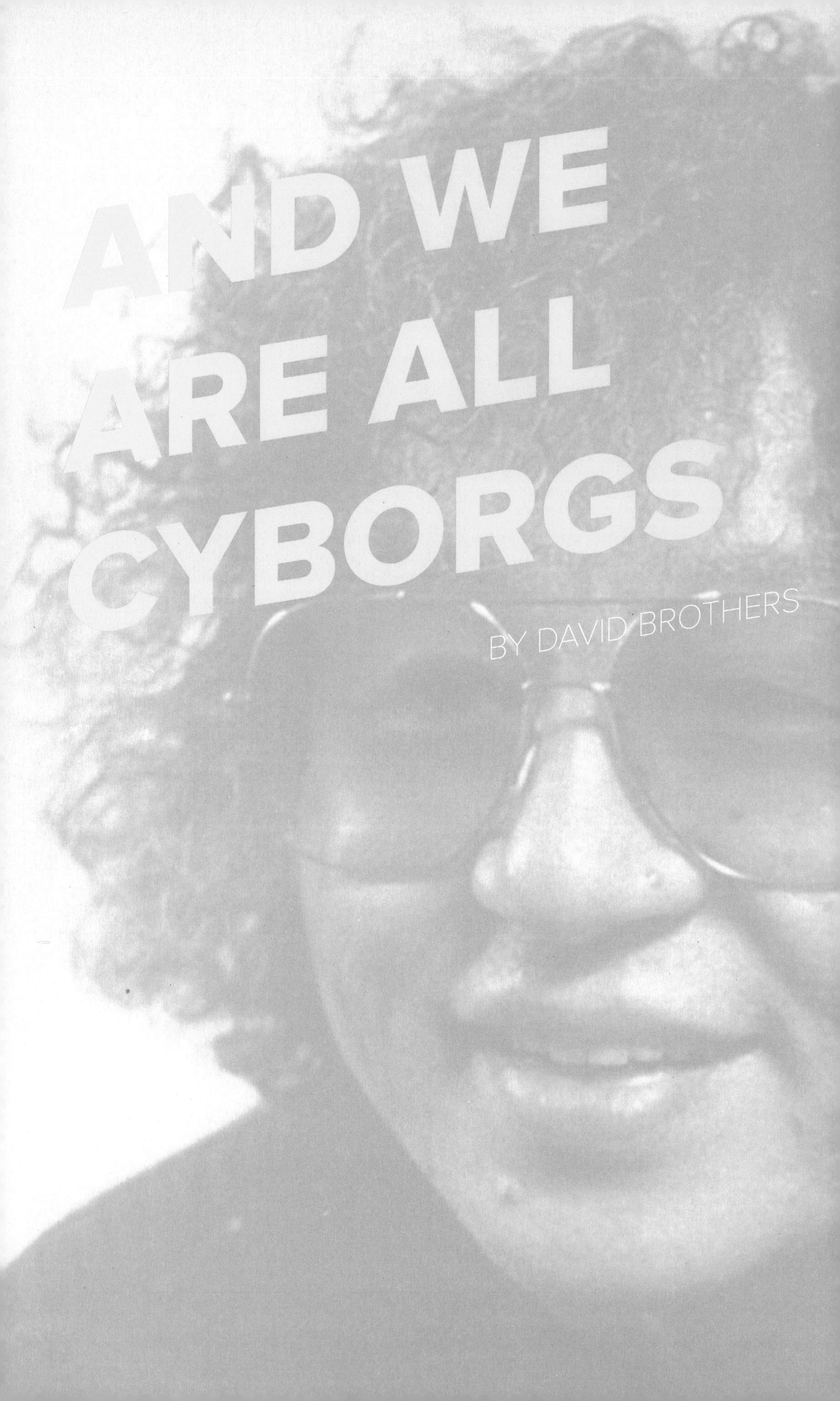

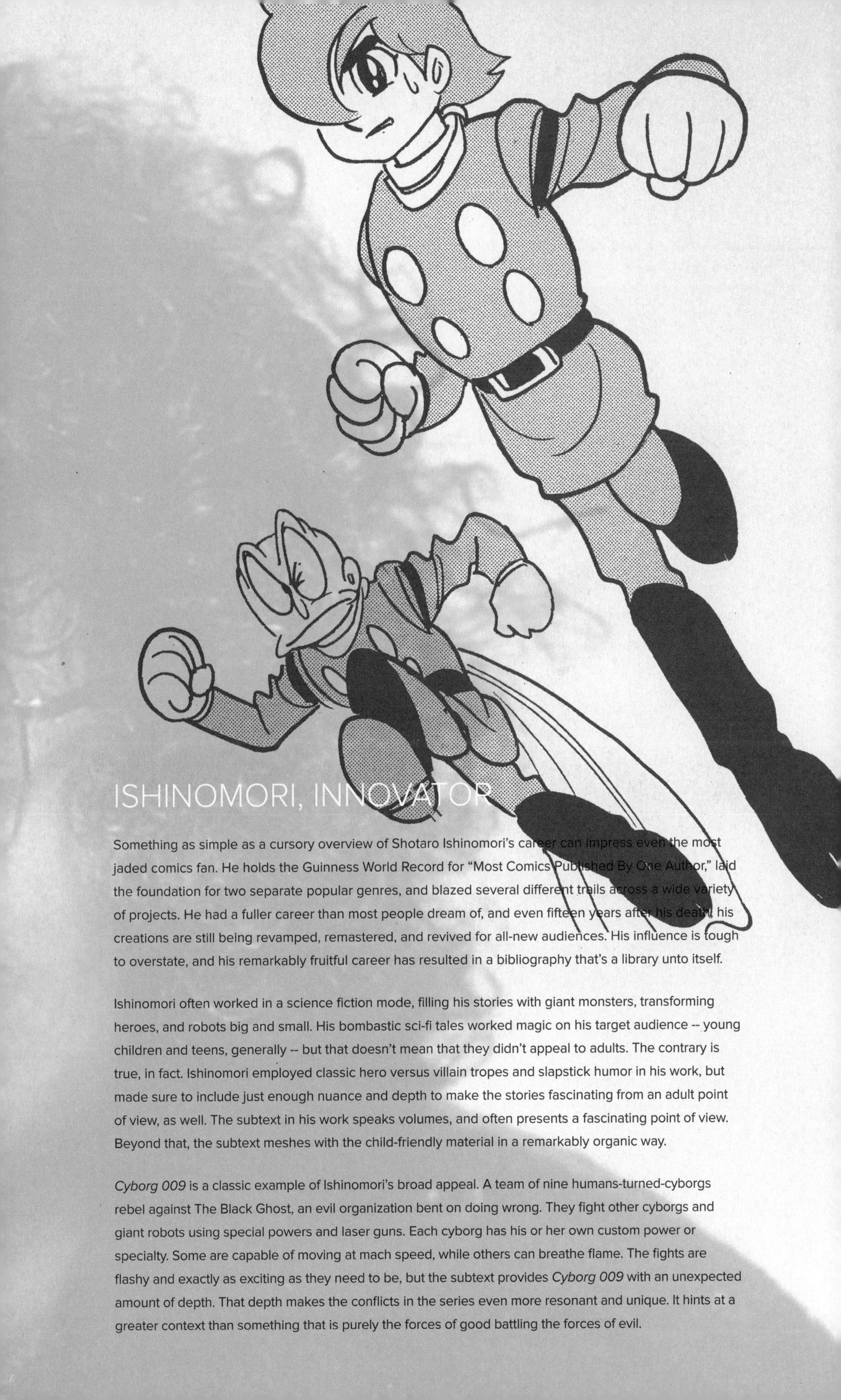

ISHINOMORI, INNOVATOR

Something as simple as a cursory overview of Shotaro Ishinomori's career can impress even the most jaded comics fan. He holds the Guinness World Record for "Most Comics Published By One Author," laid the foundation for two separate popular genres, and blazed several different trails across a wide variety of projects. He had a fuller career than most people dream of, and even fifteen years after his death, his creations are still being revamped, remastered, and revived for all-new audiences. His influence is tough to overstate, and his remarkably fruitful career has resulted in a bibliography that's a library unto itself.

Ishinomori often worked in a science fiction mode, filling his stories with giant monsters, transforming heroes, and robots big and small. His bombastic sci-fi tales worked magic on his target audience -- young children and teens, generally -- but that doesn't mean that they didn't appeal to adults. The contrary is true, in fact. Ishinomori employed classic hero versus villain tropes and slapstick humor in his work, but made sure to include just enough nuance and depth to make the stories fascinating from an adult point of view, as well. The subtext in his work speaks volumes, and often presents a fascinating point of view. Beyond that, the subtext meshes with the child-friendly material in a remarkably organic way.

Cyborg 009 is a classic example of Ishinomori's broad appeal. A team of nine humans-turned-cyborgs rebel against The Black Ghost, an evil organization bent on doing wrong. They fight other cyborgs and giant robots using special powers and laser guns. Each cyborg has his or her own custom power or specialty. Some are capable of moving at mach speed, while others can breathe flame. The fights are flashy and exactly as exciting as they need to be, but the subtext provides *Cyborg 009* with an unexpected amount of depth. That depth makes the conflicts in the series even more resonant and unique. It hints at a greater context than something that is purely the forces of good battling the forces of evil.

MERCHANTS OF DEATH

The original *Cyborg 009* manga begins with a history lesson. Ishinomori quickly summarizes World War II, including the dropping of atomic bombs on Hiroshima and Nagasaki, before introducing the idea of nuclear proliferation and the Cold War. He then immediately transitions to a meeting of the real villains of the series, creating a direct link between them and the war. Instead of being a shadowy cabal of evil magicians, scientists, or aliens, the men behind the horrors sweeping over the globe were much more mundane. They were mere arms dealers and warmongers. They put up with the dramatic overtures of The Black Ghost and produce weapons of mass destruction in order to make money hand over fist. The evil of their actions is simply an acceptable side effect of business. It's collateral damage.

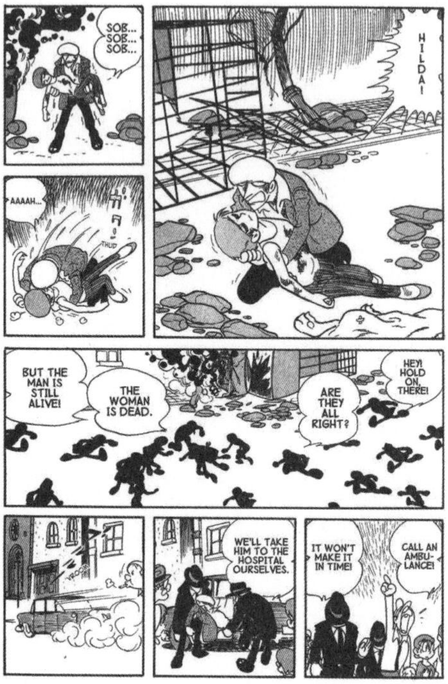
SOB... SOB... SOB...
AAAAH...
THUD
HILDA!
BUT THE MAN IS STILL ALIVE!
THE WOMAN IS DEAD.
ARE THEY ALL RIGHT?
HEY! HOLD ON, THERE!
WE'LL TAKE HIM TO THE HOSPITAL OURSELVES.
IT WON'T MAKE IT IN TIME!
CALL AN AMBU-LANCE!

Ishinomori's use of warmongers as the prime movers of the series is pointed casting considering the atmosphere at the time. *Cyborg 009* debuted in 1964. That's less than 20 years after the end of World War II and the introduction of atomic warfare, 11 years after the end of the Korean War, and square in the middle of rapidly escalating violence in Vietnam. The world was in the process of being carved up by opposing forces, and the business of war was booming. The creation of newer and more lethal weapons allowed war to become a very profitable enterprise. The predations of warmongers partially led to the overwhelming paranoia and fear that permeated the Cold War era, and nuclear panic ensured that everyone knew that the world could end at any moment.

It's telling that the villains have such a banal motivation, as well. Ishinomori's villains may employ the classically cartoonish and outlandish tactics that you would expect from an organization with a name like "The Black Ghost," but at their core, they're simply men who want more than they have and will stop at nothing to get it. They're greedy, and greed is a very human failing. The human element is what makes Ishinomori's stories so resonant, even decades after they were first introduced. The villains in *Cyborg 009* are human to the core, and it is the very human capacity for unthinkingly callous evil that drives The Black Ghost.

The cyborgs are part of an arms race. In this case, the warmongers want to create new weapons to take advantage of new battlefields and thereby avoid the peace process. They're an escalation, another result of the evolution of war. The Black Ghost's plan to turn humans into cyborgs requires the corruption of human beings. Rather than soliciting soldiers or building a volunteer army of cyborgs from scratch, the organization chooses to kidnap innocent humans from a variety of places and walks of life and turn them into cyborgs. The Black Ghost, like war, can and will reach you, no matter how far removed you may think you are from the conflict.

MAN MADE MACHINE

The international and diverse cast of *Cyborg 009* hammers that home. Our nine cyborg heroes and the cyborg villains they battle are ballerinas and chefs, actors and delinquents, privileged and oppressed, adults and children. They represent us; they represent humanity. The cyborgs are unique, both in power and personality, but they all have a great capacity for good or evil. Like most humans, they simply have to choose between their baser natures and doing good.

The concept of free will is a vital part of the *Cyborg 009* story, but Ishinomori explores coercion and the limits of free will, as well. The villainous cyborgs are under the control of evil forces but still manage to demonstrate genuinely human traits, even in the midst of battle. Sometimes they've been bullied and are lashing out, and other times they repay a kindness as best they can, even if it goes against their programming.

They are human first, even when their human identity has been stripped away. Many of the cyborgs have been altered far past the point where they can be strictly defined as human. But no matter what we go through, no matter what horrors, we are still human. We have the capability to not just adapt to our situations, but to overcome them.

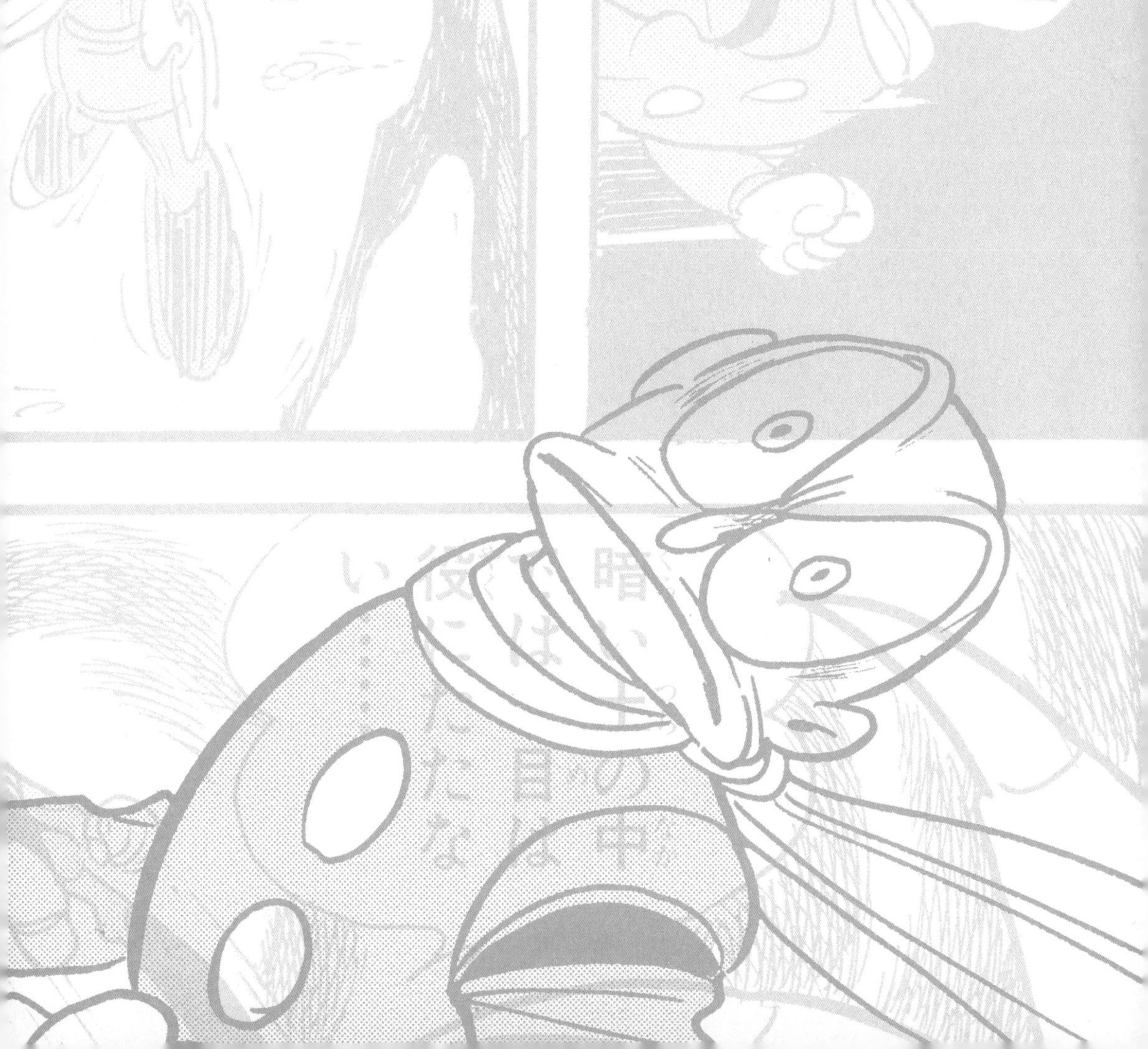

THE GOOD DOCTOR

Part of what gives us the strength to overcome adversity is our community. We find strength in groups, wisdom from our elders, and motivation from seeing people like us succeed. In the case of *Cyborg 009*, Dr. Isaac Gilmore serves as their mentor and engineers their jailbreak. Gilmore served as a scientist in the Black Ghost organization and shares responsibility for the creation of the cyborgs. He rebelled against his employers and in doing so, represents another important aspect of the human experience: repentance.

Gilmore, as an agent of the The Black Ghost, did wrong. His intentions may have been honorable, but he took part in an experiment that forever ruined the lives of more than a dozen human beings. Many of the advances in science that led to the creation of weapons of mass destruction didn't come from men and women who wanted to destroy the world. The pursuit of knowledge often comes with a catch and Gilmore was lucky enough to realize it before he progressed too far down a dark path. He chose to stop and repent for his dirty deeds, and that gives him a strength and depth that is vital for the story of *Cyborg 009*.

Making up for mistakes is an important part of the human experience. It's a way of exercising control over both yourself and your environment. You refuse to let yourself be defined by your mistakes, you work to make up for those mistakes, and in doing so, you change the world around you. You become the good person that you want to be when you seek forgiveness for your mistakes, and the knowledge that you have the capacity to slip up keeps you on the straight and narrow. You've been there before -- you don't want to go back again.

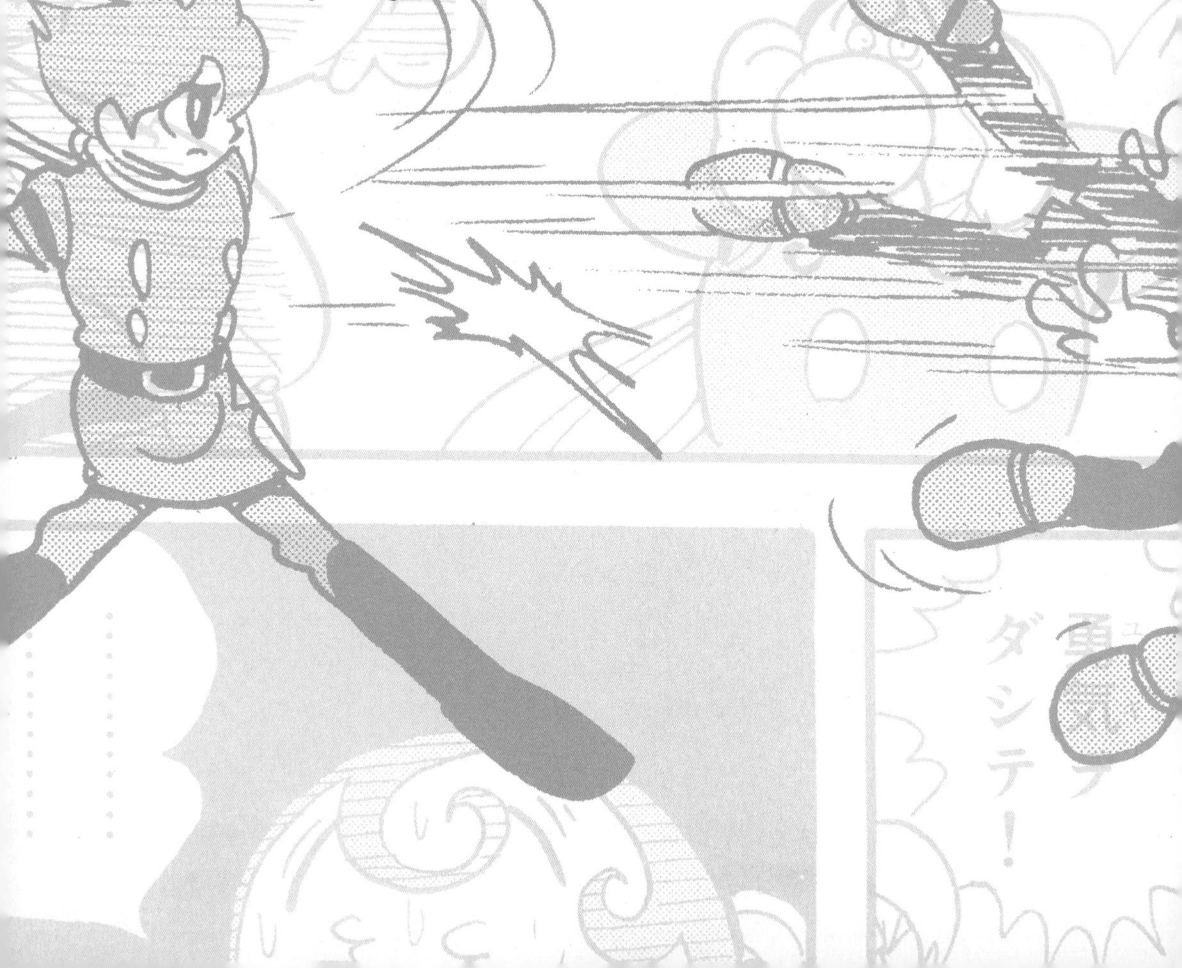

THE MORALLY UPSTANDING JUVENILE DELINQUENT

Joe Shimamura, better known as 009, is another example of a heroic character with rough edges. Originally, he was the son of a Japanese woman and a foreign father. He was considered an outcast, and he suffered for his heritage. He was bullied and teased, and he easily slipped into the life of a delinquent. He didn't become an outlaw because he wanted easy money or because he felt like being a delinquent was fun. He was forced into a corner and he adapted.

He never left behind his inner goodness, however. After becoming a cyborg and returning to Tokyo, he comes across an old friend in Shinjuku. The friend is more than willing to bully and rob another person, but 009 rejects that idea. He stops his friend and rebukes him in front of a complete stranger. This kindness is repaid later, when the stranger is revealed to be a rival cyborg in disguise and chooses to spare 009's life.

009's graciousness is another sign, and an important one. You always have a choice. If you find yourself between a rock and a hard place and you do something wrong, that doesn't mean that you're incapable of doing right. It just means that you made a choice. You can always choose differently, even if it means temporarily alienating a friend to comfort a stranger.

The fact that 009 is the titular character and the window into the *Cyborg 009* universe is fascinating. We see the world through 009's eyes, and as a result, we can't help but identify with him. 009 and the reader are both new to the world Ishinomori has created, and 009's experiences color our own experiences with the world.

Many heroes are written as if they are always morally upstanding and have never wavered in their beliefs. It's a comforting idea to think that there is someone out there who always makes the right decision, but that isn't realistic. Everyone makes bad decisions and goes through trials and tribulations. 009 is no different from anyone else. The difference is that he's made the decision to reject the negative choices he made before, and to do right from that point on.

DANSEUSE, SOLDAT, FEMME

Francoise, unit 003, is innocent and unaffiliated. Where 009 had to fight simply for the right to live life as he wanted before he became a cyborg, 003 spent her time as a ballerina. Her passion was to entertain people, to be a living work of art. In a way, her purpose in life was the opposite of what war represents. War devastates communities, destroys livelihoods, and lines the pockets of the men and women who don't care who they hurt. There are no winners when it comes to war.

Dancing, on the other hand, is meant to enrich our lives. You can experience it on a physical level, as you admire the acrobatics and contortions the dancer performs. You can also experience it on an emotional level, as the movements of the dancer spark feelings within you. Dancing is meant to create appreciation in a viewer, while war only ever creates conflict.

By drafting 003 into their war, the Black Ghost organization is doing exactly what war does: corrupting innocence. It takes something beautiful -- whether that's dancing or simply living your life as you wish -- and dashes it against the rocks. War is cruel and unfair and 003 is a perfect example of why. She's a kind and sweet person, nice almost to a fault, and she did absolutely nothing to deserve her fate.

War respects no one. It doesn't pick and choose whom it affects. It simply happens and we're left to pick up the pieces. In the case of 003, she was left enhanced by her experience with The Black Ghost, thanks to the addition of high tech communications capabilities, but is left divorced from her previous life. She can't go back, not without bringing the baggage she now carries with her. War's touch is indelible. You can move past it, but it sticks with you. You're forever changed.

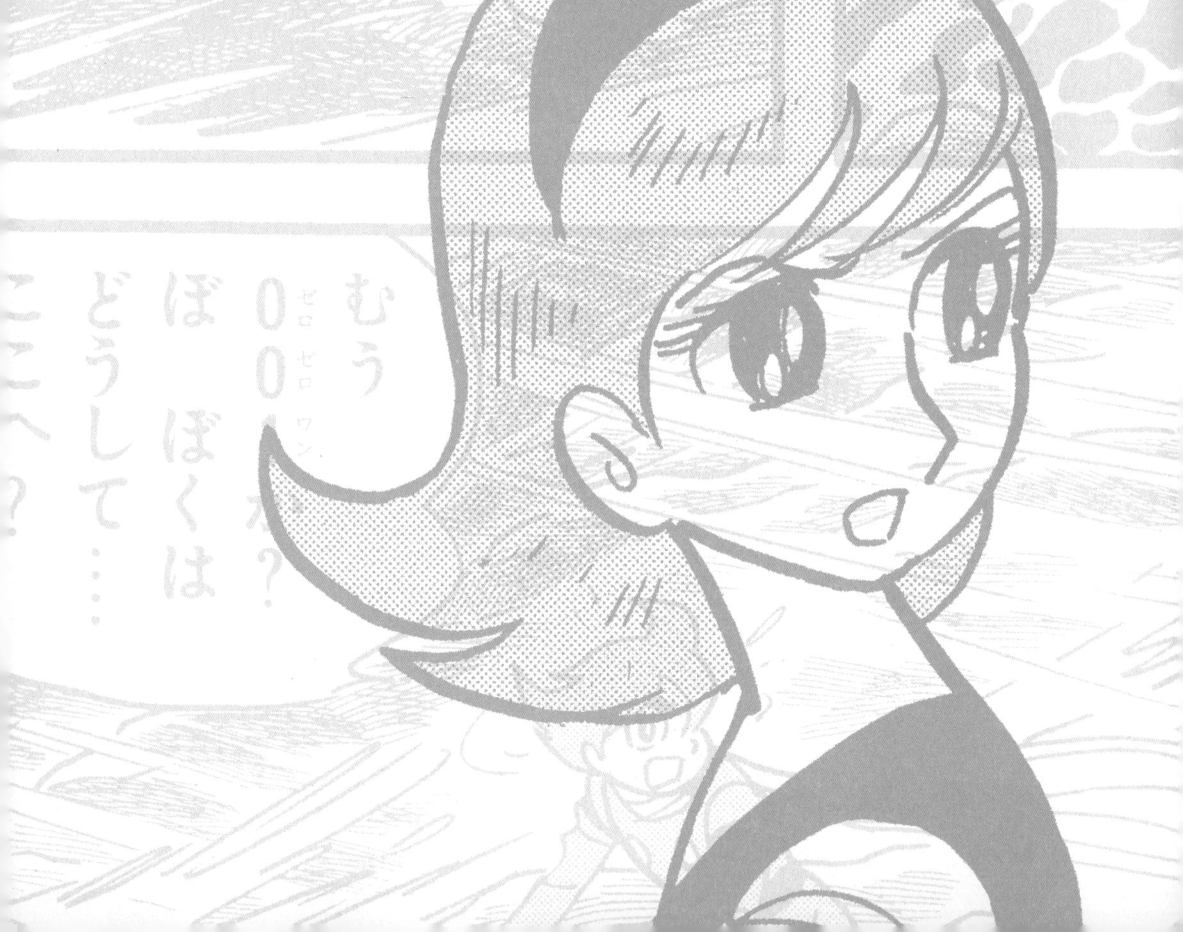

CYBORG SOLDIER, HUMAN HEART

One of the most impressive things about Ishinomori's original *Cyborg 009* stories is how resonant and relevant they remain to this day. The world has existed in a state of constant warfare for decades now, if not longer. Skimming the newspaper or Internet shows that armed conflict is a fact of life for many. There are powers beyond our control that wish to divide the Earth up, reasonable people who have been forced into bad situations, and bad people who are eager to take advantage of those situations. War is here, it is real, and sometimes it's even right outside our window.

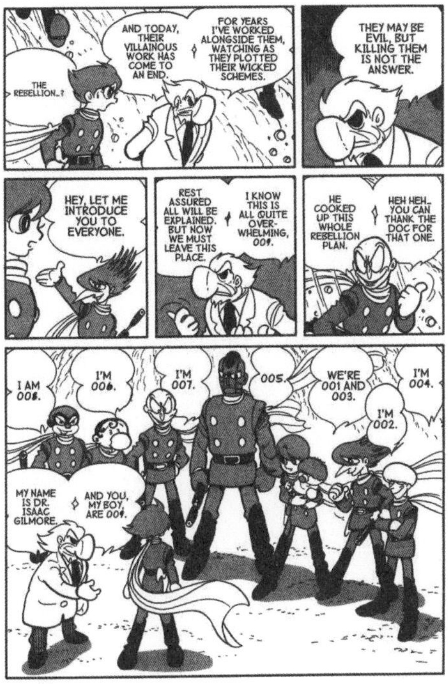
AND TODAY, THEIR VILLAINOUS WORK HAS COME TO AN END.
FOR YEARS I'VE WORKED ALONGSIDE THEM, WATCHING AS THEY PLOTTED THEIR WICKED SCHEMES.
THE REBELLION...?
THEY MAY BE EVIL, BUT KILLING THEM IS NOT THE ANSWER.
HEY, LET ME INTRODUCE YOU TO EVERYONE.
REST ASSURED ALL WILL BE EXPLAINED. BUT NOW WE MUST LEAVE THIS PLACE.
I KNOW THIS IS ALL QUITE OVER-WHELMING, 009.
HE COOKED UP THIS WHOLE REBELLION PLAN.
HEH HEH... YOU CAN THANK THE DOC FOR THAT ONE.
I AM 008.
I'M 006.
I'M 007.
005.
WE'RE 001 AND 003.
I'M 004.
I'M 002.
MY NAME IS DR. ISAAC GILMORE.
AND YOU, MY BOY, ARE 009.

Ishinomori's cyborgs represent us, but they do more than that. They encourage us. They inspire us. They suggest that someone, somewhere can stand against great evil and not just survive, but succeed. They can make a difference, whether it's pushing for nuclear disarmament in real life or battling evil cyborgs in fiction. All it takes is making a choice. The specific choices change as time goes on, but the core idea is incredibly versatile.

The cyborgs are human. Once you understand that, the meaning behind the rest of the series flows like water. Their enemies are war incarnate, men and women who would exploit the Earth for their own gain. After being touched by those enemies, the cyborgs are decidedly different than they were before, but their innate human goodness remains the same. They rage against the injustice they suffered, and they fight to make sure that that injustice is never perpetrated again.

The setting of *Cyborg 009* is a world that is constantly on the brink of being destroyed. Governments wage war, shadowy figures finance and enhance those wars, and the only thing stopping humankind from being overrun are the actions of honest and moral human beings who refuse to let the wrong side win. The cyborgs are sacrificing their lives to prevent that exact outcome. There are plenty of reasons to be afraid, but there is a reason to have hope, as well.

Seeding a comic intended for children with these ideas may seem strange at first glance, but Ishinomori pursued his allegory in such a way that the story remains perfectly appropriate for all ages. Ishinomori stops well short of becoming overbearing or preachy. There's nothing in there that's inappropriate for children. He couches the allegory in familiar ideas: a delinquent with a secret heart of gold, a wizened mentor, and a flashy and bombastic evil organization. It's only once you dig deeper that you realize the reason why *Cyborg 009* works as well as it does is because it is working with deeper themes than pure "good versus evil" or squeaky-clean generic adventures.

Born in Ishinomori, Miyagi Prefecture, Japan on January 25, 1938, Shotaro Onodera was a prodigy in the Japanese comics industry, submitting works to Mainichi Junior High School Newspaper and *Manga Shonen* magazine as early as 12 years old. His diligence and unique talent led to his first professional job in the industry as an art assistant to the legendary Osamu Tezuka, creator of the manga masterpiece *Astro Boy*. He was still in high school when he made his professional manga debut in 1954 with *Second Class Angel*. Upon his debut, Shotaro took on the professional name of Ishinomori in homage to his beloved hometown, which today is the home of a museum built in his honor.

He was a prominent figure in the manga industry for decades, working in varying genres and using his chosen medium to spread a universal message of positivity throughout the world. His tremendous impact on Japanese and worldwide entertainment was immense. Ishinomori innovated the extremely popular concept of Sentai ("battle teams") with his classic titles *Cyborg 009, Kikaider, Himitsu Sentei Gorenger* (the original version of *Power Rangers*), and introduced the world of manga to it's first anti-hero, *Skullman,* thus creating new standards in manga storytelling.

With a love of cinema and an understanding of the modern world, he branched out to the screens of Japan as one of the founders of the animation company Studio Zero and adapted several of his manga properties for live action television. His most successful creation, *Kamen Rider* (aka *Masked Rider),* was launched simultaneously as a manga and television series in 1971, making it one of the world's first transmedia properties. Over the course of 41 years, more than a thousand episodes of *Kamen Rider* and 39 feature films have been produced. It is now the number one boys merchandise seller in Japan. Ishinomori's creations have been produced in over 105 different movies and television series.

In 1980, he celebrated the amazing milestones of drawing his 70,000th page and his 25th anniversary of entering the comics industry, and his work continued until his untimely passing in 1998. Aside from *Cyborg 009,* Ishinomori's legendary body of work includes: *Flying Phantom Ship, Ganbare!! Robocon, 009-1, Transforming Ninja Arashi, Gilgamesh, Hotel, Inazuman, Miracle Giants Dome-kun, Robot Detective, Sabu to Ichi Torimono Hikae, Sarutobi Ecchan, Seiun Kamen Machineman, Space Ironmen Kyodain,* and *Voicelugger.* His work covered a vast number of genres, from sci-fi to spy, and even includes a series of graphic biographical pieces of musicians and bands.

His list of awards throughout his illustrious career include The Kodansha Children's Manga Award-winner, 2-time Shogakukan Manga Award-winner, The Grand Prix of the Japan Cartoonists Association Award-winner, The Nakada-cho Honorary Town Resident Prize-winner, The Academy Grand Prix Award-winner, The Tezuka Osamu Cultural Prize-winner, The Special Manga Award winner.

Shotaro Ishinomori is also registered in The Guinness Book of World Records for the world's largest number of comics published by a single author (770 titles and 128,000 pages of material).

Shotaro Ishinomori passed away on January 28th, 1998, in Japan.

F.J. DeSANTO is a producer, writer and creator whose recent projects include films such as *The Spirit*, the animated *Turok: Son of Stone*, documentaries on Grant Morrison and Warren Ellis, and the critically acclaimed *Smuggler's Gambit*, a live *Star Wars* radio drama. He is currently developing a television series, *Orion*, for Syfy Channel, and is working with Ishimori Production Inc., in Japan to bring the rich library of manga characters created by the legendary Shotaro Ishinomori (*Kikaider*, *Skullman*) for the entertainment space. He has written for DC Comics, Archaia, Moonstone, Tokyopop and Lucasfilm and his first creator-owned series *Insurgent* was published in 2013. He lives in New York and Los Angeles depending on what day of the week it is.

BRADLEY CRAMP is a writer and producer living in Los Angeles. His feature credits include work on such films as *Gattaca, The Truman Show, Simone, Lord of War* and the upcoming *Invertigo*.

MARCUS TO is a Canadian artist and illustrator whose credits include *Red Robin*, *Huntress*, *Soulfire* and *The Flash*. Born in Red Deer, Alberta, Canada, he has been a part of the American comic book industry since 2004. To lives in Toronto, Ontario and is a member of the Royal Academy of Illustration and Design. You can follow his adventures at MarcusTo.Tumblr.com.

IAN HERRING is an Eisner-nominated colorist. Splitting his youth between small town Ontario and smaller town Cape Breton, Ian was raised on Nintendo and reruns of *The Simpsons*. Somewhere during this time he learned to color. Now based in Toronto, Ian has worked on various titles including Archaia's *Jim Henson's Tale of Sand*, DC's *The Flash*, and IDW's *TMNT*. His work can be found at 156thmongoose.com.

Eisner Award-nominated letterer, DERON BENNETT knew early on that he wanted to work in comics. After receiving his B.F.A. from SCAD in 2002, Deron moved out to Los Angeles to pursue his career in sequential art. He quickly became a letterer and production artist with Tokyopop, but soon found himself returning to his hometown in New Jersey to raise a family. Since then, Deron has been providing lettering services for various comic book companies. His body of work includes the critically acclaimed *Jim Henson's Tale of Sand*, *Jim Henson's The Dark Crystal*, *Mr. Murder is Dead*, *The Muppet Show Comic Book*, *Darkwing Duck*, and *Richie Rich*. You can learn more about Deron by visiting his website andworlddesign.com or following @deronbennett on Twitter.

JON ADAMS was an orphan from ages two to six and then again from six-and-a-half to seventeen. At age eighteen he was able to legally adopt himself through a loophole in the Connecticut childcare system, thus becoming his own father. Still though, he was motherless. Unable to marry for the fear that whoever he chose as his bride would also awkwardly become his mother, Jon put himself up for adoption once again. Now, at least, he is free to love. citycyclops.com

DAVID BROTHERS has a day job in video games, but he spends his evenings writing about movies, comics, music, and everything in-between. He runs 4thletter.net with a friend, has contributed to The Atlantic, Wired, Kotaku, and regularly discussed comics art on the multiple-Eisner-Award-nominee ComicsAlliance. His favorite cyborg is 007, but he'll always have a soft spot for 0012.

THANK YOU: Akira Onodera, Masato Hayase, Masayasu Takigawa, Daisaku Sonoda, and Ishimori Production, Inc. for their invaluable assistance and support, Trevor Hairsine, Jack Cummins, Michael Kennedy, Becka Kinzie, Jukie Chan, Sakiko Ura, Doran Woo, Trevor Hanowski, Ryusuke Nagai, Deb Aoki, Ramón Pérez and R.A.I.D. Studios, Chong Bradish, Denise Crovetti-Cramp, Irene Bradish, Frank DeSanto, R.J. Ryan, Hiroshi Aramaki and Wataru (Candy) Ishida at Itochu Corporation.

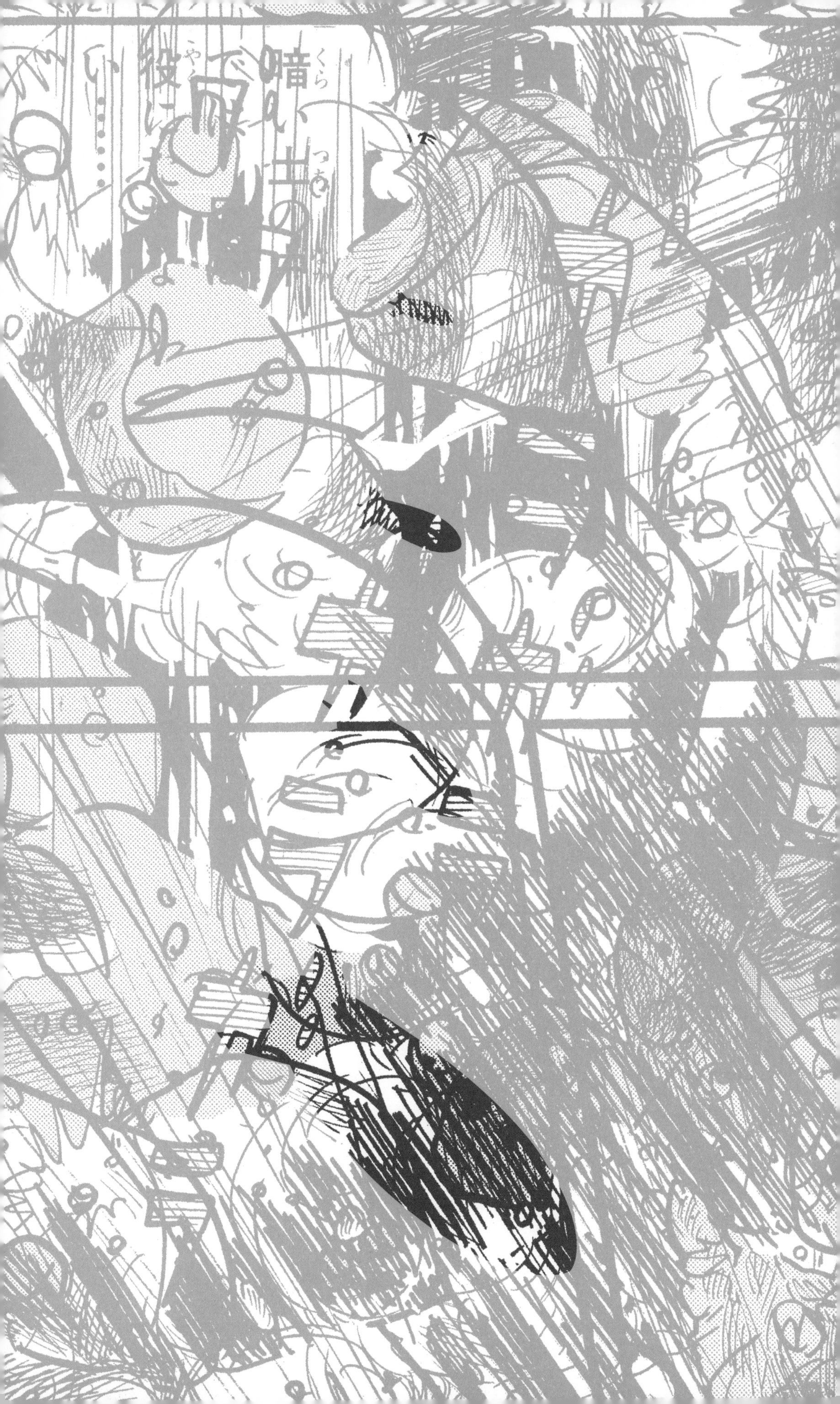

暗い土の
で、役に
い……

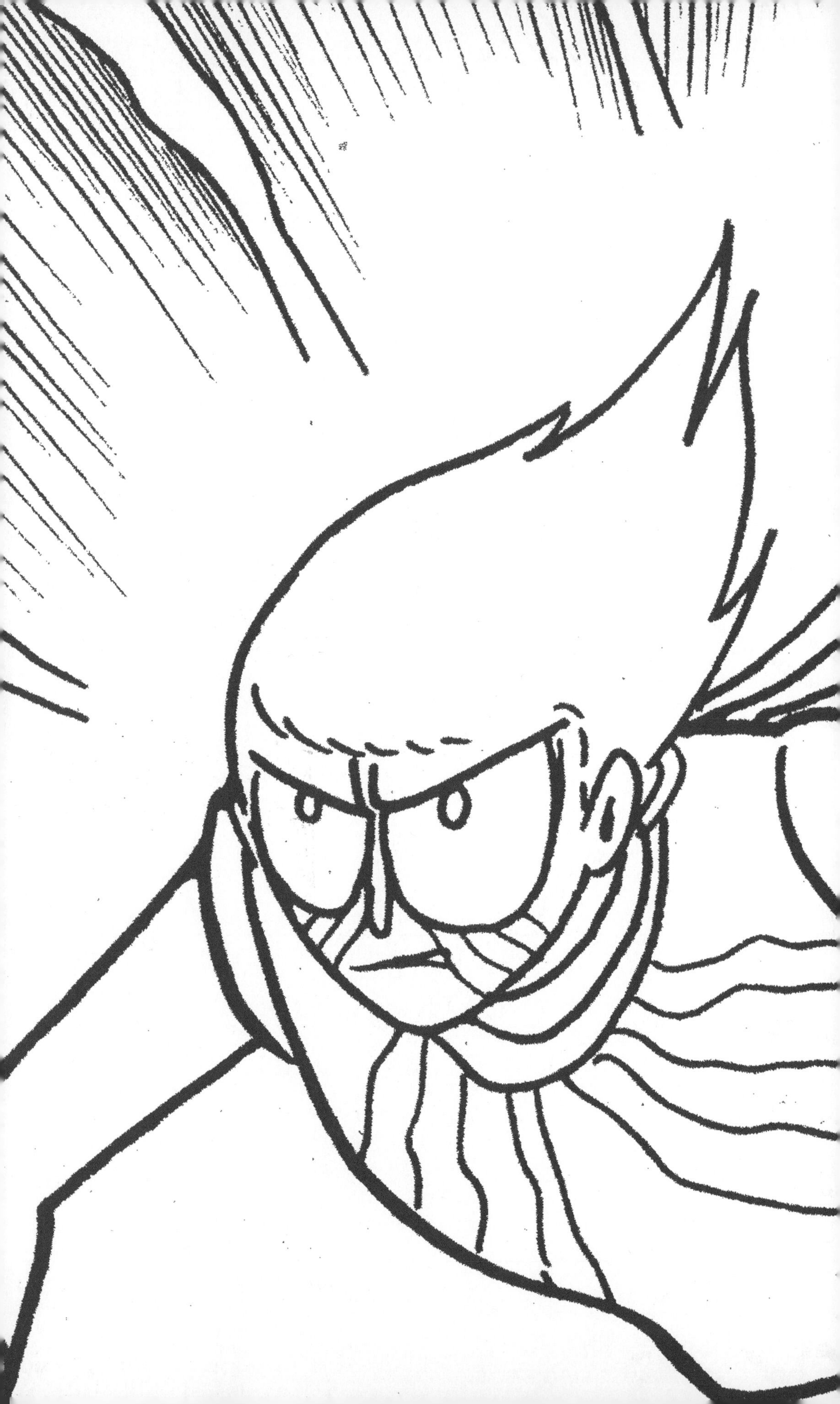